EXPLORERS, GUIDES & MEANING-MAKERS

Mission Theology for Catholic Educators

Jim and Therese D'Orsa

THE BROKEN BAY INSTITUTE
MISSION AND EDUCATION SERIES

This volume has been written in honour of
missiologist extraordinaire Fr. Cyril Hally S.S.C., who over a long and fruitful life has been a
great friend and guide to Catholic educators.

It is further gratefully dedicated to Catholic educators past and present.
Jim and Therese D'Orsa

Published in Australia by
Vaughan Publishing
32 Glenvale Crescent
Mulgrave VIC 3170

Vaughan Publishing
A joint imprint of Broken Bay Institute and Garratt Publishing

© 2011 Copyright James D'Orsa and Therese D'Orsa

Reprinted in 2012, 2013

All rights reserved. Except as provided by Australian copyright law,
no part of this publication may be reproduced in any manner
without prior permission in writing from the publisher.

Cover design by Cristina Neri, Canary Graphic Design
Text design by Ian James, JGD Graphic + Web
Cover image – Thinkstock.com

Printed by Lightning Source

9780987306029

The scripture used in this book is from the New American Bible.
Excerpt from Re-Visioning Mission: The Catholic Church and Culture in Postmodern America, by Richard G. Cote, O.M.I. Copyright © 1996 by Richard G. Cote, Paulist Press, Inc., Mahwah, NJ. Reprinted by permission of Paulist Press, Inc. www.paulistpress.com
Excerpts from Transforming Worldviews by Paul G. Hiebert, Baker Academic, a division of Baker Publishing Group, Grand Rapids, Michigan, 2008. Used by permission.

CONTENTS

FOREWORD vii
Chapter One: Orientations 1
Genesis 1
Exploring the Idea of "Frontier" 2
Grassroots Theology and Academic Theology – Differences 4
Building a Bridge 6
Living on the Frontier of Hope 7
Structure 7

PART A: FOUNDATIONS 10
Chapter Two: Developing a Missiological Imagination 12
A New Movement in Human Aspiration 12
Missiological Imagination – Reclaiming the Catholic Imagination 14
Faith and Imagination 15
Discerning the Signs of the Times 15
Traditional Understandings of Mission 18
A New Understanding of Mission 18
Missiology Anchors Theology 19
New Perspectives on Mission in School Education 20
Meaning-making and the Missiological Imagination 21

Chapter Three: Doing Grassroots Theology 23
Search for Insight 23
Thomas Groome and Shared Christian Praxis 25
The Whiteheads and Method in Ministry 27
Killen and De Beer – The Art of Theological Reflection 29
Contextual Nature of Theology 32
Doing Local Theology 35
Revised Model for Doing Grassroots Theology 36
Mission Theology as Local Theology 38
Befriending in Grassroots Theology 39

PART B: BEFRIENDING CULTURE, BEFRIENDING
HUMAN EXPERIENCE 41
Chapter Four: Culture as the Learning Place
of the Faith Community 43
Culture as a Resource in Theological Reflection 43
Classicist View of Culture 44

Modern View of Culture 45
Cultural Processes – Enculturation and Acculturation 47
Understanding the Modern View of Culture – Two Working Models 48
Model A – Culture as a Society's Design for Living 49
Model B – Narrative and Culture: The Iceberg Model 53
Culture and the Gospel – Inculturation 59
The Gospel and Culture – Evangelising Cultures 61
Culture and Theological Reflection 62

Chapter Five: Exploring Post-modern Experience....................................64
Time and Its Significance in Meaning-making 64
Worldviews and Human Aspiration 65
Understanding "Post-modernity" 66
"Post-modern" as a Period in History 67
"Post-modern" as a Sensibility 68
Post-modern Catholics 70
Developing an Interpretive Map 72
Paradigm Shifts within a Worldview – The Case of Galileo 75
The Pre-modern Worldview and Constructed Identity 76

Chapter Six: The Narrative of Post-modernity..79
The Importance of Historical Consciousness 79
The Pre-modern World..80
The European Enlightenment and Early Modernity 81
Early modernity – Its Aspirations and Development 84
Crisis in Modernity and the Beginnings of the Post-modern Experience......85
The "Second" Modernity 87
Mission in the "Second Modernity" 90
Educating in a Modern/Post-modern Environment 91

PART C: FORCES RE-SHAPING THE FRONTIER OF MISSION 94
Chapter Seven: The Many Faces of Globalisation....................................95
Globalisation as Complex Connectivity 95
Globalisation as the Knowledge Economy 97
Globalisation as "McDonaldisation" 97
Globalisation as the New Migration 99
Globalisation – Some Educational Dimensions..101

Chapter Eight: Secularisation – Friend or Foe? 104
Secularity, Secularisation and Secularism 104
Narrative of Secularisation 107
Secularisation Theory 108

Perspectives on Secularism 109
Secularisation as a Cultural Phenomenon 110
The Secularisation of Morality 111
Catholic Discourse on Secularisation 112
Secularisation – Leadership Issues 115

Chapter Nine: Contemporary Pluralism
– The Rise and Rise of Difference 118
Empirical Pluralism 118
Ideological Pluralism and the Foundations of Knowledge 119
Plausibility Structures in Pre-modernity 120
Modernity and the Principle of Contingency 121
Faith and the Principle of Purpose 123
Re-definition of "Public Knowledge" in Modernity 124
Post-modernity and the Principle of Critique 125
Ideological Pluralism and the Issue of Truth 125
Narrative of Ideological Pluralism -
The Emerging Worldview of Modernity 126
Truth in the Post-modern Worldview 129
Creating the "New Whole" 130
Ideological Pluralism – Some Educational Implications 132

PART D: BEFRIENDING OUR RELIGIOUS TRADITION 134
Chapter Ten: Befriending a Living Tradition 137
With Life comes Challenge and Change...137
Mission Theology and Mission Practice – the Connection.....................138
The Church as Universal and Local 140
Development of Mission Theology – Magisterial Documents 142
Key "Moments" in the Development of the Theology of Mission 143
First Moment – "The Church is by Nature Missionary"..........................144
Second Moment – "Making Present the Kingdom of God" 147
Third Moment – "Proclaiming a Person, Jesus Christ" 149
Charting the Church's Understanding of Evangelisation........................151
Mission as Local within the Global 152

Chapter Eleven: Gospel Communities – Then and Now 154
Going Beyond Naïve Literalism 154
Parameters of Revelation 156
Content and Process in Revelation 157
Backgrounding the New Testament Texts..159
Doing Narrative Mission Theology – The Gospel Process.....................160

The Gospels as Narratives 162
Gospel Narratives as Pastoral and Missional 163
The Lens of the Resurrection 166
Missionary Commission in the Gospels 167
Jesus' Teaching on the Kingdom – The Gospel Content 169
The Kingdom in History and Beyond History 171
The Church and the Kingdom 173

CONCLUSION 175
Chapter Twelve: Catholic Educators as Explorers Guides and Meaning-makers 175
Making Sense of the Frontier Experience 175
The Ecology of Human Growth 177
An Ecology of Knowledge 177
Ecology of Knowledge and the "Catholic Curriculum" 180
An Ecology of Relationships 183
An Ecology of Community 185
Community as Holder of Identity 188
The Place of Grassroots Theology in an "Ecology of Human Growth" 191
"The Heart of the Matter" 192

LIST OF FIGURES
Figure 1. Model for Theological Reflection 37
Figure 2. Culture as a Dynamic System 50
Figure 3. Model A – Culture as a Design for Living 51
Figure 4. A Linear Model of Culture 54
Figure 5. Model B – The Iceberg as an Analogical Model of Culture 55
Figure 6. Meaning-making in the Context of Interacting Worldviews 66
Figure 7. Schemas for Categorising Recent Historical Periods 68
Figure 8. Worldview as an Interpretive Tool 72
Figure 9. Evangelisation as the Totality of the Church's Mission 151
Figure 10. Catholic Education at the Nexus of Worldviews 175
Figure 11. The Ecology of Knowledge 179
Figure 12. Dynamics Shaping Israel's Identity 189

INDEX 194

FOREWORD

Several years ago, Jim and Therese D'Orsa knocked on my office door at Catholic Theological Union (CTU) and introduced themselves to me. They explained that they had come to CTU on sabbatical to attend classes on mission and to reflect on how they might make their own area of expertise – Catholic education – more mission-focused. Therese sat in on Tony Gittins's classes, and Jim sat in on my course in ecclesiology. As we talked during their stay, but particularly in an hour's conversation as they were about to return to Australia, I realised just how great their expertise was and how passionate their desire was to help Catholic educators understand the immense opportunity they had for Christian evangelisation in their schools and classrooms. Here were people of immense experience, and with a far-reaching vision. I could only express my admiration for them and encourage them with my support.

Jim and Therese, on their return to Australia, were appointed by the Broken Bay Institute (BBI) in the diocese of Broken Bay, New South Wales, to teach courses in mission and education. Therese was also appointed to the head of the BBI's Department of Mission and Culture. Her task is not only to teach in the area of mission, however, but also to infuse the whole panoply of courses that BBI offers with a missionary spirit. Christianity, the church, is not simply about itself, but about those outside its boundaries, witnessing to and caring for people who are unchurched and unsure about their faith, and for people of faith who are not members of any Christian church.

The D'Orsas' concern, however, is focused particularly on how teachers and administrators in Catholic schools can have such an outward-looking focus. This present volume is testimony to their concern and is truly a landmark work. As far as I know, there is no book that attempts – and succeeds – to do what Jim and Therese set out to do here. They have sought to encourage educators to engage in mission theology themselves, as well as providing necessary understanding to enable them to do this. They have digested and summarised the best of thinking on mission and intercultural studies, and have shown how such thinking is relevant and challenging to the area of Christian and Catholic education.

This book is a masterful overview of reflection on such important topics as culture, inculturation, globalisation and evangelisation, and the D'Orsas use their reflections to show educators how they can infuse their schools and classrooms with Christian values and convictions. Jim and Therese embody the title of their book. They are themselves explorers of their faith, interpreters of its meaning, and guides to exciting ways to present it and proclaim it.

Australia is a country in which Catholic education is thriving, and in which the state provides financial help for faith-based education. The D'Orsas' reflections and recommendations come from this context but they speak to a wider audience. Indeed, they are highly relevant for the situation in my own country – the United States of America. While Catholic education may not be as widespread as it once was in the United States, it is still nevertheless a vital force in American Catholic life, and has great potential for proclaiming the gospel in this country.

Teachers in Catholic schools in Australia, New Zealand, the United States, Canada, the United Kingdom and Ireland need to be inspired and challenged to explore their own faith more deeply so as to be guides and makers of meaning for the students they teach. Church leaders, ministers, teachers and parents will be grateful and delighted when they read these wisdom-filled pages.

Stephen Bevans, SVD
Louis J Luzbetak Professor of Mission and Culture
Catholic Theological Union
Chicago, USA

CHAPTER ONE

Orientations

Genesis

Catholic educators are aware that a qualitative difference exists between the way teachers and leaders operated even a decade ago and the way they need to operate now. What educators sense, and what they have conveyed to us, is *fundamental change*. In the chapters that follow, we will discuss elements of this fundamental change and the new horizon within which educators need to operate in order to be effective in terms of their mission or purpose.

Alongside broad societal and cultural change there has also been change in the Catholic culture within which educators operate. This in turn reflects a change in the students' experience of Catholic community – the majority of students have at most one parent who has any substantial commitment to the local church, and many parents who acknowledge themselves as "Catholic" often do so on their own terms.

In the conversations which took place in our own diocese, the Diocese of Sale, Victoria, Australia, during a recent major diocesan planning process,[1] this intuition was expressed in terms of the need to reconceptualise and to re-state the mission of the school in order to deal with a changed reality. Teachers and school leaders recognised that a point of discontinuity had been reached. The image of "frontier" was often invoked to express this new reality. It is an image which recognises that Catholic educators are now operating in largely uncharted territory, and there is a need to make new "maps".

Catholic schools are communities of faith.[2] They have taken life from the faith commitment of those who founded them, and they are sustained because people of faith – parents, teachers, parishioners, clergy and religious – believe in their efficacy in carrying on Jesus' mission. Given the fundamental nature of the societal and cultural changes that have occurred in the past two decades, teachers and leaders recognise that things that could once be taken as givens can no longer be assumed. People's beliefs have become less easy to predict and so controversy arises more readily than formerly. Also their motivation in associating with a Catholic school is more complex. This means that developing

---

[1] Catholic Diocese of Sale Pastoral Planning Document, *Journeying Together*, 2002.
[2] Evelyn and James Whitehead in their classic work *Community of Faith* (Minneapolis: The Winston Seabury Press, 1982) provide a basic understanding of community as a group linked by common goals, shared values and mutual commitments. Within this image of community, individuals have degrees of association. See especially Chapter Two "Community Is a Way to Be Together", 21–33.

a vision and working towards common goals to which people are committed is something that demands more time and effort than was once the case. One consequence is that educating adult members of the community, including staff, becomes an important pre-condition for educating students.

Our own conviction is that two types of conversation about mission need to be brought into systematic contact with each other. Firstly, there are the conversations of professional theologians, which are occurring predominantly, though not exclusively, in mission institutes and academia. Secondly, there are conversations about mission, which might be termed "grassroots theology",[3] taking place in the variety of contexts where people engage in mission. The latter conversations occur between people with very mixed levels of theological training – members of local school, parish and diocesan communities – who are trying to make sense of their present situation. This second type of conversation, grassroots theology about mission, will be referred to as "grassroots missiology".[4] It is important to note that, while not generally professionally qualified as theologians, those engaged in grassroots missiology are likely to be highly qualified in a variety of other professional areas.

Having promoted missiological conversation among educators through the present volume, we are presently seeking to promote a further, related, conversation in a subsequent volume – *Walking with Mystery: Education as Evangelisation*. The present volume deals more specifically with the dialogue between missiology and education. Set at the interface of missiology and education, this dialogue is pursued at the level of the disciplines themselves. The work is designed to demonstrate that much practical insight is to be gained when the disciplines of missiology and education meet in a substantive way.

Exploring the Idea of "Frontier"

In this book an image, that of the "frontier", is used to evoke the newness of the contemporary environment in Catholic education. The image of the frontier or an associated term has currency in a number of "New World" countries such as the United States of America, Canada and Australia. The image, though widely used, is far from innocent. As originally used in the United States the frontier marked the division between "settlement" – the known world – and "wilderness" – the unknown world. However, this world was not unknown

---

[3] James and Evelyn Whitehead provided something of a primer on "grassroots theology" in *Method in Ministry* (New York: The Seabury Press, 1981). A less structured, but equally perceptive treatment is found in Clemens Sedmak *Doing Local Theology* (Maryknoll New York: Orbis, 2002).

[4] Missiology is, in broad terms, the field of study incorporating how the Christian community understands and pursues its mission and so continues the mission of Jesus. The place of missiology within the formal structure of tertiary studies tends to differ from one Christian denomination to another. In Catholic tertiary institutions in recent years its place is tending to move from the area of applied theology to a more central and integrating position within the overall curriculum.

to the native peoples who lived there. The white European settlers' "frontier" proved to be the "skirmishing line" for native peoples as they attempted to resist the intrusion of unknown people into their lands. The frontier in the United States, and the bush in Australia, are symbols which have become integral to what Cote calls the "dynamic myth" of the cultures of these respective peoples. In both cases the myth is ethnocentric in its origins.[5] In the case of the United States, Frederick Turner argued that the frontier experiences provided the furnace in which key aspects of the American character were forged.[6] The bush played a similar role in Australia. In both cases the gaining of a shared identity on the part of the white settlers resulted in a corresponding loss of identity of the native peoples. Both images carry with them considerable ethnocentric baggage.

However a symbol can have value beyond the historical circumstances in which it was generated. Today we talk readily about the frontiers of knowledge, of science and medicine. By this we indicate the limits of what we know and can imagine.

The contention of this book is that today Catholic educators find themselves at another type of frontier – a frontier of meaning. The meanings that have characterised Catholic "settlement" fail to make sense to an increasing number of people inhabiting the new wilderness created by globalisation, secularisation and modern/post-modern pluralism. If our students are to live out the destiny to which God calls them, they will have to learn how to make sense of this new situation. They will struggle to do this if those who teach them, and those who lead them, have not first journeyed into the unknown territory themselves and made sense of the journey. Having done so, they can then help others make meaning, acting as guides and interpreters. They and their students will then be in a position to be serious contributors to bringing the contemporary "wilderness" within the realm of God's Kingdom, and therefore advancing God's mission.

Teachers quickly raise questions, such as those below, when asked to explore the frontier image:
- What is the nature of the frontier? How and why does it challenge old certainties?
- How does one orient oneself in this new and challenging environment?

---

[5] For a larger discussion of this with reference to the United States see Richard G. Cote *Revisioning Mission: The Catholic Church and Culture in Post-Modern America* (New York: Paulist Press, 1996), 116ff. For a discussion of the same issue in the context of Australian culture see John Thornhill *Making Australia: Exploring our National Conversation* (Newtown NSW: Millennium Books, 1992), 143ff.

[6] Cote,117.

- How does one construct a Catholic identity these days, and why are there so many ways of doing this?
- How can we assist educators to understand, adapt to, and be effective in this emerging environment?
- What help does the Church offer in addressing these questions?
- How is the changing environment shaping the way we assess human need and respond as Christ's disciples?
- Is it still possible to talk meaningfully of a Catholic culture?
- How do we as a group conceptualise and articulate mission?
- As we re-imagine what we are doing, how do we invite others to share the vision and work towards achieving the goals?
- Are there any emerging certainties to replace what is being lost?

These are not everyday staffroom questions, be the staffroom located in the bishop's chancery, parish, school or tertiary institution, but the way in which they are answered will have a great impact on the day-to-day delivery of education. This is because, in educational institutions, such as schools and colleges, people are generally working towards a common purpose, share a common identity, and feel the sense of achievement that comes from doing something that is perceived to be worthwhile. Mission, when it is authentically conceptualised and carried through into daily living, *is an integrating force in community endeavours.* It is life-giving and provides direction as the community confronts, and is confronted by, questions such as those outlined above.

Doing theology in a frontier situation requires a particular set of understandings and skills. If the understandings and skill-set possessed by leaders and educators were adequate for the current environment there would, in all likelihood, be no sense that something fundamental has changed, and therefore no angst about the present and the future.

Grassroots Theology and Academic Theology – Differences

A premise of this book is that the essential skill in coping with the "frontier" is the ability to "do theology" so as to enable the Catholic educator to develop a mission theology which can underpin a communal sense of mission. Like other branches of knowledge, theology involves both content and process. It is an ongoing endeavour of people within a faith community to make sense of their experience, individual and collective, from the perspective of faith. To the extent that we reflect on our experience in the light of faith, *we are all grassroots theologians.*

Many people see theology as a body of knowledge to be mastered rather than as a process to be followed. A common misconception is that theology is what you know, not what you do. It is learned from experts. This is a very limited understanding of theology. Such a view does not take into account how theological knowledge is constructed in the first place. Certainly, there is a legitimate field of study which involves accessing the work of the great theologians of our tradition, but there is much more to theology than that. Great theologians have tended to systematise and codify, and in the process render abstract, reflection on human experience that was originally concrete, and bound by the exigencies of context and history.

Grassroots theology differs from professional academic theology in that *it is carried out in a more or less informed way at the local level*. This form of theologising is common in school communities, in parishes, in diocesan settings and, in the case of communities of religious, at the congregational level. Its focus is on particular contexts and the issues to which they give rise. This is its strength. A characteristic of grassroots theology is that it is often episodic, unsystematic, focused on the immediate, and stops once the issues have been dealt with. It can become partisan and needs to be complemented by, and open to, the insight generated by accessing the experience of others. The fact that it is not approached systematically is its weakness.

The practitioners of grassroots missiology are rarely professionals in theology and often struggle to understand much of the language of the professional conversation. Many would be unaware that the conversations they engage in can be described as "theologising". For most, theology is more a noun than a verb; it is understood as content rather than process. Very importantly, however, these practitioners bring to their conversations commitment and a depth of knowledge born of experience. They are the people who carry out God's mission in particular contexts which they know intimately and in which many of them are quite expert. They are therefore not only worthy, but essential, partners in a broader conversation about mission.

In summary, professional missiology is driven in the main by academic concerns and draws its momentum from these concerns. Grassroots missiology, on the other hand, is driven by the challenges, hopes, angst and energy of lived experience in particular settings. As both Tanner,[7] writing from a Protestant background, and Rohlheiser,[8] writing from a Catholic background, point out, these two conversations need to be brought together if the high energy currently invested in each is to be productive. Grassroots missiology needs to be better

---

[7] Kathryn Tanner "The Nature and Task of Theology" in *Theories of Culture* (Minneapolis: Fortress Press, 1997), Chapter 4, 61–92.
[8] Ronald Rolheiser *Secularity and the Gospel* (New York: The Crossroad Publishing Company, 2006), 24.

informed and put on a more substantial footing; professional missiology would benefit from taking up some of the concerns of grassroots missiology as these emerge from particular contexts such as from Catholic schools and parishes, which constitute a major area for applied missiology. The question then is – how do we do this?

Building a Bridge

The present study seeks to answer this question in a particular setting – that of Catholic schools and colleges and the networks in which these are embedded. More specifically, our focus is Catholic schools, colleges and educational systems in western cultures. Our own immediate context is Australian Catholic education and, by travel and association, Catholic education in the United States, Canada, New Zealand, the United Kingdom and Ireland. We believe that the Australian context is in many ways privileged in that schools and colleges there are substantially supported financially by government, but with limited interference in their organisation and operation. This support ensures there is now minimal financial dependency on parishes or dioceses to meet running costs or a significant proportion of capital costs. Despite some hardship due to the poor funding levels of some state governments,[9] teachers are paid at rates comparable to their colleagues in the public systems, so teaching in a Catholic school is seen as particularly desirable from a range of perspectives. The Australian Catholic school context, therefore, has its unique characteristics, while sharing many common elements with Catholic schools in other countries.

Our experience of grassroots missiology has come from working with a large number of schools, parishes and dioceses as they have developed or renewed their understanding of mission and have endeavoured to live this out. It has come from being part of innumerable conversations about mission and mission issues in these settings. A second level of involvement has come from working with school leaders both in professional development programs and basic theology programs. Perhaps the major involvement, however, has been in our own ministry as leaders in Catholic school systems, with the unique entree this gives to discussion about mission at the grassroots level.

Our participation in the professional conversation about missiology has developed out of a long association with the Columban Fathers and their work in the field, particularly in cross-cultural mission situations. This book deals with many of the major themes being addressed with our tertiary students, teachers

---

[9] In Australia the major portion of school funding comes from the Australian government, but a significant portion also comes from state governments. The differences in funding levels between the states is currently significant.

and school leaders who are engaged in day-to-day ministries, predominantly in Catholic schools. We believe our experiences ensure we are well placed to take on a bridge-building role, joining the broader professional conversation about mission to that of grassroots discussions about mission in various Catholic educational settings.

Living on the Frontier of Hope

When a community sets out to consider its mission or to re-vision that mission, whether it recognises it or not, it is constructing a "local theology" and providing a solid basis for hope. The local theology can provide a foundation for spirituality, community prayer, and the unique way in which the Gospel is lived out in a particular context. Identifying this theology is important in sustaining both hope and mission, since *hope is the lifeblood of mission.*

As we have indicated, many teachers in Catholic schools are conscious of living and working on a missional frontier. Sustaining hope in such situations is critical.[10] A feature of life on a frontier is that there are no pre-existing roads or bridges. In this respect being on a frontier differs from being at a crossroads, which is another metaphor often applied to Catholic education. At a crossroads the choice is between two ways that are known. On the frontier the choice is between the known and the unknown. Also, on the frontier there are no fully developed maps to consult except those that are created as the journey proceeds. To move forward, map-making and bridge-building skills are needed, along with a depth of faith and hope. Improving the quality of grassroots missiology is vital in this regard.

This book is for school and system personnel and other Church leaders – lay, religious and clerical – with whom school leaders relate in living out the mission of the school. Hopefully, it also gives professionals in the field of missiology a better understanding of mission issues surfacing in school contexts, and how missiology finds application in the Catholic Church's efforts to educate young people in school settings. While the focus of our concern is Catholic school education, discussion with colleagues in other education sectors within the Church, as well as those involved in parishes, welfare and health, indicate similar patterns exist in these fields of mission as well.

Structure

The book is organised in five major sections. Part A deals with *foundational* issues. Having named the concerns that need to be addressed in Chapter One, Chapter Two suggests that developing a missiological imagination is an

---

[10] Therese and Jim D'Orsa "Mission and Catholic Schools: Grounding Hope in Uncertain Times" in Anne Benjamin and Dan Riley (eds) *Catholic Schools Hope in Uncertain Times* (Mulgrave: John Garratt, 2008), 32–44.

essential requirement in addressing them. Our strong belief is that such an imagination is developed through theological reflection. Chapter Three outlines in narrative form the development since the 1970s of theological reflection as a resource for those engaged in the mission of the Church. It focuses on both models and methods.

Theological reflection involves bringing together a number of key elements – personal and communal experience, social and cultural analysis, scripture and Christian tradition – all of which can be considered resources in the process. Each of these resources has an important contribution to make in how we, as individuals and as communities, understand and place a value on mission. Part B deals with two of these resources – *culture and human experience* – treating them as interrelated elements in how teachers understand their present context and the concerns to which this gives rise.

Context has its historical roots, its current manifestations in personal and communal experience, and its cultural expressions. It is part of an ongoing narrative in which we are embedded. Culture is a powerful, though often poorly understood resource, in making sense of the world of experience. This aspect of context is explored in Chapter Four. "Post-modernity" is the subject of the next two chapters. Chapter Five provides perspectives on the exploration of post-modernism and Chapter Six deals with post-modernism's narrative. As people of faith we believe this narrative has a trajectory and is meaningful.

In Part C we recognise that, while the narrative is ongoing, it is shaped by global processes such as *globalisation, secularisation and pluralisation* which have particular salience in our time. Understanding these influences is important in interpreting our expedience as well as in planning our work as educators (Chapters Seven, Eight and Nine).

Part D explores the contributions our religious tradition, in which we also include scripture, can make to grassroots theological reflection. Ours is a *living tradition* and there has been considerable theological development with regard to how the Church understands its mission and its place within God's mission since the Second Vatican Council 1962–65 (Chapter Ten). The process by which the Gospels came to life within the early New Testament communities has much to offer those who seek to re-create such communities in the present time in a variety of educational environments (Chapter Eleven).

In Chapter Twelve we seek to bring the various themes of the book together. The overall thesis of this book is that the intuition of many teachers and leaders that something fundamental has changed in Catholic schooling is correct. The "something" is a combination of changing context and changing frameworks of understanding both within culture and within the Church. In the demanding context of the frontier such changes demand a response which, in turn, entails reconceptualising important aspects of the mission of the Catholic school, and living with the consequences of this work. It is a call to be not just map-readers, but also to become map-makers, thus sustaining the hope of those we lead.

PART A

Foundations

A major challenge in dealing with the frontier situation and the difficult issues it raises for educators is developing *the imaginal capacity to respond to the new and unexpected.* "Imaginal capacity" is the ability to imagine and think creatively using images. We all approach the frontier situation within our existing imaginal horizons. Dealing with the new and unexpected often demands seeing things within a new horizon, using the wider perspective this provides. As long as the horizon of the possible is fixed, options are limited. How then does one shift the boundaries of imagination so that old situations can be seen in a new light and new situations within a wider perspective?

Chapter Two suggests the need to develop what Stephen Bevans calls a "missiological imagination". This means giving our Catholic imagination a new orientation, one that places mission as the centre of our thinking. In a broad sense mission is about choosing directions with others and for others, and moving with a firm hope in those directions. Mission constantly poses the questions: which directions, with whom, for whom, how, and for how long? In pursuing mission one also needs to know what hopes or aspirations drive the group forward. It is impossible to have aspirations without imagination since hope deals with what is not yet but is desired. As a group moves in its chosen mission direction, new perspectives open up, new possibilities arise and aspirations change. If we are wise, we learn as we move forward. As Christians we believe that this process, while it may not always represent "progress", is not random, but is guided by God's spirit. *Mission and learning, therefore, go together.*

If leaders and educators are to effectively address the many challenges that face them in the contemporary Catholic school, they need insight so that they can help make sense of new and challenging situations, not only for themselves but also for those they lead and instruct. They need to be able to *do theology in a way that is appropriate to their situation.* Another way of saying this is that they need to be able to engage in systematic theological reflection as leaders and educators, and have the capacity and confidence to bring teams and schools communities into this process of meaning-making. We call this doing "grassroots theology" from a mission perspective.

To do grassroots theology systematically it is necessary to have a *model* which sets out the basic elements in such reflection, and a *process* people can follow that guides reflection and leads to action. Chapter Three traces *the emergence of processes of theological reflection* developed in the main for lay leaders and educators since the 1980s. This corresponds to developments in the wider field of theology which stress the *contextual nature of all theology* and the importance of "local" theology in the unfolding of our theological traditions. Across the past three decades these two streams of thought have interacted to help clarify the essential elements in a model, as well as options with respect to process.

CHAPTER TWO

Developing a Missiological Imagination

A New Movement in Human Aspiration

We live in a world and culture wherein, paradoxically, the one predictable reality is change. Educators are aware that the rate of change their students will face as they grow up will be even greater than the often bewildering rate they themselves have encountered, and this worries them. The situation is seen as an assault on human consciousness and on human aspiration. Leadership in this context is problematic particularly for an organisation such as the Church which, by nature and practice, must conserve its tradition, as well as respond to the changing context in which its communities survive and seek to thrive.

Educators also find the current environment challenging because they are expected to mediate society's aspirations for the next generation, yet these aspirations are, at best, only dimly defined. It is a daunting task to prepare young people to live in a world where the contours are poorly defined. It comes as no surprise then that writers such as Parker Palmer speak of "the courage to teach"![11] Catholic educators find themselves particularly challenged given both the aspirations of the body that sponsors their work and the often countervailing aspirations of parents and students. The latter are substantially shaped by a secular culture that tends to determine how they see the future and its possibilities.

An important thesis of this book is that educating effectively in such a situation requires that educators develop a new way of imagining this future. We see this as involving what missiologist Stephen Bevans refers to as "missiological imagination".[12] Coupled with this, educators require the capacity for theological reflection, a capacity which involves both the *knowledge and skills* not only to make sense of experience in new ways and to think differently, but also to think beyond the limits imposed by our social or cultural position and the age in which we live. Theological reflection is a necessary means for surviving in our current context. A missiological imagination enables educators not just to survive, but to thrive.

Imagination is the human capacity to mentally reconstitute the elements of experience, both personal and collective, in order to arrive at new possibilities and new expressions, and to find new meanings in our experience. Through

---

[11] Parker Palmer *The Courage to Teach* (San Francisco: Jossey-Bass, 1998).
[12] Stephen Bevans "Wisdom from the Margins: Systematic Theology and the Missiological Imagination", *Australian e-Journal of Theology*, August 2005, Issue 5.

imagination we can project ourselves beyond the limits of our experience be they limits of place or time. Using imagination we can suspend beliefs that lie at the core of our interpretive system and inhabit and make sense of the "worlds" created by literature, art, dance, music, film and religious ritual. Imagination also enables us to transform the perspective through which we interpret experience – to stand in another's shoes. Culture plays an important role in the process of imagining because it provides us with the images, symbols, categories, narratives and so on that we use. Culture both aids and limits the use of imagination depending on the range of resources it makes available to us.

Writers such as Charles Taylor refer to the collective resources open to a people in imagining possibilities as the "social imaginary". There is nothing theoretical about the social imaginary as Taylor uses it. He describes it as consisting of "the ways in which they imagine their social existence, how they fit together with others, how things go on between them and their fellows, the expectations which are normally met, and the deeper normative notions and images which underlie these expectations".[13]

It is the social imaginary which imposes a limit on what people see as possible. We use a concept similar to Taylor's social imaginary in referring to thinking, planning and working within an "imaginal horizon". People can see their options out to a certain point, but not beyond that point. They are often unaware that they view possibilities within an imaginal horizon. In creating meaning it is necessary to help people identify the limits of this horizon in order to transcend it. When this happens, what was once seen as not possible, or beyond the bounds of possibility, becomes through a transformation of perspective, a new option. Thus it is possible to think beyond the limits imposed by our individual or collective imaginal horizon provided we acknowledge the existence of that horizon. We are able to transcend our social imaginary.

In a pluralised world, people have access to alternative imaginaries. Developing a missional imagination involves going beyond the social and ecclesial imaginaries which shape most of the thinking in both Church and society. It calls for the radical transformation of perspective that is required when mission is thought of not only as what the Church does in the world to advance the Kingdom announced by Jesus, but also what God does to achieve that result.

---

[13] Charles Taylor "Modern Social Imaginaries" in *A Secular Age* (Cambridge Massachusetts: The Belknap Press of Harvard University Press, 2007), Chapter 4, 155–211 and in particular 171.

Missiological Imagination – Reclaiming the Catholic Imaginary

Some years ago sociologist Andrew Greeley observed that there was something unique about the way Catholics looked at life, and began to delineate the "Catholic imagination".[14] His was a significant insight, highlighting the existence of a Catholic imaginary and pointing up the way Catholic culture has provided people with the images, symbols, rituals and narratives with which it is possible to make sense of religious experience. The secularisation process has the effect of eroding this Catholic imaginary. Greeley's contention is that it needs to be reclaimed.

With his emphasis on missiological imagination, Bevans provides an important complement and counter-balance to Greeley's more "sacramental" view of the Catholic imagination. As we shall see, one of the major mission challenges for Catholic education is to evangelise the social imaginary within which the students make sense of their experiences and their lives. Imagination operates at the interface between culture and life. Culture is a key area in the study of mission, and for this reason we will devote a full chapter to it. For the present, however, we note the importance of culture to human existence in that it enables people to live together more or less harmoniously and more or less productively.[15] On the other hand culture, for all its benefits, renders human existence safe by limiting the possibilities in living. Unless challenged, "our way" becomes "the way" to the unthinking exclusion of all other ways. Culture creates an *imaginal horizon* which people living within the culture rarely recognise.

The task educators face in addressing the challenges posed by rapid change in human aspiration is knowing how to expand this imaginal horizon so that new perspectives, and the possibilities these create, can emerge. To lead in this way means *seeing the task of education in a new context*. This is a context in which the imaginal horizon is moving within both Church and society so that, in consequence, new missional possibilities can arise, and new coalitions be formed. Imagination provides the key for tapping into the resources of human aspirations and the energy associated with these aspirations.

The challenge we have set ourselves in teaching and writing is to help school leaders and their educator colleagues re-imagine and re-assess the significance of their work within the expanded understanding of mission now held within the

---

[14] Andrew Greeley *The Catholic Imagination* (Berkeley: University of California Press, 2001).

[15] Among the many definitions of culture, one which has stood the test of time is that of Louis Luzbetak in his book *The Church and Cultures* (Maryknoll New York: Orbis, 1988), 157. Luzbetak defines culture as a more or less successful plan for living which is widely adopted by a people in response to life in a particular physical, social and ideational environment.

Catholic community. Specifically, what we are exploring are the consequences of a change in perspective. We are aware that the Catholic experience parallels in many respects similar shifts in other Christian traditions.

Whether they are considering the renewal of the vision/mission of a school, the rationale for a department, pastoral initiatives, revision of policies, the curriculum, or community-building, educators have the opportunity – we would say the responsibility – of reflecting on the imaginal horizon within which they customarily operate so as to assess its adequacy. At issue are the following questions. How does this horizon limit and curtail our hopes? Are we thriving or merely surviving within our current understanding of what is possible? This kind of reflective practice, when carried out in the light of our faith tradition, is the form of meaning-making that Catholics know as theological reflection – faith seeking insight and meaning in the events of our personal and collective lives. When applied to the dynamics at work in a changing context, it is known as "reading the signs of the times".

Faith and Imagination

To be meaningful, faith needs both *practical and symbolic* expression. The original Gospels were just such expressions of faith. They came into being as a consequence of theological reflection on the story of Jesus as carried in the memory of particular communities and re-interpreted in the light of the new experiences of those communities. The Gospels have to be interpreted at the level of Christian practice, and also at the symbolic level, because they are highly symbolic in terms of the material which has been woven into the narratives of Jesus. As theological reflections the Gospels are far more complex than at first seems to be the case.

Today's Christians construct and express a similar theology in the narrative and celebration of their own faith communities. They can create this attentively and skilfully if they have the imagination to realise what is happening and the courage to develop the necessary skills with which to express faith adequately. This book seeks to equip educators with the perspectives necessary to engage productively in purposeful reflection about their work, to see its significance in a new light, so as to make better decisions with respect to priorities. It provides, hopefully, a point of entrée in developing a missiological imagination.

Discerning the Signs of the Times

An approach to doing theology which takes context and Jesus' teaching about the necessity of reading the signs of the times seriously (Luke 12:54–56) was given official blessing during the Second Vatican Council and has continued to influence enormously the way theology, especially local theology, is done.

Sometimes called the *theology of the signs of the times*, the method has a different starting point, and uses a different process from traditional theology.[16] Within the Council its major impact can be seen on *Gaudium et Spes* (*Pastoral Constitution on the Church in the Modern World*). In *Gaudium et Spes* attention is being given to this new way of doing theology because its impact has been significant in the development of the Church's understanding of its mission at both global and local levels. Other types of contextual theology followed suit in the period after the Council, generally focusing on more specific contexts than that of *Gaudium et Spes*, which was global in focus.

The nature of this new theological methodology is well set out in the introduction to *Gaudium et Spes* (#4):

> In every age, the church carries the responsibility of reading the signs of the times and of interpreting them in the light of the Gospel, if it is to carry out its task. In language intelligible to every generation, it should be able to answer the ever recurring questions which people ask about the meaning of this present life and of the life to come, and how one is related to the other. We must be aware of and understand the aspirations, the yearnings, and the often dramatic features of the world in which we live...[17]

The document then goes on to enumerate and discuss a whole variety of such "signs of the times" and the effects which they are having socially, culturally and religiously.

Theological method is closely tied to theological vision. As we have endeavoured to point out, vision is something that is imaginatively created and re-created in the light of a fresh discernment of the circumstances of the community and of its environment. During the Second Vatican Council such discernment was taken very seriously, with a special sub-commission established to work on what was then termed "the signs of the time".[18]

The discernment process follows a series of steps:

- **Sociological Exploration** The major phenomena affecting society are identified and available data assessed, often with the help of professional expertise.

- **Anthropological Exploration** The question is asked: how are these phenomena impacting on what it means to be human?

---

[16] Bernard Haring *Evangelization Today* (Middlegreen Slough: St Paul Publications, 1990), 6–21.
[17] Austin Flannery, ed., *Vatican Council II* (Northport New York: Costello Publishing Company, 1996), 165.
[18] See:http://www.vatican.va/jubilee_2000/magazine/documents/ju_mag_01051997_p-28_en.html for Pope John Paul II's recollections of his own membership of this sub-commission.

- **Theological Exploration** The faith community attempts to discern in the light of scripture and the broader range of Christian experience how, through particular experiences, God's Kingdom is being made present on earth.[19]

This new theological method was used by Pope Paul VI in some of the influential documents he wrote subsequent to the Council, for example, the encyclical *Populorum Progressio* (*On the Development of Peoples*, 1967) which was a Catholic response to the first United Nations Development Decade. It was also used in the apostolic exhortation *Justice in the World* issued from the 1971 synod and more recently in Pope Benedict XVI's social encyclical *Caritas in Veritate (Charity in Truth*, 2009*)*. It has also been used in the development of many local mission theologies.

Of particular interest to educators is its use in the 1997 document on Catholic education produced by the Congregation for Catholic Education, *Catholic Schools on the Threshold of the New Millennium*.[20] This document sets out in some detail elements of the socio-cultural environment affecting students in Catholic schools in our time, before addressing what this environment demands of Catholic schools as they seek to respond in mission. As the Congregation for Catholic Education teaches very clearly in this document, a school community engaged in a "signs of the times" theology seeks to be a discerning, saving community. This means it has, or seeks to develop, its own grassroots theology of mission.

In using a signs of the times theological method, *the community acknowledges God's Spirit at work in the world, as well as within the Church itself*. It is therefore a theology that tends to project the faith community towards a respectful and collaborative relationship with other churches, other faiths, and the broader society. This relationship involves various forms of dialogue.

The community seeks to remain open to the Spirit who helps the community unmask false ideals and ideologies both personal and collective. Given that Christians, like their Jewish forebears in the faith, believe that God reveals Godself within human history, the importance of what is termed here the signs of the times methodology can scarcely be over-estimated. It is vital in developing an understanding of mission in the local context – the goal of grassroots missiology.

---

[19] A particularly insightful lecture on this methodology by Catalino Arevalo S.J. entitled *On the Theology of the Signs of the Times* was delivered to the Catholic Broadcasters and Catechists of the Christian Communities Program, Baguio City, Philippines, February 16, 1972. Unpublished source material.

[20] Congregation for Catholic Education *The Catholic School on the Threshold of the Third Millennium* (1997).

Traditional Understandings of Mission

The word "mission" comes from the Latin work "mittere" meaning "to send" so it means literally "what one is sent to do". In general English usage "mission" equates with purpose. This is the meaning used, for example, in regard to organisations and is frequently heard in connection with mission statements particularly of service organisations. In Christian communities "mission" also has to do with purpose, purpose being understood as continuance of Jesus' mission in the world.

This purpose has been construed in modern times to mean bringing the Gospel to people who have not yet heard it and, in consequence, establishing the Church firstly as a faith community and later as parishes and dioceses. In this way national churches have been established across the globe, each with its own variant of Catholic culture and associated identity. Catholic schools were integral to the modern "church-building" phase of mission.

From apostolic times onwards such missionary initiatives came to carry, in due course, the official sanction of the Church. If one were to ask "who is responsible for mission?" the answer was "the Church". In a word, the Church "owned" mission in the religious sense.

A New Understanding of Mission

Beginning in the 1920s and developing through the decades to the Second Vatican Council (1962–65), a renewed and deeper understanding of mission began to emerge and gain acceptance. This understanding continues to open up new imaginal possibilities when many of the issues now before Catholic educators are considered in its light.

The key to this new understanding is a return to the original truth about mission. *Mission is located in the life of God*, a life of overflowing love. Given that through baptism Christians enter into God's life, they also begin to share in God's creative will or purpose for humankind. Jesus and his mission carry forward God's mission or purpose in the world in a unique and definitive way. Christians, in their turn, are mandated to carry out Christ's mission by virtue of their baptism. The key insight of the Second Vatican Council was that *the Church, as the community of Christians, is missionary, not as a matter of strategy, but by its very nature* (c.f. *Ad Gentes* 2).

The changed realisation, common across the Catholic Church and many Protestant Churches is that the order contained within the statement *"God's Church has a mission"* is wrong. The order, and perspective, should be *"God's mission has a Church"* because primacy rests with God's mission or purpose and not with the Church.[21] The Church is a principal, though not exclusive, means by which God achieves God's purpose in the world. God's mission predates the Church and continues to take place on a canvas much more extensive than the Church. The Church is intentionally, indeed of its very nature, at the disposal of God's mission.

This change in understanding has major significance not only for how Catholics think about mission, but also how they think about themselves and others in relation to mission. It affects how they view matters such as ecumenism, inter-religious dialogue, work for justice and peace, the place of religion in a secular society, reconciliation, and engagement with the modern world, to name but a few. While the change was recognised officially in the documentation of the Second Vatican Council, a change we will chart in some detail in Chapter Ten, the major developments in thinking have occurred in the period since the Council. The educational implications of these advances in our understanding of mission are still to be explored fully.

Missiology Anchors Theology

The change in perspective described above arose as a consequence of theological reflection on the experience of mission throughout the twentieth century. This reflection involved a re-appropriation of the Christian tradition about the Trinity, the nature of God revealed in Jesus, and the Spirit at work in our world. Because mission is what God does, and cannot be thought of exclusively as what the Church does, this has an important bearing on key questions about the Church's mission and its effectiveness in carrying out this mission. From the perspective of schools it has a bearing on who can become engaged in the mission of the school and how this is to be done.

The changed understanding of mission and the imaginal possibilities it opens up also have implications for the formal study of theology and for all forms of ministry, including education. Connolly[22] argues, correctly in our view, that the theology of mission should have a more central and integrating place in theological education. Others, among them Bevans[23] and Oborji[24] share this view. Change, however, is occurring slowly. In Catholic teaching institutions missiology, as the multi-disciplinary study of mission, has in recent years begun to be relocated from the theological periphery. In the past missiology has been regarded as an aspect of applied theology, whereas today its significance is being re-conceptualised. Mission, understood as God's mission, and its associated study of missiology is being recognised as the integrating principle

---

[21] See for example the discussion in Roger Schroeder *What is the Mission of the Church?* (Maryknoll New York: Orbis, 2008), 15.

[22] Noel Connolly "Mission Mother of the Church and of Theology" in *Compass* (Vol. 40: No. 1, 2006).

[23] Stephen Bevans 2005, 13–30.

[24] Francis Oborji "The missionary role of missiology in theological education" in Omnis Terra (Vol. 344: 2004), 55–68.

for the whole of theological studies.

New Perspectives on Mission in School Education

While the transformation of perspective outlined above has been worked through at many levels in the Church, its impact in educational circles seems quite limited. At the time of the Second Vatican Council, the Catholic school was a taken-for-granted institution in most western countries, one that commanded very little attention in Rome. Consequently, there was little produced by way of normative documentation. No formal statement of principles had been made since Pius XI's encyclical on Christian Education in 1929 (*Divini Illius Magistri*), so there was considerable ground to be covered, particularly given the changed stance key Council documents took concerning the Church in the modern world.

In the years following the Council, Catholic schools found themselves becoming the focus of frustration as a long-standing Catholic culture began to unravel. Leaders were required to deal with twin challenges – to *teach* students in a way consistent with the principles and perspectives of the Second Vatican Council, which were still only partially grasped, while a major battle raged within the Church over the actual meaning of the Council's documents; and to *negotiate* the very significant change from systems of schools led and staffed by religious to systems lead and staffed by lay people.

History records that the educational leaders of the time generally dealt with these challenges effectively, so that support for Catholic schools continues strongly, but at a price. Whereas at the beginning of the era Catholic schools functioned effectively as an integral part of a strong Catholic culture, socialising young people into the life of a Church in which their parents and siblings were already members, by the end of the 1980s and for a range of reasons, this socialising role had largely dissipated.

Questions were therefore asked about the effectiveness of Catholic schools once they could no longer play their traditional role in stabilising a Catholic cultural world that was quickly disappearing. The grief that people felt at the demise of this long cherished culture was, in part, directed at the schools and the new group of people leading them. School leaders found powerful support during this era from their bishops.

If in the period prior to the Second Vatican Council there had been a dearth of official commentary on the Catholic school, the situation changed in the decades after the Council with several documents published, beginning in 1977 with *The Catholic School*. By this means the Vatican Congregation for Catholic Education sought to affirm the work of the schools and the people who lead them.

This commentary, while welcomed by school leaders, was largely written from within a framework that continued to interpret Catholic education quite narrowly. Schools continued to be envisaged predominantly as a vehicle for the Church's mission, rather than from within the broader framework of God's mission as envisaged in the Council's *Declaration on Christian Education* (*Gravissimum Educationis* 1965). This document departed significantly from the 1929 papal document in that it interprets the Church's role in education in terms of *the intrinsic value of education in affirming the dignity of the human person*, a goal that it sees is often achieved in collaboration with others who share this commitment.[25]

Meaning-making and the Missiological Imagination

Just as the understanding of the nature of mission has its implications for theological education, it also has implications for meaning-making in the current context in which Catholic schools operate. Many teachers have an intuitive sense that there is currently a significant point of difference between the demands of mission as they experience them and the expectations of the worshipping communities that sponsor the schools. This is especially so as many worshipping communities remain confused about their own fundamental identity and purpose. The mission of the parish, for instance, is often so taken for granted that it is rarely articulated. This sometimes makes it difficult for parishes to interact constructively with other Church bodies if and when these bodies have a clearer conception of mission both in the broader sense of purpose and in the sense of a specific interpretation of the Church's role in carrying out Jesus' mission in the world and their place within it.

The situation in some parishes continues to reflect the limited imaginal horizon that characterised a disappearing Catholic culture. Members of these communities find themselves prisoners of their imaginal horizon, one which offers an inadequate vision for a future already breaking in upon them and which presents challenges that now need to be addressed. Understanding mission as God's mission is important at the imaginal level.

God pursues God's mission both within and outside the Church Community. However, the mission remains the same – the realization of God's dream for humanity, the project which was central to Jesus' life and mission, and which he described by using the metaphor "the Kingdom of God". Such an understanding of mission makes it possible to find *common cause with others* across indifference, hurt, lack of understanding, differing cultural and religious beliefs, and the many other barriers which divide people. This

---

[25] Cf. *Declaration on Christian Education* (*Gravissimus Educationis* #3, 1965) in Austin Flannery (ed.) *Vatican Council II* (Northport New York: Costello Publishing Company, 1996), 578–579.

understanding of God's mission also underpins all forms of dialogue that can be undertaken in the confident knowledge that it is God's Spirit who acts to effect God's purpose.

Understanding mission in this way expands the imaginal horizon, opening up new possibilities for leaders to engage members of the school community in the school's core tasks. This is why we claim that a missiological imagination is indispensable for effective leadership in Catholic schools today. It enables new perspectives on mission to be translated into *the language and practice* of school communities in a way that builds energy and a sense of common cause. It liberates the energy that flows from hopes that are shared.

How does the leader develop a missiological imagination, one that can help construct a grassroots theology and build hope within a school community? Put more simply, how does one do grassroots theology? This is the question to which we now turn. We look at how the process of theological reflection has developed across the past three decades and then propose a model for reflection capable of being used in a wide variety of contexts. On this basis we conclude by identifying key understandings for leadership in mission.

CHAPTER THREE

Doing Grassroots Theology

The development of a missiological imagination is a goal of leadership which needs to be pursued purposefully. A key question in this regard is how do you expand your imaginal horizon? Central to the task is a search for *insight*, that is, finding a vantage point from which it is possible to make sense of things in a new way.

Search for Insight

Most leaders and educators seek insight because they wish to channel the energy generated by local aspiration. Howard Gardner suggests one way in which this can happen:

> The transformational leader creates a compelling narrative about the missions of her organization…; embodies that narrative in her own life; and is able, through persuasion and personal example, to change the thoughts, feelings and behaviours of those whom she seeks to lead.[26]

How do you create this compelling narrative? Are there other options that channel the energy generated by local aspiration? How do you raise the level of local aspiration in the first place? These are important questions for both school leaders and for educators seeking to inspire their charges. Responding to them requires both imagination and effort.

The aspiration the Church has for its schools is that, for all members of the school community, there needs to be an integration of faith and life and of faith and culture.[27] However, for most teachers the routine work of teaching is taken up by a lesser form of integration – the integration of life and culture that often proceeds outside the realm of faith and which is increasingly dictated by the intrusion of government agendas shaping not only what is taught in schools, but also how this is done. A secular orientation stands as both the default option and locus of organisational drift in Catholic schools unless leaders are proactive in addressing issues of purpose.

The pressure for compliance in education, a move often driven by public policy settings, can choke local aspiration. As governments seek increasing levels of accountability in education, outcomes are often shaped not by the needs of students or by the nature of education, but by national economic and

---

[26] Howard Gardner *Five Minds for the Future* (Boston: Harvard Business Press, 2008).
[27] Congregation for Catholic Education *The Catholic School* #44 (Homebush: Society of St Paul, 1977), 36.

political agendas. This pressure for compliance is embedded in the progressive articulation of demands in the form of professional requirements. In such an atmosphere education easily becomes the victim of political ideology. Catholic school leaders and educators sense the need to resist the impact of this essentially secular ideology. But how?

School leaders and educators seeking to tap the energy contained in local aspiration – that hope for students and society which underpins why teachers do what they do – also have to deal with limitations in both the faith community and the culture in which this community educates. This raises questions such as what is going on in our society? How do people experience their lives today? How is this experience shaping the attitudes that students, teachers and parents have about what the school stands for and what its mission should be? What is positive and what is negative in this situation?

Questions such as these are best addressed systematically. They suggest the need for a suitable model to enable systematic critical reflection on issues of concern, a model which can generate genuine insight into, and make sense of, how people feel and what they think. Teachers and leaders often ask: *is there a suitable model for critical reflection on mission and its associated challenges – one capable of generating the level of insight needed to assist us in feeling more confident in meeting those challenges?*

While there is wide agreement on the need for theological reflection as a means of "reading the signs of the times" with sensitivity and thoroughness, there is no simple answer to the above question. Several influential writers have dealt with the topic, and an emerging consensus draws a distinction between *model* and *process*, between the "what" and the "how" of critical reflection on mission issues.

Two strands of development converge on this issue. The first began in the 1980s with the work of seminal figures such as Thomas Groome,[28] James and Evelyn Whitehead,[29] and Patricia O'Connell Killen and John de Beer.[30] The efforts of these writers were largely directed to the work of lay people in pastoral ministry. A second strand arose from within professional theology. Beginning at about the same time, theologians such as Stephen Bevans,[31] Lode Wostyn, Joe De Mesa[32] and Robert Schreiter,[33] among many others, drew attention to

---

[28] Tom Groome *Christian Religious Education: Sharing Our Story and Vision* (Melbourne: Dove Communications, 1980).

[29] James and Evelyn Whitehead *Method in Ministry* (New York: The Seabury Press, 1980). A revised and updated edition was published by Sheed and Ward, Oxford, 1995.

[30] Patricia O'Connell Killen and John de Beer *The Art of Theological Reflection* (New York: Crossroads, 1994).

[31] Stephen Bevans *Models of Contextual Theology* (Maryknoll New York: Orbis, 2002).

[32] Lode Wostyn and Joe De Mesa *Doing Ecclesiology* (Quezon City: Claretian Publications, 1990).

the fact that theology *is contextual and local before it is universal*. Their efforts reclaimed an aspect of our religious tradition that had been largely lost – the value, purpose and benefit of what we have called grassroots theology. In more recent times Clemens Sedmak[34] has synthesised much of the work done by these two groups of theologians, rendering it readily accessible to educators.

In order to identify the "what" and the "how" of grassroots theology in the context of recent developments, we now briefly review the seminal work referred to above. From this review it is possible to identify with some confidence the elements of a model and options in a workable process. We do so from a missiological perspective, one which of its nature is multi-disciplinary, bringing to the interpretation of human experience the meaning-making frameworks of our religious tradition and our culture.

Thomas Groome and Shared Christian Praxis

The concept of *critical reflection* became a dominant theme in education in the 1980s under the influence of critical theorists such as Habermas, and through the work of the Brazilian educator Paulo Freire. The aim of critical reflection was "action upon the world in order to transform it".[35] Critical reflection was seen as a means to emancipation from that which oppresses people. Freire's work on literacy among Brazil's poor was so effective in transforming their situation that he was regarded as subversive and forced to flee the country.

Groome placed critical reflection at the core of Catholic education. In his view,[36] the mission of the Catholic educator is to enable those being educated to name their world and, through dialogue, come to understand it and engage creatively with it. Critical reflection, in Groome's sense, is a *process of knowing* carried out in a community. It begins with concrete historical experience and leads to action capable of changing that experience. The process is cyclical in that action leads to further experience from which more learning can be derived.

Groome developed the theory and methodology of "shared Christian praxis" initially as a basis for Christian Religious Education. However, his methodology had a much wider application. It provides a sound basis for doing grassroots theology and is dealt with in some detail below. There are five "moments" in Groome's process of critical reflection.

The first three are:

1. **Naming the present in a non-evaluative way** The first phase seeks to name present experiences: the "who", "what", "where",

[33] Robert Schreiter *Constructing Local Theologies* (Maryknoll New York: Orbis, 1985).
[34] Clemens Sedmak *Doing Local Theology* (Maryknoll New York: Orbis, 2002).
[35] Paulo Freire *Pedagogy of the Oppressed* (London: The Continuum Press, 1970), 36.
[36] Groome, 176.

"how", and "when".

2. **Reflecting critically on present experience and seeing it in its narrative context** Critical reflection involves the use of *reason* to evaluate the past, *memory* to assess the impact of the past on the present, and *imagination* to recognise the limitations constraining present actions, and to see the opportunities that may exist if one moves beyond the current frame of reference. In Groome's approach critical reflection is a matter of both *the heart and the head*.

3. **Engaging in dialogue with the community** Any action proceeding from critical reflection needs to be the work of the community. *Dialogue is a means by which a sense of community is developed*. In dialogue people become aware of, open to, and see value in, the experience of others. Through dialogue the possibilities and parameters of transformation can be identified. Dialogue is about listening and being heard.[37] To this point there is nothing particularly Christian about the process. In the context of a Catholic school, however, it is virtually impossible to name present experience, recount the community's stories, or imagine the future, without in some way touching on aspects of the religious tradition, so closely is this woven into the fabric of all that happens. The two further "moments" in the critical reflection process tap into this reality.

4. **Situating present experience within the faith tradition and story** The local community does not exist in isolation, but as part of the broader Christian community, which in Groome's words "has made a pilgrimage through history". The *narrative* of this pilgrimage has to be remembered, retold, and in a certain respect re-lived, by each successive generation. The narrative underpins and in a sense guarantees the practices and attitudes that shape our religious identity. *How individuals in the community view this tradition is a major determinant of future action*. It determines whether or not a course of action is seen as continuing the trajectory of the Christian story begun in the mission, teaching and person of Jesus, that is ,whether or not the action has a mission dimension.

---

[37] Dialogue in Groome's work refers to discussion. We use the term in a much broader sense later when we refer to "dialogue" as a modality of evangelisation (see Chapter Ten).

5. **Developing the local vision and translating it into action**
   In Groome's view, the Christian tradition and story are never neutral; *they demand that a response be made* in the context of new issues and challenges.

Groome's understanding of theological reflection places considerable emphasis on acknowledging present human experience, and seeing it within its narrative context. This enables the present to be judged against values that have currency within the community, the authenticity of which is determined, not by ideology, but by reference to a lived narrative. However, the process does not rest there; it also seeks to critique those values in the light of the Christian narrative and its mission imperatives. In this way local vision is developed that is capable of guiding action. Groome's five-step process has a strong basis in critical theory and provides an important entrée into doing grassroots theology from a mission perspective, one that has stood the test of time.

The Whiteheads and *Method in Ministry*

In the year following the publication of Groome's *Christian Religious Education*, James and Evelyn Whitehead published their seminal work on theological reflection in Christian ministry, *Method in Ministry*. The Whiteheads approached the task of theological reflection from the perspective of pastoral ministry. Their aim in outlining both a *model* and a *method* of theological reflection was to bring the resources of faith to bear on reflection in the various areas of Christian ministry in such a way as to have an impact on *practical decision-making*. While they acknowledged that theological reflection is not new, they saw that the situations in which pastoral decisions had to be made were becoming increasingly complex.

> This exciting but often bewildering complexity in contemporary Christian life heightens the need for a method of reflection: a systematic way to approach the various sources of religious information, one that leads not to theoretical insight, but to pastoral decision. Christian ministry today requires a method of reflection that is at once theological and practical. As theological, it must attend confidently and competently to the resources of Scripture and the historical Tradition. As practical, it must be more than theoretically sound; it must be able to assist a wide range of ministers in their efforts to reflect and act in complex pastoral contexts. This method must be sufficiently clear and concrete that it can actually be used by persons and groups in ministry. And it must be focussed on action…[38]

Their model identifies the sources of information that need to be considered in systematic theological reflection leading to pastoral action. Their method

---
[38] Whitehead and Whitehead, 2.

indicates how this information can be brought to bear on pastoral decisions. In developing their model the Whiteheads identify three important sources – *Christian tradition, human experience and cultural information*.

In considering the *Christian tradition*, the Whiteheads highlight the continuing, formative presence of the Spirit in the Church.[39] Hence they understand the Christian tradition as a living tradition, the outcome of a traditioning process that is dynamic and ongoing, and which, of its nature, is conditioned by exigencies of time and place. Their model also emphasises the pluriform nature of this tradition. In commenting on this they note:

> This level of pluriformity, so familiar to the professional theologian, remains a scandal for many believers and a source of confusion for many ministers. The method of reflection we discuss here assumes an understanding of Christian pluralism, not only as a scandal and sign of disunity (which it has been), but also as a sign of richness.[40]

The attitudes and feelings people bring to considering their religious tradition have an important bearing on the weight they give it in deciding on courses of action. For many Catholics, the Whiteheads note, there is a "pervasive sense of distance" from their religious tradition. What they see as needed is a means of "befriending the tradition".[41] By this they mean humanising it – developing greater appreciation of how the tradition reflects the strengths and weaknesses of the people who, under God's mysterious direction, have brought it to its present state of development.

The third element the Whiteheads stress is that the tradition exists not only in scripture and Church teaching but also *in the life of the believing community*. In Catholic theology this is known as the *sensus fidelium* – an active and intuitive sense among believers of what is to be believed, which often comes to expression in quite different ways in different communities. It is recognised as a manifestation of the Spirit at work in the people of God.[42]

In referring to *human experience* as a pole in theological reflection, the Whiteheads mean the personal experience of the minister and the collective experience of the community. This experience has two dimensions: how things are experienced in the here and now, and how present experiences relate to the narrative of the community. Is there continuity or is there dissonance?

Cultural information refers to the fact that pastoral decisions are made in the context of the assumptions of Western culture and have application within the particular culture of a community. Western culture provides a formidable

---

[39] Ibid, 14.
[40] Ibid, 15.
[41] Ibid, 16.
[42] Ibid, 18–19.

array of resources in terms of intellectual disciplines for analysing situations and experiences. How are these resources to be accessed and used? If decisions made as a result of theological reflection are to lead to effective action, there needs to be a degree of cultural fit in the local context. How is this to be accomplished if culture is not included in the reflection process?

In terms of process, the Whiteheads opt for a version of the "see, judge, act" methodology developed by Cardinal Cardijn and used by the Young Christian Workers' movement over several decades. This method continues to be widely valued as a tool of personal and communal formation and as a method of discernment which delivers insight.

While Groome was the first to understand and articulate an understanding of theological reflection as a *learning process,* the strength of the Whiteheads' work is their analysis of the *sources* that must be attended to if pastoral decision-making is to be effective.

Killen and de Beer – *The Art of Theological Reflection*

The pioneering work of the Whiteheads is taken a step further by Patricia O'Connell Killen and John de Beer in the early 1990s. They adopt the model used by the Whiteheads – seeing the three poles of theological reflection as human experience, culture and religious tradition – but develop an alternative process. In doing so they point out that many Christian denominations, among them Catholic, have historically been reluctant *to give due weight to human experience* as a pole in theological reflection, and seek to redress this deficiency.[43]

Killen and de Beer provide a descriptive definition of theological reflection which is helpful.

> Theological reflection is the discipline of exploring individual and corporate experience in conversation with the wisdom of a religious heritage. The conversation is a genuine dialogue that seeks to hear from our own beliefs, actions and perspectives as well as those of the tradition. It respects the integrity of both. Theological reflection may confirm, challenge, clarify and expand how we understand our own experience and how we understand the religious tradition. The outcome is new truth and meaning for living.[44]

For Killen and de Beer the movement towards insight and practical action is the same in theological reflection as it is in the normal process of coming to wisdom. Here they are in agreement with Groome.

Re-iterating a point made by the Whiteheads, Killen and de Beer warn

---

[43] Killen and de Beer, ix.
[44] Ibid., viii. While the pole of culture is not explicit in this definition, it is implied.

that the attitude people bring to theological reflection shapes the quality of the outcome, and here they identify two extremes. The first is the *attitude of certitude*, where the pole of scripture and tradition is over-emphasised to such an extent that the pole of human experience is given little or no authority.[45] This attitude can easily lead to a fundamentalist position that makes any form of dialogue impossible. The second extreme is an *attitude of self-assurance*, which gives so much authority to human experience that it tends to discount scripture and tradition as being largely irrelevant. Between these poles they identify a third position, an *attitude of exploration*. This respects the authority of scripture and tradition on the one hand, and human experience (including culture) on the other. This stance seeks to balance competing claims and bring them into dialogue.

As well as attitude, *readiness* has a part to play in grassroots theology. Members of the school community are often characterised by their underdeveloped familiarity with scripture, or by some degree of alienation from the religious tradition. Many lack appreciation of the strengths and limitations of their local culture, and so fail to understand the impact that its deficiencies can have on how people customarily think and react. A good deal of preparatory work has to be done to address these matters if people are to engage effectively in any form of critical reflection, including grassroots theology.

Writing in the context of a new millennium Killen and de Beer see special urgency in the need for theological reflection.

> Today, living on the verge of a new millennium and faced with personal, social, geopolitical and environmental choices and challenges not even imagined thirty years ago, let alone a hundred years ago, the consequences of our reflections on questions of meaning and value are momentous. The choices we make about how to live have significant impact not only on ourselves but for future generations and the planet on which we walk. Because so much is at stake we need to pay attention to the character and quality of our reflective processes.
>
> Traditionally human beings asked questions of meaning and value in relationship to a religious tradition: for Christians, their Christian religious tradition. Today our pluralistic situation and the political and communal activities of certain Christian groups raise an additional question: Does the Christian tradition have anything to offer in finding answers? Is Christianity a viable wisdom tradition as the twenty-first century dawns?[46]

When it comes to *process* Killen and de Beer suggest that the normal process of reflection proceeds in four "moments":

---
[45] Ibid., 4–9.
[46] Ibid., 2.

- when we enter into our experience, we encounter how we feel
- when we pay attention to how we feel, images arise[47]
- when we consider and question our images, insight is sparked
- insight leads, if we are willing and ready, to action.[48]

The critical element here is getting in touch with *how we feel*, acknowledging that this as an important source for theological reflection. In opening his book *Doing Ecclesiology*, Wostyn gives a good example of this.

> Meaningful theologising can never be insulated from the vicissitudes of life. Let me therefore introduce the exciting process of doing ecclesiology by stating that I am angry. Yes I am an angry theologian…I am a theologian who experiences indignation and sadness because I believe that twenty-five years after Vatican II our Church is on a restoration course…I feel anger and sadness because we are on a restoration course…which will lead us nowhere.[49]

There is no particular problem in feeling the way we do. The issue is what do we do about it. In writing his book Wostyn directed the energy which his angst released to good effect!

In developing their process for theological reflection Killen and de Beer match the four "moments" in the more general process of seeking wisdom outlined above to four "moments" in theological reflection. They see theological reflection as the communal extension of the process by which we come to personal wisdom. Their four moments are:

- *focusing* on some contested aspect of communal experience and entering into this experience
- *describing that experience in non-judgmental ways*, thus seeking to identify the *heart of the matter*[50]
- *exploring the heart of the matter* in conversation with the wisdom of the Christian heritage
- *identifying* from this conversation *new truths and meanings for living*.[51]

Getting to the "heart of the matter" and understanding it are the keys to effective action. Often the heart of the matter is not the presenting issue, rather the assumptions from which we work in assessing what we think is the heart of the matter. It is very helpful in exploring the heart of the matter to test whether

---

[47] The question here is why do these particular images arise for me? What is their significance?
[48] Ibid., 21.
[49] Lode Wostyn *Doing Ecclesiology* (Quezon City: Claretian Press, 1990), 1.
[50] At the "heart" of many contested communal experiences lies the necessity to re-balance the legitimate tensions that arise in pursuing competing goods. Such situations are very common in schools.
[51] Killen and de Beer, 74.

or not we are working from valid assumptions. In a context of complex change even long-held assumptions can lose their validity. Addressing the presenting issues effectively often means interpreting what is happening within a different framework, one built on more realistic assumptions.

Contextual Nature of Theology

The conversation among professional missiologists shifted in the 1980s and 1990s as an emphasis developed that saw theology more as a *process to be engaged in than a product to be consumed*. De Mesa and Wostyn reflect this changing emphasis and the active nature of theology in their books *Doing Theology* (1982),[52] *Doing Christology* (1989)[53] and *Doing Eccelesiology* (1990).[54] For these writers *theology is something that ordinary people can do in the context of their culture, and that it must make sense in that context.*

Missiologist Robert Schreiter[55] highlighted in the 1980s a second development which was occurring – a shift in theological perspective in regions where Christianity was relatively new, for example in Africa and Asia. This development sprang from "a growing concern that the theologies being inherited from the older churches of the North Atlantic community did not fit well into these quite different cultural circumstances".[56] He suggested that the reason for this shift had a number of sources. Firstly, new questions were being asked for which there were no ready traditional answers. Secondly, old answers were being imposed on new situations that left people in those situations feeling that their questions were not being taken seriously.

Schreiter discusses this situation in terms of the emergence of a new kind of Christian identity. In his view the theology behind this new identity has particular sensitivity to three areas: context, procedure and history.[57] Rather than imposing a universal theology on local contexts, the new approach was to develop a theology out of the context. The most obvious example of this process at work is the development of various theologies of liberation in South America. As the new approach developed momentum, it was realised that *people make meaning in different ways in different cultural contexts and this needs to be taken into account in doing theology*. What is appropriate in the North Atlantic may not be as appropriate in another cultural setting.

---

[52] Jose de Mesa and L. Wostyn, *Doing Theology: Basic Realities and Process*. (Manila: Maryhill School of Theology, 1982).

[53] Jose de Mesa and Lode Wostyn *Doing Christology: The Re-appropriation of a Tradition* 3rd Edition (Quezon City: Claretian Press, 1993).

[54] Wostyn, 1990.

[55] Robert Schreiter *Constructing Local Theologies* (Maryknoll New York: Orbis, 1985).

[56] Ibid., 1.

[57] Ibid., 3.

Finally, Schreiter points out that local theology created through such grassroots endeavours will reflect the *local narratives* which in turn will reflect the ambiguities of history. The transformation of the present therefore often requires a reconstruction of our understanding of the past.[58] That is, *we need to know our story*. This is not always the case in Catholic school communities.

Within the Christian tradition, all theology began as *local theology*. It therefore reflects in some way the different contexts in which it developed. This is why writers such as the Whiteheads can refer to the plural nature of the tradition, a point we take up in Chapter Eleven when dealing with scripture as a resource in theological reflection.

The issues that Schreiter notes as arising in Africa and Asia also began to surface in Western countries by the late 1980s and have become characteristics of the frontier experience of mission today. Some of the first people to notice this shift in religious sensibility in the West were missionaries newly returned home from cross-cultural situations and working in local ministry.[59]

By the early 1990s greater understanding had developed about the historical process through which the Christian tradition has evolved, together with greater appreciation of the impact culture has had in the development of this tradition. Two significant contributors here are mission historian Andrew Walls (1996)[60] and Church historian Justo Gonzalez (1999).[61] As a consequence of advances in biblical, missiological and historical studies, the notion that theological knowledge was somehow "universal" came under increased critique. This critique was not particular to theology, but part of a wider reaction to the tendency to view Western experience as normative of what it means to be human.[62] Missiologist Stephen Bevans could therefore begin his seminal study of the contextual nature of all theology with the provocative statement "There is no such thing as 'theology'; there is only contextual theology…".[63]

In commenting further on this theme he observes that

> contextual theology understands the nature of theology in a new way. Classical theology conceived theology as a kind of objective science of faith. It was understood as a reflection in faith on the two *loci theologici*

---

[58] Ibid., 4.
[59] For instance John Walsh *Evangelisation and Justice* (Maryknoll New York: Orbis, 1982), Vincent Donovan *The Church in the Midst of Creation* (Maryknoll New York: Orbis, 1989), Richard Cote *Re-visioning Mission* (New York: Paulist Press, 1996).
[60] Andrew Walls *The Missionary Movement in Christian History: Studies in the Transmission of Faith* (Maryknoll New York: Orbis, 1996).
[61] Justo Gonzalez *Christian Thought Revisited: Three Types of Theology* (Maryknoll New York: Orbis, 1999).
[62] See discussion in John Tomlinson *Globalisation and Culture* (Chicago: University of Chicago Press, 1999), 81–97.
[63] Bevans, 3.

(theological sources) of scripture and tradition, the content of which has not and never will be changed, and is above culture and historically conditioned expression. But what makes contextual theology precisely contextual is the recognition of the validity of another *locus theologicus*: present human experience. Theology that is contextual realizes that culture, history, contemporary thought forms, and so forth are to be considered along with scripture and tradition, as valid sources of theological expression. And so today, we speak of three sources or *loci theologici*: scripture, tradition, and present human experience – or context.[64]

There is a convergence here between the model of theological reflection developed to guide pastoral decision-making and the emerging understanding of contextual or local theology, thus putting the former on a firm theological base. As Bevans further observes:

As our cultural and historical context plays a part in the construction of the reality in which we live, so our context influences the understanding of God and the expression of our faith. The time is past when we can speak of one right unchanging theology, a *theologia perennis*. We can only speak about a theology that makes sense at a certain place and in a certain time. We can certainly learn from others…but the theology of others can never be our own.[65]

One of the principal attractions of grassroots theology is the need to help those engaged in mission develop a theology of mission which they can own. It is a characteristic of the frontier situation that this will happen first in the local context, if it is to happen at all!

Adding context (culture and narrative) to the sources in doing theology is not a matter of correcting a limitation in traditional theology; it changes the whole situation. It also draws attention to the fact that both scripture and tradition are themselves *the products of particular contexts* and have to be read and understood within those contexts.[66]

In the case of a school community there is a need for a *local theology* reflecting the local experience, culture and narrative, and expressed in a form that is meaningful for those involved.

Beginning in the 1980s two ideas have grown in importance and, taken together, represent important "signs of the times". The first is the idea that *theology is an active pursuit,* related to making sense of experience in the contexts in which we live, and not something done only by professionals. As

---

[64] Ibid., 3–4.
[65] Ibid., 4–5.
[66] Cf. Ulrich and Thompson "The Tradition as a Resource in Theological Reflection – Scripture and the Minister" in Whitehead and Whitehead, 33. Cf. also Bevans, 5.

Clemens Sedmak puts it, "theology is an invitation to wake up: to be mindful and attentive".[67] The second is the idea that *theology is a serious reflection on human experience and God's ongoing presence to that experience*. Those "doing theology" are really seeking to discern this presence as a source of empowerment in mission. Doing grassroots theology is not about technique; it is something far more substantive.

Doing Local Theology

Because grassroots theology is about meaning-making, it involves asking questions. Good theology implies that we ask the right questions, that is questions which prompt exploration into important areas of personal and/ or communal meaning. Many people teaching in Catholic schools seem ill-prepared for this task and have few expectations that it is a task for them.

Schreiter makes an important point when he notes that in most instances the "hard yards" of making sense of things generally falls to groups within the community that process and interpret the experience of the whole community.

In many instances it is helpful to make a distinction between the role of the whole community of faith, whose experience is the indispensable source of theology, and whose acceptance of a theology is an important guarantor of its authenticity, and the role of smaller groups within the community who actually give shape to that theology. In other words the role of the whole community is often one of raising questions, of providing the experience of having lived with those questions and struggled with different answers, and of recognizing which solutions are indeed genuine, authentic, and commensurate with their experience.

> …Significant members within the community, often working as a group, give voice to the theology of the community…[68]

However, Schreiter also points out that such meaning can never be imposed. To be authentic *it must be received by the community*. His comments provide some important guidelines in answering the question: who should be involved in grassroots theology at the school level?

Finally, Clemens Sedmak, in line with Bevans and Schreiter, suggests that grassroots theology involves rediscovering *the way Jesus did theology* and emulating it. With reference to the Gospels he argues that the way Jesus did theology can be set out as a number of theses. These can be summarised as follows:

- **Jesus did theology *with authority that was not his own***
  The basis of Jesus' theology was his relationship with God.

---

[67] Sedmak, 1.
[68] Schreiter, 17.

That is why he sought out spaces for prayer and solitude.
- **Jesus was doing theology *with common sense.*** He invited people to use their own judgment and trusted in the capabilities of human reasoning.
- **Jesus did *"situational theology"*** He had an eye for detail, the small things and the "little" people. Jesus used occasions to do theology and he respected the dynamics of particular situations.
- **Jesus did theology *to build up community*** He called everyone into community, a community that is constantly "on the move".
- **Jesus did theology *with self-respect and with respect for others*** He did theology "as if people matter". Healing and feeding, and forgiving and teaching formed a unity in Jesus' way of doing theology.
- **Jesus talked about the criteria for good theology** The most obvious of these is that of good fruit, but he also saw this fruit as coming from modest beginnings. Jesus did theology according to the criteria of *sustainability, appropriateness empowerment and challenge.*[69]

Jesus is presented in Sedmak's work as the grassroots theologian *par excellence.*

Revised Model for Doing Grassroots Theology

The strands of the discussion so far can be summarised as follows:
- There are three poles to a model of theological reflection: our human experience seen in its context, our cultural situation and our religious tradition.
- Human experience can be personal or collective. This experience never exists in isolation but as part of a narrative deriving meaning within a particular culture.
- Our religious tradition develops as new circumstances and new situations arise. It evolves over time. It is local before it becomes universal.
- Our culture frames both how we make meaning and what we think is possible. It is the least well understood of the three poles, partly because, as we shall see in the next chapter, much of culture lies out of our awareness.

[69] Sedmak, 25–42.

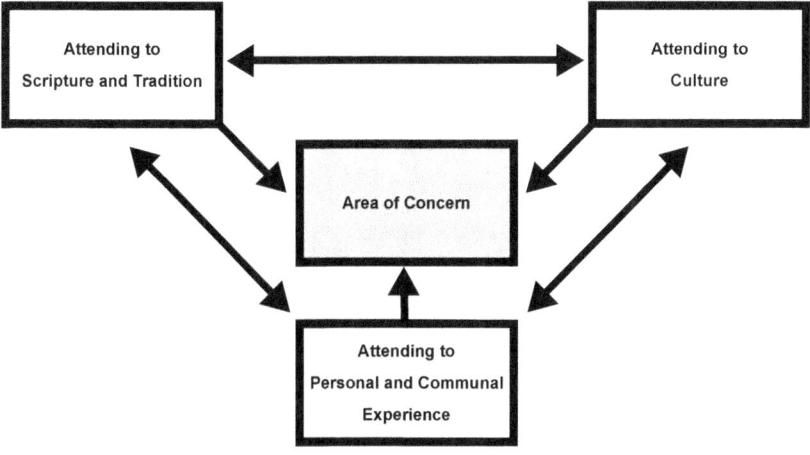

Figure 1 sets out these propositions schematically as a model.

Figure 1. Model for Theological Reflection

Grassroots theology seeks to create meaning or make sense of *specific issues* that arise in the life of a community. The principal purpose for engaging in grassroots theology is to build up and stabilise the identity of the community and re-affirm the value of its mission.

People engage in this form of theologising mainly when there is an area of concern that becomes the focus of attention. This issue usually presents itself in the form of personal or communal experience that challenges the status quo, or the values that are presumed to underpin the status quo. The pole of human experience covers not only how we experience the issue now, but also how the issue sits within the narrative of the community. This gives the issue a *context in time*. As a pole in theological reflection, culture requires that we use the tools that it puts at our disposal in understanding situations as well as exploring how the issue fits into our sense of "the way things are done around here" – the local culture of our organisation or community. Local cultures change over time as people change and attitudes evolve. This happens imperceptibly and is often a major source of the concerns that arise in schools. Our religious tradition, as the third pole in theological reflection, invites us to consider where the issue sits in relation to the Gospel and the narrative of the tradition itself. People often have fixed ideas which mask the nature of the tradition as a living tradition.

An effective process in grassroots theology enables us to uncover "the heart of the matter". Sometimes this is the group's inability to imagine new alternatives to culturally-framed positions. Sometimes it is a lack of appreciation of the history of the situation or perhaps of what the religious tradition actually requires of us in regard to the matter. Sometimes it is the complex nature of the issue itself. Most commonly, however, the heart of the matter is that the assumptions we hold, which we use to assess the issues, have lost their validity. Engaging with an issue from multiple perspectives generally generates new options for dealing with new questions. These options form the basis for *informed action*. To be helpful, the process of theological reflection needs to draw systematically on the three resources of theological reflection – human experience, culture and the religious tradition. It also needs to interrogate these resources effectively if it is to result in effective action. The action itself will generate a new round of experience, leading to a further cycle of reflection and action, hopefully built on greater insight into the situation and its missional demands.

Mission Theology as Local Theology

Doing grassroots theology is not new. It is reclaiming what has always been part of the Christian heritage in order to meet new situations and new needs. It has been a feature of Christian communities from the beginning. In the New Testament, for example, the writers of each of the four Gospels *did not write for a universal audience*; each wrote for particular communities faced with particular difficulties in local contexts. The work of modern scripture scholars has opened up new insights as those working with the scriptures come to understand more fully the contexts in which the books were written.`

Local or grassroots theology seeks to make the Kingdom of God, the core element in Jesus' mission, present in the here and now. The commitment to engage in mission has, therefore, to be realistic. It needs to flow from a belief that ordinary wounded people, when they join in community can, through the action of God's Spirit, rise above their sufferings, doubts, and shortcomings, to achieve goals that make God's Kingdom present. Woundedness is part of our collective story, something that has always to be acknowledged and addressed. It is also part of any compelling narrative of mission. Mission invites us to go beyond ourselves, to engage in heroic effort. However, it also invites us to deal with the reality of "this" Church without imposing an impossible ideal as a condition of actively participating in its mission.[70] The Spirit can handle imperfection!

Mission flows from hope and gives coherence to an agenda. The leader has

---

[70] Richard Lennan develops this theme well in *Risking the Church: The Challenges of Catholic Faith* (Oxford: Oxford University Press, 2004), 122ff.

constantly to keep in mind the advice of Peter (1 Peter 3:15) that we always need to be able to respond to people's questions about the hope that drives us on. When this hope is shared, it unifies a community. Mission involves sharing and sustaining the hope of all in the community. It is about knowing how to read "the signs of the times". Effective leaders and good educators look at the same reality as others, *but perceive it differently*. They see new or different possibilities and so can offer a basis for hope that enables the community to move beyond where it has been. If having a missiological imagination is the *sine qua non* for moving beyond the frontier, being able to "do theology" provides the essential skill for survival.

Catholics are far from alone in carrying on the mission of Jesus and thereby contributing to the coming of God's Reign or Kingdom. This becomes particularly clear to us when we join with others, both Christians and people of other faiths, in what Pope John Paul II called a "dialogue of life and action".[71] In charting our way forward on the new missional frontier, ecumenical and inter-faith dialogue are essential elements in pursuing God's mission. Not surprisingly, God's mission brings people together in a way few other aspects of Church life can.

In navigating on the frontier, Catholic school leaders and educators are sharing in the kind of experience that has been common to those working in cross-cultural mission. The study of missiology has gained in importance as people have come to realise that it now provides an essential scholarly scaffolding for those ministering in Western cultural situations. Educators have much to learn from contemporary missiology, the study of the mission of a Church community whose very reason for being is mission.

This chapter set out to explore the nature and process of theological reflection seeing it as an important tool in the meaning-making leaders are increasingly expected to provide. It has traced developments in the field across the last thirty years and, in the process, identified a model for understanding what theological reflection involves, as well as options for engaging in the process itself. It has also tried to place these developments within the context of broader developments in theology. The model illustrated in Figure 1 creates a framework for the rest of the book.

"Befriending" in Grassroots Theology

We conclude this chapter by noting as James and Evelyn Whitehead do that to do grassroots theology effectively, it is necessary to *befriend* our religious tradition, our culture and our human experiences. These are the human foundations from which God's Spirit launches God's mission. By "befriending" we mean "being

---

[71] John Paul II *Redemptoris Missio* #57 (1990).

at home with" as distinct from "being alienated from". Friendship can survive the disagreements and misunderstandings that arise from time to time!

Part B of the book explores two important aspects of our present context – culture and narrative. Culture provides a means of interpreting much of human experience *in the here and now*. This is both its strength and its limitation. Narrative on the other hand *exists across time and gives meaning to time* as well as to what people do within time. It represents the depth side of human experience. These two dimensions of what it means to be human must be considered together in "befriending culture" and as a way of "befriending human experience".

In subsequent chapters we will examine three of the major influences impacting on all cultures and narratives at the present time – globalisation, secularisation and pluralisation. In the light of this, we will then explore what it means to "befriend our religious tradition" as a *living* tradition, particularly its significance in the meaning-making processes in which leaders and educators engage with, and on behalf of, young people.

PART B

Befriending Culture – Befriending Human Experience

Culture plays an important part in meaning-making. It provides us with a cognitive framework as well as language, concepts and images. Within a given society, culture is shared and its form at any point in time is determined by the interplay of competing claims about "how things are done around here". There is a dynamic dimension to culture as groups within a society vie for dominance.

The word "culture" is used in a variety of ways and this leads to much confusion. Culture can refer to the great achievements of European art – ballet, music, literature and so on. It can refer to the way of life of a people such as in "Aboriginal culture" or "North American culture". Leadership programs increasingly talk of "organisational culture" and "cultural leadership". When football teams are performing badly the cause is often attributed to the "culture of the club". Again in educational discourse we hear references to "school culture", to a "culture of evidence", or a "culture of learning". Given its wide range of usages, the challenge is to determine what people mean when they refer to "culture".

In Chapter Four the aim is to provide some precision to the notion of "culture" so that when we propose that "culture" is a resource in grassroots theology, we know what we mean. The chapter explores in some depth the anthropological or "empirical" understanding of culture, often called simply the modern understanding of culture, and contrasts this with the "classicist" view.

Organisational theory employs the term "culture" by adapting the empirical understanding of culture and using it *metaphorically*. An organisation such as a school is thought of as if it were a culture. "Culture" can therefore be employed in a *macro sense* – referring to whole societies – or a *micro sense* – referring to units within society. The latter usage of the term proves useful in understanding some of the dynamics that operate in school communities, school systems or local churches. When using it in the micro sense, we refer metaphorically to what cultural anthropologists call "sub-cultures".

The term culture is also applied to the Church. People often refer to "Catholic culture". This can mean many things. In the macro sense, it can refer to universal characteristics shared across the global Catholic community. At a more limited level it may refer to the culture of the local Church such as the parish or diocese, or it can refer to the culture of groups within the Church as in "the culture of the clergy" or "the culture of the religious congregation".

Culture has become an important concept in theological discourse, first in relation to missions and more recently in relation to evangelisation. The term is used extensively, if somewhat ambiguously, in the Second Vatican Council's document *The Church and the Modern World (Gaudium et Spes)*. In more recent times it is used primarily in its anthropological sense. Official Church documents relating to Catholic education seem to retain the ambiguous usage of *Gaudium et Spes*, so that the term "culture" needs to be interpreted. When we say that Catholic education is about the integration of faith and culture and faith and life, what do we mean by "culture"? The implication here seems to be that there can be "life" without "culture". This would be a contradiction in terms.

In Chapter Four the aim is to explore the various meanings of culture before focusing on the significance of culture as an issue in evangelisation, and by implication, in Catholic education. Culture exists *in the here and now* shaping perceptions, the interpretation of events and so on. It is underpinned by a *worldview* that gives it both depth and coherence. This worldview has evolved over time and has to be conveyed to successive generations if the culture is to survive. This is achieved imaginatively by "telling the story" of the people. This story is referred to as the *narrative of a people*. Every people has its narrative, which unfolds in history, underpins its identity, and is a principal tool in meaning-making. Narrative is not the same as history. A people's narrative encompasses *both* historical facts and its highest aspirations.

The narrative structure for people living in Western cultures has them presently living in a *post-modern world*. This world is defined in relationship to the *modern world*. The modern world, in turn, is seen in relationship to the *pre-modern world*. This way of categorising recent history indicates the pivotal role the modern world plays in the development of our cultural consciousness. As we shall see, these "worlds" are not just points in history, they carry within themselves distinctive ways of perceiving reality and defining identity. Chapters Five and Six explore aspects of our contemporary period, and the transitions that have occurred within Western cultures in moving from the pre-modern world to the post-modern world. In this context they explore the various meanings attached to "post-modern" and the implications these meanings have for educators and leaders. These chapters provide important background for considering modern pluralism which is taken up further in Chapter Nine. Culture and narrative, when brought together, provide us with a way of understanding the *context* in which human experience unfolds.

CHAPTER FOUR

Culture as the Learning Place of the Faith Community[72]

Culture as a Resource in Theological Reflection

Attending to culture is one of the three poles of grassroots theology. However, this presents a difficulty in that our culture is like the air we breathe; *we are so immersed in it that much of it is out of our awareness.*

Cultural anthropologist Paul Hiebert[73] provides an interesting example of this phenomenon. He suggests that people living in Western cultures are conditioned to the belief that "floors are dirty places". As a result of this belief, they prefer not to sit on them, lie on them, sleep on them, and definitely not to eat on them. In consequence, their homes are full of beds, chairs, recliners, lounges and tables – all of which achieve the purpose of keeping them off the floor. A Japanese person, by way of contrast, coming from a culture that does not share this implicit cultural belief about floors, thinks the Western approach to household furniture excessive. *Culture illuminates our life, but it can also blind us.*

Culture shapes both what we see as important, and why we see it as important. Culture has a *macro* dimension which gives us access to the major interpretive frameworks developed by humans to explain and understand the world. It also has a *micro* dimension in that it shapes what we see as legitimate in responding to particular situations and particular contexts. Such is the nature of culture, however, that we are often unaware of when we encounter it. Understanding culture and its significance is, therefore, important to all forms of leadership. "Attending to" our culture is essential if we are to appreciate its power both as a resource and as a limiting factor in negotiating life on the frontier.

Conceptions of Culture

The word "culture" is often used in very imprecise ways and, as the literature of cultural anthropology makes clear, the concept is notoriously difficult to define. At its simplest level, culture is a *marker of identity*. It is something that members of a society share that distinguishes their society from others. It helps define "us" against "them". There are various ways of thinking about what this "something" is, and because of this, definitions of culture take a variety of

---

[72] The title of this chapter was inspired by an essay by Andrew Walls entitled "Culture and Coherence in Christian History" in *The Missionary Movement in Christian History: Studies in the Transmission of Faith* (Maryknoll New York: Orbis, 1996), 16–25.
[73] Paul Hiebert *Anthropological Insights for Missionaries* (Grand Rapids: Baker Book House, 1985), 43.

directions. What is undeniable is that culture both includes and excludes.

Religion provides an interpretive framework and is an element of most cultures. Faith is an essential component of only some religions, so the relationship between faith and culture is complex. The mission narrative of the Catholic Church reflects this complex relationship between faith and culture on the one hand, and religion and culture on the other. As Osborne points out, there is an inherent tension in Catholicism between claims to be supra-cultural and the need to understand and express its central messages within the confines of particular cultures.[74]

Persons do not exist in the abstract. To be human is to be a *person-in-culture*, as this is the only form of existence there is. Furthermore, each human grouping has a right to its own culture.[75] Cultures are wholes that encompass a way of life. They do not exist as collections of parts thrown together that can easily be tampered with. At the same time, as a human construct, culture has its inherent limitations and, like the humans who construct it, is capable of renewal and development. Another way of saying this is that cultures, too, are subject to the salvific grace of God.

Culture shapes how we, as individuals and as members of society, understand the world and the rules, written and unwritten, that enable people in society to live together more or less harmoniously. Culture shapes what we think is "proper" in terms of thought, speech and behaviour. Culture also sets the opportunities and constraints within which we express how we feel, think, imagine and act. This means that there will be profound links between culture and faith, particularly with respect to how faith is understood, appropriated and acted upon.

As noted in the introduction to Part B, "culture" has become a fashionable concept and is often used imprecisely. This leads to much confusion. It is therefore necessary to clarify the meaning of the term, to the extent that this is possible.

Classicist View of Culture

In considering the meaning of culture, the basic distinction between what Shorter calls the "classicist" and the "empirical" views of culture needs to be understood.[76] The classicist view links culture to the notion of "civilisation". The notion of civilisation persisted in European/Western thinking from Roman

---

[74] For discussion of these see Kenan Osborne *Orders and Ministry: Leadership in the World Church* (Maryknoll New York: Orbis, 2005), 28.

[75] Expatriate missionaries often find themselves at the forefront of the struggle to defend the right of indigenous people to their culture in the face of various forms of cultural oppression.

[76] Aylward Shorter *Toward a Theology of Inculturation* (London: Geoffrey Chapman, 1988), 17–23.

times till the end of the Age of Empires. In the classicist view, the world is divided into two groups – those who are "civilised" and those who are not, the latter being variously known as "barbarians", "savages", "aborigines", "primitives" and so on. To the classicist mindset as it came to exist in the West, "civilisation" was synonymous with the trappings and forms of the culture adopted by European/Western elites.

"Culture" is thus associated with the way a privileged group of people understand and organise the world, and is seen as superior to the way others do it. Of course, such an ethnocentric view of the world is not unique to the West, as even a limited study of the history of either China or Japan readily reveals. In the broader context of history, who are the "civilised" and who are the "barbarians" is very much a matter of perception.

The classicist view of culture views the dominant culture as an ideal to which all other peoples should strive. In the West, this "high" culture became synonymous with the best expressions of European culture, whether in the arts, sciences, literature, government, music, religion and so on. The "white man's burden" in the Age of Empires was interpreted as accepting responsibility for inducting other peoples into classical European ideals. This belief was part of the mythology of colonialism.

Once Christianity became the dominant religion in the West, the concepts of "civilising" and "Christianising" became intractably fused, particularly in the Age of Discovery beginning in the fifteenth century. The evangelisation of South America, for example, was blighted in its origins by this mistaken linkage. The classicist understanding of culture remained dominant not only in Western society, but also in the Church, well into the middle of the twentieth century.

Modern View of Culture

In the modern view,[77] culture is seen as the *defining characteristic of a people*. In this sense all peoples have a culture. The modern view no longer represents culture as a universal ideal; rather it talks of cultures. Cultures are forged in the processes which a people uses to cope with its particular environment. Cultures can, therefore, be the subject of empirical research. Cultural anthropology is the social science which has culture as its main field of study. A derivative field is mission anthropology.

The rapid development of cultural anthropology during and after the Second World War helped clarify the modern conception of culture,[78] and this development has had important benefits for missiology.[79] Cultural

---

[77] The terms "modern", "empirical" and "anthropological" can be used interchangeably to refer to this understanding of culture. "Modern" is adopted in the balance of the text.

anthropologists were in demand in this period because of high level cross-cultural interactions occurring between Westerners and peoples of other cultures in reconstruction efforts following the war. The needs of the time brought to prominence the work and methods of the various schools of anthropology. As Louis Luzbetak notes, the great achievement of anthropologists in the first half of the twentieth century lay in clarifying the empirical, or modern, understanding of culture.[80] The period also saw the beginning of mission anthropology. This latter development reflected the need to answer questions such as what is the significance of the emerging empirical study of culture for the work of missionaries and for our understanding of mission itself?

A major difficulty facing anthropologists in the 50s and 60s was the lack of an agreed frame of reference for analysing cultures.[81] Anthropologists divided into various schools of thought, each with its own orientation. In this period missionaries were often viewed by cultural anthropologists as the enemies of culture. As a blanket judgment this was unfair. While some missionaries were clearly iconoclastic in their treatment of local cultures, others played a vital role in recording the languages and customs of many indigenous peoples. Without such pioneering work many indigenous cultures would be impoverished today, some irrevocably.

Within the Catholic sphere, Louis Luzbetak SVD became a seminal figure in the new field of missionary anthropology. His book *The Church and Cultures* first published in 1963, proved important in forging a new synthesis between more traditional approaches to mission work and the emerging social science of cultural anthropology. Published on the eve of the Second Vatican Council, it anticipated many of the conclusions reached at the Council with respect to culture. As a primer on missionary anthropology the book was substantially re-written and was re-published in 1988 as post-conciliar theological themes regarding mission became clearer. Again it provided a powerful synthesis of theology, anthropology and mission history.

The classicist view of culture has had a significant impact on theories of education and associated conceptions of what constitutes a "good" education. In more recent times, the modern view of culture has also played its part in shaping notions of appropriate approaches to education, particularly as societies have become more multi-cultural and multi-faith in character. Because modern views of culture do not hold with classical assumptions, the battle lines are

---

[78] Edward T. Hall *The Silent Language* (New York: Anchor Books, 1973), 23–27.

[79] For a comprehensive treatment see "Missiological Anthropology" in Louis Luzbetak *The Church and Cultures: New Perspectives in Missiological Anthropology* Revised Edition (Maryknoll New York: Orbis, 1988), Chapter Two, 12–63.

[80] Louis Luzbetak *The Church and Cultures* Revised Edition (Maryknoll New York: Orbis, 1988), 133.

[81] Edward T. Hall *The Silent Language* (New York: Anchor Books, 1973), 26–28.

often drawn, particularly with respect to curriculum. In reality, curriculum development needs to take into account elements of both approaches in order to do justice to the educational needs of young people. Our students have a right to access both their cultural heritage and their contemporary culture as they engage in the process of knowledge construction, which lies at the heart of education.

Cultural Processes – Enculturation and Acculturation

In working with culture, it is important for educators to understand two basic cultural processes in particular – enculturation and acculturation.

Enculturation

Humans are not born with culture; culture is acquired through a process of socialisation. For example, a baby absorbs its family's culture in the process of growing up. This happens through a variety of means – modelling, punishment and reward, repetition, correction, repeated exposure to images, as well as through conscious learning. Anthropologists name the process by which the individual is incorporated into his/her culture "enculturation". Schools are important vehicles of enculturation.

Acculturation

When people from different cultures interact over time, they learn from each other and in the process cultural change is likely to occur within both cultures, although not necessarily to the same degree. This process of *mutual change* is known in cultural anthropology as "acculturation". The rapid and unprecedented movement of people today under the impact of modern globalisation makes acculturation an important contemporary social phenomenon. That *acculturation is a two-way process* is very obvious, for example, in the way cuisines, dress styles and music styles change as cultures intersect.

The classicist view of culture assumes that when cultures come into contact, the "superior" culture will swiftly achieve a position of dominance. In such a perspective acculturation is a one-way process, a view reinforced by the social theories derived from Darwinism. In the face of the Western imperial onslaught, however, many native cultures, caught up in the colonial expansion, simply went underground only to reappear in modified form in the post-colonial period. A similar phenomenon was associated with the imposition of communist regimes in Eastern Europe. The fall of communism saw the re-emergence of religion functioning, inter alia, as a marker of a lost cultural identity. An obvious conclusion seems to be that culture is a very deep part of a people's identity and is capable of resisting attempts to subvert it.

Given that one of the important benefits of culture is that it confers social identity, there is growing resistance to the erosion of social identity through the rapid acculturation that globalisation is perceived as causing. This is clearly not a freely chosen form of acculturation. On the other hand, multiculturalism, when understood as expanding the parameters of the local cultural identity through the freely chosen inclusion of people from other cultures, represents a consciously chosen form of acculturation at least on the part of governments. Even when such acculturation is government policy, the important issue is the extent to which the local population comes to accept the inclusion of others, that is the extent to which the acculturation process is received positively within the broader society.

The larger processes of culture – enculturation and acculturation in particular – are important phenomena for mission. In a later section of this chapter another of these processes, the theological process of *inculturation*, will be discussed. However, to explore these processes in any depth, it is necessary to have a clearer understanding of the modern view of culture.

Understanding the Modern View of Culture – Two Working Models

Culture is a complex phenomenon, best understood in terms of "working models". Gerard Egan[82] provides two basic criteria for an effective working model – it must be sufficiently complex to account for the principal features of the reality it attempts to describe or portray, and at the same time it must be sufficiently simple to direct action.

Models of culture tend to fall into two categories – *conceptual* models and *analogical* models. Conceptual models link abstract components into a comprehensive framework. The models used by Hall, Hiebert and Luzbetak, cited previously, fall into this category. Analogical models use a dominant image to bring the various elements of culture together. This approach is adopted by missiologists such as Shorter,[83] Cote[84] and Gallagher.[85] In this chapter two working models of culture are explored in order to explain the dynamism and importance of culture. One uses a conceptual framework and the other an analogical framework. These models are representative of the many similar models in each category. For ease of reference these are referred to as Model A and Model B.

Model A is a conceptual model derived from the work of Louis Luzbetak.[86] In

[82] Gerard Egan *Change Agent Skills in Helping and Human Service Settings* (Monterey: Brookes/Cole Publishing, 1985), 6.

[83] Alwyard Shorter *Theology of Mission* (Cork: Mercier Paperback, 1972).

[84] Richard Cote *Re-Visioning Mission: The Catholic Church and Culture in Postmodern America* (New York: Paulist Press, 1996).

[85] Michael Paul Gallagher *Clashing Symbols: An Introduction to Faith and Culture* (London: Darton, Longman and Todd, 2003).

this perspective, culture is a society's *plan or design for living*.[87] The essence of culture is embodied in the meanings that underpin its cultural forms. Culture is studied as a construct of the mind. Model B is an analogical model which uses an iceberg as a metaphor to aid understanding of the concept of culture. The model focuses on the pervasive nature of culture and highlights the fact that much of culture is out of our awareness. The model is derived from the work of Richard Cote.[88] Both models provide a frame of reference in which it is possible to take a "snapshot" of a particular culture *at a point in time*. This gives them their empirical power. Because both models deal with the culture of a people, they deal with culture *at the macro level*.

No one model covers all aspects of the empirical concept of culture. When considered together, however, the two models throw considerable light on the concept and its central importance in any process of reflection on human experience that attempts to make meaning and sense of that experience.

Model A – Culture as a Society's Design for Living

In Luzbetak's treatment, culture, understood in a very broad sense, provides a society's plan for living. It is a dynamic reality in that the plan is constantly in the process of development as the environment changes. More specifically, "culture is a plan according to which a society adapts itself to its physical, social and ideational environment".[89] Cultures survive because this plan is, to greater or lesser degree, successful.

The *physical environment* in which a culture evolves determines a set of primary needs for food, housing, transport, technology, health care and so on. In responding to these needs, a society develops its *technological system*.

The *social environment* reflects how people in the culture choose to relate as members of society. It also includes what they regard as correct and proper in interpersonal and group relations and interactions. Over time a set of norms, standards and ideas develops with respect to group life. These encompass areas such as politics, kinship, various forms of care, family, communication, leadership, social organisation, law, justice and so on, which are translated into unique structural arrangements. Social environments result from the desire and wish within a society that people live together harmoniously. The needs involved here are *derived needs* and meeting them gives rise to a society's *social systems*.

The development of a culture's technological and social systems is guided by *a set of master ideas which provide meaning and a sense of cohesion*. People

---
[86] Luzbetak,156–159.
[87] Ibid., 156.
[88] Cote, 105–122.
[89] Luzbetak, 157.

in a culture have access to a complex of ideas that constitute its *ideational environment*. The uniquely human demands for coherence and meaning give rise to what Luzbetak terms "integrative needs". In identifying the operation of social systems and the meaning systems which give significance and bring cohesion to behaviours, a society creates what is called in Model A its "symbolic system". The symbolic system reflects the norms, standards and ideas relating to magic, philosophy, art, religion, ideology, economics, science and so on as the latter confer meaning on actions. Many models of culture focus exclusively or predominantly on this dimension.

The dynamism of culture comes from the ongoing interplay of environment, needs, and cultural systems. Changes in one element bring about developments or reactions in the others. As an example of this dynamism, modern communications technology, which is part of the technological system in our culture, is altering the ideational environment of many societies by facilitating the rapid exchange of ideas. This change generates new needs through the recreational, educational and social networking opportunities it opens up. The resulting changes in behaviour affect the culture as a whole. The relationships at work here are represented in Figure 2

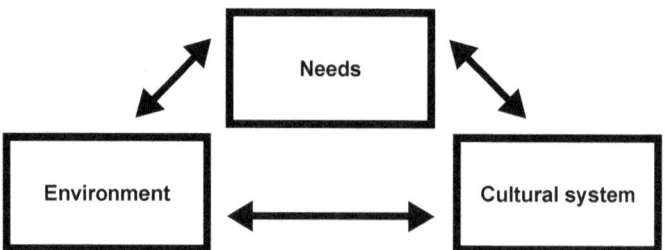

Figure 2. Culture as a Dynamic System

Cultural systems evolve in response to changing needs. In the case noted above, the culture of many Western countries has adapted by improving the technology in schools, developing protocols for the use of the internet, developing laws to control what people have access to on the internet, preventing cyber bullying, protecting against piracy, protecting intellectual property rights and so on. Different societies address the challenges of the internet in different ways depending on their existing cultural systems. This is because different societies place varying constructions on what "liberty" means in practice.

The conception of culture in Model A is represented schematically in Figure 3.

Environment	Needs	Cultural System
Physical	Primary	Technological
Social	Derived	Sociological
Ideational	Integrative	Symbolic

Figure 3. Model A – Culture as a Design for Living

Model A emphasises an important element in the understanding of culture. *Culture is a complex whole in which the parts exist in relationship to one another.* Some parts of culture are seen as more important, and thus less easy to change, than others. The symbolic system of a culture represents its depth dimension. Destroy an important element here and you begin to undermine the identity of a people, generally with catastrophic effects.

An instance of this is the way indigenous peoples and white settlers viewed land in the early European settlement period of Australia. In the cultural understanding of the early European settlers, land was a commodity to be developed and traded. The concept of individuals owning land was, however, quite foreign in aboriginal cultures. In these cultures land was considered a tribal possession. The land existed in its own right, and embedded within it was the mythology of the people. The land did not belong to people; people belonged to the land. Clearly, land had a different value in the ideational systems of aboriginal and settler cultures.

From the settlers' cultural perspective, since the aborigines were not cultivating the land, they had no proprietary rights over it. So, if the land was required for farming or mining purposes, the aborigines were removed. If they resisted, the settlers invoked their legal system. Quite often aborigines, resisting the take-over of their land with its sacred sites, were branded as criminals, or in more extreme cases, they were declared to be "vermin" and exterminated. Without their land, which played a central role in defining their cultural identity, many native peoples simply ceased to exist as a people. The best hopes of well-intentioned whites to address this situation by "civilising" them failed badly. While, with instruction, some did master the settlers' technological and social systems, including learning how to play cricket,[90] most did not. The well-intentioned efforts of liberal-minded whites could not restore a lost cultural identity and simply compounded the misery of the aboriginal peoples.

---

[90] An Aboriginal cricket team from Australia toured England in 1868 and proved to be quite competitive. This came as a great surprise to the English professional cricketers against whom they played.

It is only in recent decades that Australian governments have begun to grasp the significance of land in aboriginal cultures, and have commenced systematically to redress this matter through recognition of their land rights. Furthermore, as the need to protect the environment has become more obvious, a new appreciation has developed of the need to care for the land, a significant value in aboriginal cultures. Quite belatedly, some acculturation is taking place on this issue.

Luzbetak highlights another important dimension of culture, the insider/outsider phenomenon. This has an important bearing on the empirical study of cultures. Outsiders to a culture can study the *forms of culture* without necessarily coming to grips with their inner symbolic meaning. Mastering the latter is notoriously difficult, because an "outsider" always looks at culture through the lens of his/her own culture that, more often than not, is assumed to constitute "normality". "Insiders", on the other hand, learn their culture through enculturation. In part this process occurs well below the level of consciousness, so the capacity of insiders to explain their culture is often quite limited. It is only when important elements in a culture are challenged that these are brought to conscious attention.

An example of how cultural forms can be confusing is the story of the woman who, while putting flowers on her mother's grave in the local cemetery, noted that in the Chinese section across the pathway a man was placing food on a grave there. Somewhat bemused she asked, "When do you expect your loved one to eat that food?" to which the reply came "About the same time that your mother comes up to smell the flowers!" Most Western people would struggle to explain precisely why it is that we put flowers on a grave. This is a cultural form that an outsider can observe and an insider has difficulty in explaining. While the reason has been lost in history, insiders know that it is an appropriate thing to do, and that other insiders accept and expect this.

The key components of a culture exist in interrelationship, so cultures are never static. They adapt continuously to offer members at least the promise of success in coping with the demands of living together. Living cultures persist tenaciously over time because they are seen to deliver on this promise, so people have developed faith in their culture's capacity to continue to do so. Because of this, culture provides a *plan for living* that is held to tenaciously, not least because the alternative is failure.

Culture facilitates understanding, but at the same time provides a people with an *imaginal horizon* beyond which they cannot see. The struggle for the recognition of human rights is replete with examples of societies operating within horizons limited by culture. For instance, for centuries people in the

West took slavery as a cultural "given".

Model A suggests why culture holds various aspects of society together by providing meaning and cohesion to the norms, standards and ideas which influence how people perceive the reality around them and how they act. It provides a useful basis for comparing cultures. The emphasis in Model A is on culture as "a thing of the mind", and the distinction between culture and cultural forms is an important feature of the model.

Model B – Narrative and Culture: The Iceberg Model

Model B is an example of approaches to culture that use a dominant image, in this case an iceberg, to convey central ideas. It differs markedly from the previous model in the emphasis it places on the role of narrative (and mythology) in a culture. In commenting on this feature of the model Cote observes that

> the roots of every culture run deep into the dark background of a people's dreams and originating experiences when they first became aware of being a distinct or peculiar people and this "founding" experience is initially shaped and accompanied more by images and social imagination than by abstract ideas. Indeed the role of social imagination is not only determinative in the "birthing" and formation process of a culture, but also for the interpretive analysis of that culture.[91]

This phenomenon is seen clearly in the Old Testament account of the Exodus event and the formation of the nation of Israel in the wilderness years.

With its emphasis on the way social imagination, narrative and ideals come together in creating the deepest levels of culture, Model B provides a corrective to the more abstract analysis of Model A. Culture maps the imaginal horizon of a people precisely because their narrative encompasses what they can imagine when reality and ideals are brought together – the result is the dialogue between "roots and horizons" to which Gallagher draws attention.[92]

In Model B, culture is understood as an orderly whole with *inter-related layers of meaning*. The relationship between these layers is seen as linear with influence exerted both upwards and downwards as Figure 4, which draws on the work of Hiebert,[93] shows. The image that best conveys this relationship is the iceberg, which has a small proportion of its mass visible above the sea while a greater mass giving the iceberg stability lies under the sea, out of sight and potentially threatening.

---

[91] Cote, 105.
[92] Gallagher, 172.
[93] Paul Hiebert *Transforming Worldviews: An Anthropological Understanding of How People Change* (Grand Rapids Michigan: Baker Academic, 2008), 33.

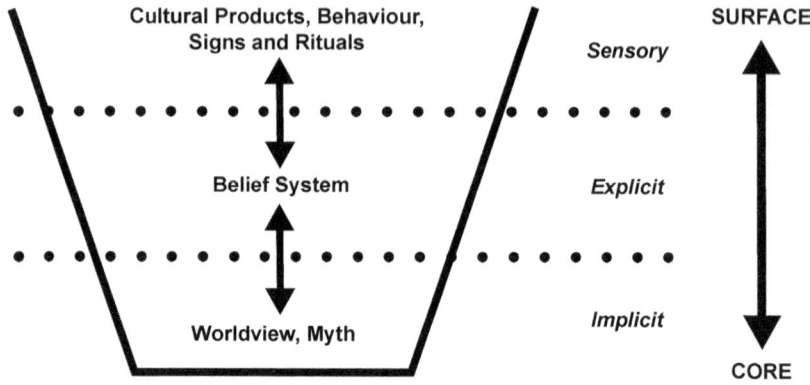

Figure 4. A Linear Model of Culture (after Hiebert, 2008)

The parallel here is between those aspects of culture which are within the realm of the conscious, thus accessible to the observer/outsider, and those which reside in the sub-conscious of a people and are therefore out of awareness for "insiders" and out of sight to "outsiders". Arbuckle[94] invokes Freud's theory of the unconscious mind to suggest that accessing the unconscious dimension of a culture needs forms of analysis comparable in quality to psychotherapy!

As with a ship near an iceberg, the outsider needs to be wary of the potential hazard this sub-conscious dimension of culture can represent. Some of the major catastrophes of mission history have been the result of foundering on the ice below the surface of an unknown culture, where the missionary made the mistake of thinking that what an "outsider" sees is all there is to see and comprehend. Even insiders recognise some important aspects of their culture only when it is attacked and so brought to consciousness. Until that happens, their responses to new circumstances can seem to outsiders as being reactive and non-rational, sensing a lack of fit, because they are unable to articulate why they feel the way they do.

In analysing cultures Cote suggests they have two major domains, that within awareness and that out of awareness. He divides the *conscious domain* of culture into two levels – the expressive level and the semiotic level – the "semiotic" being the level of signs and rituals. Both of these levels are accessible to the outside observer. The "out-of-awareness" domain also has two levels, that of fundamental values[95] and the deeper level of "dynamic myths" (see Figure 5). Cote does not include "worldview" as an element at the core of culture and this seems a deficiency in his model.

---

[94] Gerald Arbuckle *Refounding the Church* (Homebush: St Paul Publications, 1993), 37.

Explorers Guides and Meaning-makers

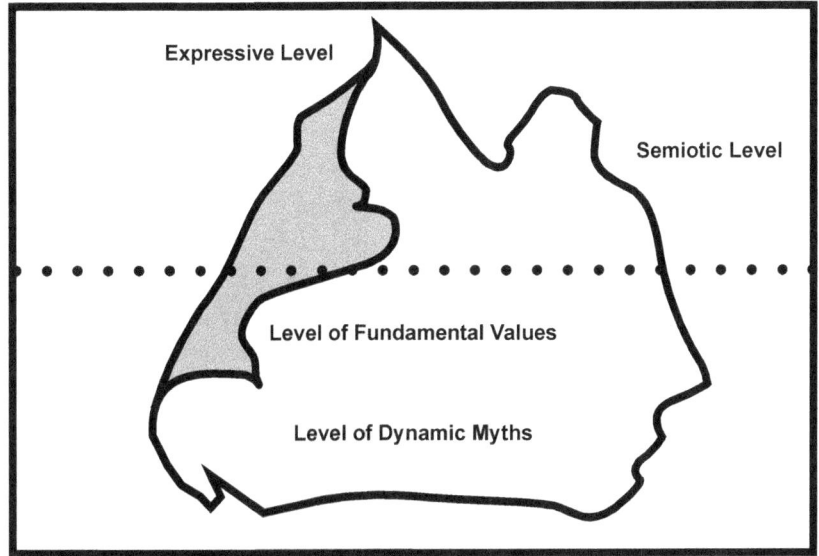

Figure 5. Model B – The Iceberg as an Analogical Model of Culture (adapted from Cote, 1999)

"Myth" in Cote's model is used as a story-symbol. Myth provides meanings central to cultural identity which, when conveyed in narrative form, encompass the core ideals and hopes of a people. Myths have a crucial place in culture as they provide the images that bring people together and hold them together *emotionally*. They can liberate great energy among a people particularly when invoked in times of crisis or challenge. The meaning of these myths can often be misconstrued by outsiders as the following example demonstrates.

Each year in Australia there is a national holiday on ANZAC day.[96] Associated with this celebration of national identity are large parades of veteran soldiers, which take place in all capital cities and throughout the country. At the level of historical fact the holiday commemorates the military disaster that befell Australian and New Zealand troops at Gallipoli in Turkey during the First World War. To the outsider, it often seems that only a nation with an ironic sense of humour could celebrate a defeat. An Indian priest, newly arrived in Australia on secondment to one of the Australian dioceses, so misinterpreted this event as an outsider to Australian culture, that he was moved to preach against what he saw as "the glorification of war". His efforts somewhat stunned

---

[95] There is a current tendency in popular usage of the word "culture" to treat it a synonymous with cultural values. This can occur to affirm values, such as when educators talk of "a culture of evidence", or to critique values as in "a culture of dependence".

[96] ANZAC is an acronym for Australian and New Zealand Army Corps.

the locals. For them, the celebrations mark the fact that at Gallipoli Australians fought together for the first time as a nation, and did so extremely bravely, winning the respect of the Turks, who were fierce adversaries. In the crucible of battle, values important to Australian identity were forged, particularly the value of caring for one's mates. For insiders the celebration is about the birth of a nation. What is celebrated relates to mythology and goes far beyond any historical "facts".

A contention of Model B is that change is easier to achieve and more readily legitimised in the surface layers of culture than in its core levels. The deepest level of culture, dynamic myth, is so tightly bound to the cultural identity of a people, that is to who they are, that it is virtually impossible to change. Change at this level can be catastrophic, as the example of aboriginal peoples in Australia amply illustrates. Yet it is the level to which mission is directed. It is indeed timely that serious consideration is currently being given, within at least some local churches, to what is involved in the inculturation of the Gospel.

Cote's contention is that for too much of its history the Church has been content to address its mission to the surface levels of culture without being conscious of the need to bring the Gospel into the deeper levels of value and myth. In consequence, the evangelisation of people, even in "Christian lands", has often been superficial and incomplete and therefore unable to withstand the challenges posed by modernity.

The important insight of Model B is that culture is not just a codified response to needs generated in a particular environment, but is also shaped by *the social imagination of a people*. That is, a culture has associated with it a constellation of images that grow out of shared experiences which art, in its many forms, often evokes. Art is a provider of images and symbols to which leaders can appeal in developing a "compelling narrative of mission". As Cote observes:

> Many of these social "imaginings" when strong enough come to be translated and concretized in people's habits, customs or rites as well as in…customary law. Cultural myths – like all myths – provide unquestioned assumptions about the forms of behavior appropriate to various broad fields of behavior and activity within a culture. They give rise to fundamental value orientations and indeed the most important values of the culture.[97]

The notion of myth is related to that of narrative – the story of how a people came to be and to think of themselves as a distinct people with a particular destiny. A people's narrative covers its origins, its "founding" aspirations and so on. Cultural narratives can facilitate a collective awakening to new

---

[97] Cote, 109.

possibilities. When invoked, they are dynamic in their power to orient and energise. This helps to explain why each year many thousands of mostly young Australians and New Zealanders gather on 25 April at Anzac Cove in Turkey to take part in a dawn service.

Narratives serve a number of major purposes. They confer on important values and on social structures the mantle of being sacred, and in so doing assist in conserving these aspects of the culture. At the same time, they continually invite people to see beyond what is, to what could be, involving the use of the imagination. For a narrative to hold its power *it must be given a contemporary expression*; it must link past and present experiences. The narrative underpinning culture is never complete because new chapters have yet to be written. In this sense the narrative has dynamic power because successive generations can find a home in it.

Cultural narratives also have the capacity to reduce fear in the face of adversity when people are made aware, at least to some degree, of their dynamic myths. Through them people come to know that others in their society, when faced with adversity, have been able to cope and cope well. They reveal the deeply held convictions of a people. They unify people in the face of challenges that could easily divide them and they highlight the resilience of a people confronted with challenge. When invoked wisely, myths can act as a catalyst for change.[98]

Narrative is not history. It is an interpretive schema that provides the imaginative constructs used to make sense of the events of history. Much of the New Testament experience, for instance, is interpreted in terms of the mythology (story symbols) of Israel. While history can track the flow of events, and historians can adduce effects and causes, history of itself lacks the compelling power of a people's narrative which blends fact and interpretation into a meaningful whole, reflecting both collective imagination and collective aspiration.

By emphasising the importance of imagination and narrative, Model B complements Model A. It also makes sense of the insider/outsider problem in assessing culture. Insiders are often unaware of the deeper structures of their culture and because of this underestimate its power and value. As a consequence, outsiders have great difficulty in accessing these structures and often misread the culture. Model B poses significant questions about the place culture has in mission.

Hiebert suggests that at the core of every culture there is a particular way of viewing the world.[99] He provides a useful working definition of worldview, which we adopt, describing worldview as "the foundational cognitive, affective,

[98] Cote, 111.
[99] Hiebert, 15.

and evaluative assumptions and frameworks a group of people makes about the nature of reality which they use to order their lives".[100] While the worldview can be analysed in conceptual terms, it is rarely conveyed in those terms. The worldview of the culture is embedded in its narrative and conveyed from one generation to the next through narrative. The term "worldview" is used broadly in the literature to apply to a number of areas of human life. In our view, it can be appropriately extended to the cognitive, affective and evaluative assumptions and frameworks used by individuals to make sense of their world. It is similarly appropriate to apply it to faith traditions (cf. Chapter Twelve).

The discussion above refers to culture in the macro sense. It can be equally applied in the micro sense to the culture of an organisation such as a school. Questions such as the following can be asked: how aware are the members of your school of the myths that underpin its culture, what are its dynamic values, how well is the message of the Gospel integrated into these levels of the culture, what use does the school make of symbols and rituals, and how open is the culture of the school to renewal? The answers to such questions throw up significant issues for leadership.

The two models outlined above, when taken together, indicate why culture is such a "slippery" concept. Equally, however, when taken together they suggest how important the modern concept of culture is in making sense of human experience, particularly in its collective dimensions.

The modern view of culture tends to suggest something that is sharply defined. However, the contours of living cultures are dynamic. In a living culture there are values that are widely affirmed as core to the culture, and a field of contested values that lie at the periphery of the culture and which various groups in the culture seek to have acknowledged as core.

The processes of globalisation, secularisation and modern pluralism exacerbate this dynamic in most western cultures, with migration becoming a touchstone issue for assessing core cultural values.[101] Debates about migration tend to bring to the surface aspects of culture that are often held below the level of consciousness. Such debates provide an opportunity for acknowledging, assessing and re-affirming core values and for re-defining the contours of a local culture.

---

[100] Ibid., 25–26. The full discussion in Chapter 1 ("The Concept of Worldview") and Chapter 2 ("Characteristics of Worldviews") is particularly helpful.

[101] As the field of contested values has expanded commentators such as Kathryn Tanner suggest the need to re-frame the modern conception of culture to take this blurring of boundaries into account. This reconstructed understanding of culture she calls the "post-modern view of culture". Cf. Kathryn Tanner *Theories of Culture: An Agenda for Theology* (Minneapolis: Fortress Press, 1997), 56–58.

Culture and the Gospel – Inculturation

If, as Luzbetak has suggested, culture can be construed as a "set of norms, standards and associated notions and beliefs…organized into a dynamic system of control",[102] then one of the principal tasks of mission in any society is to ensure the Gospel message is made present within the culture, and expressed in terms that make sense in that culture. In Catholic circles, the process by which this occurs is called "inculturation".[103] The nature of this process is much debated.

For Luzbetak[104] one of the principal tasks in inculturation is the development of a communal answer to the question "what would Jesus teach, and how would he behave if he were born today…not two thousand years ago, but today, here and now?" The empirical view of culture provides a useful tool in responding to this question.

> Whenever God deals with human beings, whether in the Bible or in our own times, he deals with them as cultural beings. (From this it follows that) every Christian community must experience Christ not as a foreigner who somehow after two thousand years appeared in the community's midst, but as "one of us", as someone sharing the community's culture and therefore possessing its very soul.[105]

Within this general understanding of the significance of Christ

> (inculturation) is the process by which a local community integrates the Gospel message (the "text") with the real life context, blending text and context into a single God-intended reality called "Christian living".[106]

It follows from all that has been said then, that "Christian living" can no longer be seen as a universal ideal independent of the culture in which it occurs. Such a notion would be "classicist" in its cultural orientation. What constitutes "Christian living" has to be worked out in the dynamic context of culture, respecting, and at the same time challenging, the integrity of that culture. *In this sense the message of Jesus is open to all cultures and cannot be identified with any one culture.*

Debate about the process of inculturation centres on whether or not this process is two-way like acculturation or one-way. People tend to part company here depending on whether they hold classicist or modern ideas about the nature of culture. In the modern perspective, there is a reflexive side to the process of inculturation and this flows from the fact that God's creative Spirit is present

---

[102] Luzbetak, 156.
[103] An alternative term, "contextualisation", is often preferred by Protestant missiologists.
[104] Luzbetak, 133.
[105] Ibid.,134.
[106] Ibid., 133.

in all cultures. Evangelisers themselves gain greater insight into the Gospel in the process of evangelising. People of a classicist bent do not necessarily hold this to be the case.

Quite ancient teaching of the Church, attributed to Justin Martyr in the second century, is that "the seeds of the Word" are present in all cultures.[107] Therefore, while the Gospel, as understood by the evangelisers, provides a critique of the culture to which the missionary has come, the people whose culture it is can, in turn, provide a critique of the particular understanding of the Gospel that missionaries bring. Insight can, and often does, flow both ways. This is why dialogue has such a prominent place in mission.[108] Anyone who has taught teenagers Religious Education in a Catholic school will be aware of this dynamic in action!

Inculturation, understood as a theological process in which the Gospel engages seriously and systematically with culture, has opened up a new approach to mission. This shift in perspective helps explain why ideas such as the "local Church" and "local theologies" have achieved such currency in recent years and why, increasingly, people critique the previous "classicist" presentations of theology as Euro-centric, unappealing and not addressing the needs of people in other cultures.

Shorter[109] argues that at the heart of any culture lies a worldview implicitly or explicitly addressing fundamental questions such as what does it mean to be human, and how do people interpret the realities of life, death and suffering? The worldview, according to Shorter, places religion or the potential for religion, close to the heart of any culture. Religious faith brings a new dimension to this worldview, imparting added conviction and motivation to action. Writing in an African context, he concludes that religious understanding is at the heart of culture itself. It lies at its ideational centre, and from there influences all levels of culture. Seen from this perspective, a purely "secular" African culture would be a contradiction in terms.

The adoption of the modern concept of culture in Catholic theological discourse, while not universally accepted, offers the prospect of a Church more open to growth because of its closer connection to living cultures and the needs and aspirations of people belonging to those cultures – a primary locus for the

---

[107] Obviously, the Greek apologist Justin Martyr did not have the modern construct of culture with which to work, but in his bridge-building work between Christianity and the broader Graeco-Roman world, he recognised the workings of God in classical philosophy. See discussion in Stephen Bevans and Roger Shroeder *Constants in Context: A Theology of Mission for Today* (Maryknoll New York: Orbis, 2004), 84.

[108] Dialogue and proclamation are the two basic modalities of mission. Cf. Pontifical Council for Inter-religious Dialogue *Dialogue and Proclamation* 1991.

[109] Shorter 1988, 37.

working of the Spirit.

Model B has much to say about the "how" of inculturation. In the first instance it suggests the necessity of being in contact with the narrative of a people and understanding the relationship between this narrative and the values it conveys. It suggests also that we can misread, or lack adequate appreciation of, the message of the Gospel both in terms of the limitations of our own culture and the lack of understanding of the limitations in the cultures in which the texts themselves were written.

The Gospel and Culture – Evangelising Cultures

Model B suggests that a process of evangelisation that operates only at the superficial levels of culture, which has often been the case throughout mission history, can easily unravel. Imposing one society's cultural expressions of the Gospel on another is likewise a fraught strategy.

Pope Paul VI was the first pope to formally write about mission in terms of "the evangelization of cultures". In *Evangelii Nuntiandi* (1975) he identified the need to

> evangelize man's culture and cultures not in a purely decorative way as it were, by applying a thin veneer, but in a vital way, in depth and right to the roots…[110]

Commenting further he stressed that

> every effort must be made to ensure the full evangelization of culture or more correctly, cultures. They have to be regenerated by an encounter with the Gospel. But this encounter will not take place if the Gospel is not proclaimed.[111]

In *Evangelii Nuntiandi* Pope Paul VI is clearly writing from within the modern or empirical conception of culture.

For most Catholics, and many Catholic educators, the idea that evangelising culture is part of the mission of the Church is quite new and its implications for Catholic education still remain to be spelled out in full. Church historian Andrew Walls has conducted a number of important studies in this area[112] which point to the fact that the Church has learned much and continues to learn from its engagement with cultures.

The evangelisation of culture as a goal of mission seeks to reshape/renew the values and worldview of a culture in a way that is *received as authentic by insiders*. Yet in very few Religious Education curricula in this or, we suspect,

---

[110] Pope Paul VI *Evangelii Nuntiandi* #20 (*On the Evangelization of Peoples*, 1975).
[111] Ibid.
[112] Cf. Andrew Walls *The Missionary Movement in Christian History: Studies in the Transmission of Faith* (Maryknoll New York: Orbis, 1996) and *The Cross-cultural Process in Christian History; Studies in the Transmission and Appropriation of Faith* (Maryknoll New York: Orbis, 2002).

other countries, is the local culture viewed as in any way seriously relevant to Religious Education. At best it is given only superficial recognition as either locus or vehicle of evangelisation. Analogical models of culture such as Model B, suggest that people engaging in mission need to have some awareness of the values, narrative and worldview of their own culture and the impact these have on their own religious understanding. They likewise suggest the importance of understanding the cultural values, narrative and worldviews encountered in the Old and New Testaments so that understanding of the Gospel goes beyond a kind of naïve literalism.

Finally, since God wills the salvation of all peoples, God is at work in their narrative and therefore Kingdom values are to be found in all cultures. This perspective is important to all forms of inter-religious dialogue. A vital task of mission is to help people discern the presence of God in the narrative of the community to which they belong, be the community the family, the parish, the school or even the nation.

Culture and Theological Reflection

Culture is a complex but important reality. In this chapter we have endeavoured to explore its various dimensions using two "working models". Each model adds something unique to the picture. The models are derived from the field of missionary anthropology. Their common concern is the engagement between culture and the message of the Gospel – how this engagement is best construed and pursued. The cultural processes of enculturation and acculturation were also discussed. The discussion in this chapter has drawn attention to the theological notion of inculturation, the complex dialogue between the Gospel carried in a community and a culture, that results in the recognition of the Spirit present in the culture, and which makes possible deeper incorporation of the Gospel message within the culture.

Attempts to live out the Christian message in a new cultural situation, or in a situation of cultural change, sometimes provide new models of Christian living that become resources for the global Church community and therefore open up a new chapter in the narrative of that community. The Church as a whole benefits ultimately from new models of Christian living and from greater insights into the message of the Gospel. This is well illustrated in the development of liberation theologies in South America and of inter-religious dialogues in Asia. The engagement of Western European churches with the secularised cultures in which they now exist has also become a significant project in exploring the relationship between the Gospel and culture, one close to the heart of Pope Benedict XVI.

Historically speaking, culture has been, and continues to be, the learning place of the Church. Christian living on the frontier, at the beginning of the third millennium, is about living in a learning Church. This learning process began in earnest when Paul undertook his missions to the gentiles and, through various peaks and troughs, has continued ever since. It is a history marked by conflict, misunderstanding and slow progress, but progress nonetheless. Put simply, a Church that does not appear to learn, lacks credibility as a teacher. Inculturation must therefore be central to its mission.

In theological reflection culture is a resource that cannot be taken for granted, nor can we rest satisfactorily with a situation in which major aspects of our cultural understanding remain out of awareness. The modern approach to culture provides a useful tool to explore and understand our way of life, one which is shaped not only by the Gospel narrative but also by the narrative of modernity. Western culture in particular provides us with an amazing array of intellectual tools for use in analysing human experience and therefore contributes to "grassroots theology". No process of critical theological reflection could be taken seriously if it were to ignore culture as a vital resource.

CHAPTER FIVE

Exploring Post-modern Experience

Time and Its Significance in Meaning-making

In the previous chapter we discussed the modern notion of culture using two models, one conceptual and one analogical. The models allowed us to take a "snapshot" of culture without any real necessity to ask how or why the culture evolved to the point that it has. However, cultures change and evolve over time and this development has a trajectory. Any sound explanation of human experience has to take this into account. Time, its accumulation as history, and the recall of significant events as narrative, are all crucial issues in interpreting human experience and provide the focus of this chapter.

Our understanding of where we are in time is an important part of our human consciousness. For example, St Paul, who died in AD mid-60s, was of the view that "the end of days" was near. He thought this way because in the Jewish culture of his time "the end of days" was associated with the coming of the Messiah. Paul's understanding of where he was in time gave added urgency to his sense of mission. However, by the time the author of John wrote his Gospel some two or three generations later any sense that Jesus' return would be immediate had begun to fade. The Gospel writer had to think of time and its significance in a new way.

This raises the question of where in time we are today. Are we still perhaps in the early ages of the Christian experience? From science we learn that our planetary system is about halfway through its natural lifecycle and has about 4.5 billion years to go before the expansion of the sun renders life on earth unsustainable. We also know from the fossil record that humans in many ways similar to ourselves have inhabited the planet for about 60,000 years. Human history on earth therefore could continue to unfold for another 4.5 billion years! Looking at time from this perspective means that it is at least possible that we have not reached the 0.002% mark of human history! Such considerations put our human experience and our understanding of history in a new and unaccustomed perspective. If human life were to continue for the duration of the life of the planet, then we are certainly living in the early ages of the Christian experience, in the very early stages of the life of the Church. What we do know is that the present is *our time,* a unique interval in that history, and it is this to which we have to give some meaning. Many interpreters name our time as being "post-modern" and claim we live in an era

called "post-modernity". What does this mean?
To explore this question in any meaningful way we need to:
- outline what we mean by "post-modern"
- develop a *conceptual framework* within which to explore the journey from pre-modernity to post-modernity
- trace the journey that people in the West have made from pre-modern to post-modern times
- explore the changes in human aspiration that have characterised this journey, their significance for mission in general, and for the mission of the Catholic school in particular.

This chapter deals with the first two elements of this agenda. Chapter Six deals with the third and fourth elements.

Worldviews and Human Aspiration

In the previous chapter we examined culture and saw that in the depth of a culture, at its core, lies a "worldview". The *worldview of a culture* is conveyed from one generation to the next via its narrative which operates at the macro level bringing together both the history and myth of a people. Cultures influence human conduct *in the here and now*. Cultures are, in turn, strongly influenced by the *worldview of the age* in which they exist. This particular worldview incorporates those elements used to interpret and give meaning to life shared across contemporaneous cultures. The two worldviews, that of the culture and that of the age, *exist in ongoing interaction.*

The Church has been an important part of the human journey from pre-modernity to "post-modernity", particularly in the West. As we shall see, the Church developed its own interpretive tradition as this historical transition occurred. This gives rise to a *religious worldview* which has come to sit alongside, influencing and being influenced by, the worldviews of culture and of the age. We therefore need to examine the role of the Church in Western society as it has made its journey from pre-modernity to post-modernity.

Making sense of human experience means understanding the major worldviews that are at work at any point in time as well as the narrative of how these developed. Figure 6 depicts the relationships between worldviews as the modern period unfolded. The picture remains largely unchanged today.

People, individually and collectively, make sense of human experience with reference to three interacting worldviews, those of their culture, of their age, and of their faith tradition. The three worldviews identified in Figure 6 develop and evolve, so their interactions over time are quite complex. Worldviews reflect the collective aspirations people have for the future. These aspirations have their sources in culture, religious faith and changing human experiences.

Explorers Guides and Meaning-makers

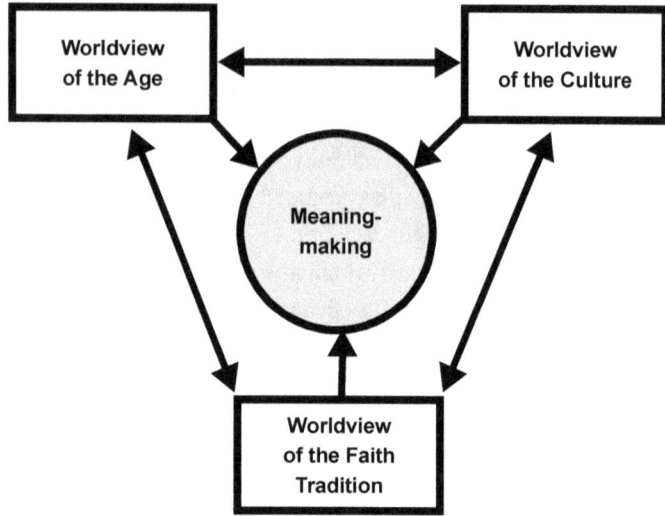

Figure 6. Meaning-making in the Context of Interacting Worldviews

Schools operate at the intersection of the three worldviews noted above. Understanding them and the aspirations embedded in them is of critical importance to both meaning-making and sound education. The school is both an agent of enculturation and of informed choice. In this chapter the focus is on the worldview associated with the spirit of our so called "post-modern" age. As we shall see, this is a "mixed" age in which the modern and the post-modern stand side by side.

Understanding Post-modernity

For several generations now in the West the media and, in more recent times, governments have endeavoured to enculturate people into a worldview that leads them to define and understand themselves mainly as *the producers and consumers of goods and services*. In this context education, which can and should provide some much needed balance in this process, is increasingly treated as a product to be consumed by hopefully "happy" parents and students – "happy" in the sense that the student and the school s/he attends get higher standardised test scores than others. High test scores, while not unimportant, now seem for many people to be equated with "good education". As this view of education becomes dominant, the links between education and human development are becoming increasingly blurred. Education is seen in instrumental terms and its critical role is diminished.

Religion is also seen as a product that people are free to consume or not – one choice among the myriad in the "culture of choice"[113] that characterises our post-modern environment. The emerging sensibility is well caught in the story of the student who, when challenged on a matter of Catholic teaching, replied "Well, that's just God's opinion". Leading and educating in such an environment is uniquely challenging! Knowing how people construct the worldview they use to interpret and make sense of their experience is important if teachers are to make sense of teaching in a Catholic school in our "post-modern" era.

The term "post-modern" is used in two senses – to denote *a period in history*, and to denote *a sensibility*. Thus we can talk of "post-modernity" and "post-modern sensibility". The quotation marks indicate that the terms are used in a number of ways and their meanings need to be clearly specified.

"Post-modern" as a Period in History

As a period in history the post-modern period is presumed to have begun in the early 1970s. Used in this sense "post-modern" can be interpreted as:

- the historical period *after modernity*[114]
- *a state of transition* between modernity and the period following modernity
- a *later stage in modernity*, as in "high" modernity, or "late" modernity[115] in which the major themes of modernity have reached a new stage in their historical evolution
- *a new configuration of modernity* caused by the major re-alignment of some, but not all, of its major paradigms, as in "global modernity",[116] the "new" or "second modernity".[117]

The underlying uncertainty here is whether the post-modern period, referred to as "post-modernity", is a new period in history, a further development within the existing period, or a state of transition between periods.

---

[113] For a discussion of this see Dean Hoge, William Dinges, Mary Johnson, & Juan Gonzales *Young Adult Catholics: Religion in the Culture of Choice* (Indiana: University of Notre Dame Press, 2001), 218–226.

[114] For instance, Martin Albrow speaks of "the global age" in *The Global Age: State and Society beyond Modernity* (Cambridge: Polity Press, 1997), 6.

[115] Cf. Anthony Giddens *Modernity and Self-Identity: Self and Society in the Late Modern Age* (Cambridge: Polity Press, 1991).

[116] John Tomlinson Globalisation and Culture (Chicago: University of Chicago Press, 1999), 33.

[117] Robert Schreiter sets out this perspective in a four-part article in *New Theology Review* under the title "A New Modernity: Living and Believing in an Unstable World" *New Theology Review* February, May, August, November, 2007.

The interpretive options found in the literature seem to fit somewhere in a spectrum between Schema A or Schema B in the table below.

Schema A	Schema B
Pre-modernity Modernity Post-modernity	Pre-modernity Enlightenment Modernity Post-modernity Second Modernity

Figure 7. Schemas for Categorising Recent Historical Periods

Schema A interprets post-modernity as a *new epoch* in history, the one following modernity. Schema B sees post-modernity as a *transition period*. What is clear is that "post-modernity" is always interpreted in relationship to the period known as modernity. It is not possible to understand or make sense of post-modern experience unless we understand the worldview of modernity and the currents of thought that shaped it.

In the chapters which follow we adopt the view that "post-modern" is best understood *as a transition period from which we are emerging as we enter into a second phase of modernity*.

"Post-modern" as a Sensibility

The second usage of "post-modern" refers to a *perspective, sensibility or stance*.[118] There seems broad agreement that, beginning in the mid-1970s, a new sensibility developed among people in the West. This sensibility now characterises many of the parents, teachers, and particularly students, who make up Catholic school communities and often provides a default position in trying to understand the attitudes they bring to participation in the life of this community.

Sociologist Mark Taylor provides a useful summary of the principal characteristics of post-modern students as seen on American tertiary campuses.[119]

- **Consumer-oriented** They grow up, or have grown up, in a culture of choice. They expect to make their own choices and not to have the range of choices open to them constrained. Such constraints are interpreted as a

---

[118] Some writers use "post-modern" to refer to the sensibility and reserve the term "post-modernity" for the historical period.

[119] Mark Taylor, 'Generation NeXt Comes to College: Meeting the Post Modern Student,' 2004. Retrieved 14 May 2009 from www.taylorprograms.org/images/Gen_NeXt_article_HLC_06.pdf.

denial of freedom or of their "rights". The "right to choose" is seen as the most fundamental of all "rights".

- **Entertainment oriented** From an early age post-moderns are socialised into the view that learning and life should be entertaining, fun and easy. Their focus in living is on the now. They have little understanding of delayed gratification or reward achieved through sustained effort.
- **Value-free** From an early age post-moderns have been exposed to multiple and competing value systems. The consequent relativising of value systems that occurs makes it difficult for them to evaluate the propriety of their actions or the impact their behaviours have on others. They appear to lack civility. Post-moderns do not seem to suffer from guilt in the same way that previous generations have. Value confusion underpins much of the parody and irony that post-moderns use to minimise the importance of things others hold dear. Caring for others is not seen as fashionable.
- **Adaptable and pragmatic** Post-moderns are adept at adapting to situations and changing expectations. They have grown up in an era of change where adaptation is the price of survival. They have learned to appreciate what works, as distinct from what people tell them should work.
- **Self-absorbed** Post-moderns expect to take care of themselves, having done so from day-care onwards. They can be quite assertive in meeting their own needs.
- **Sceptical with respect to truth claims** Incessant exposure to advertising and political spin make post-moderns sceptical of truth claims – seeing most as self-serving. They place more store on subjective and personal experience than on what they are told, being prepared to challenge most forms of authority.
- **Cynical/distrustful of institutions** Post-moderns have low levels of trust in social institutions, which are judged untrustworthy or even corrupt. This includes the institution of marriage.
- **Reluctant to commit** In a culture of choice it is not seen as "cool" to limit the range of future choices by making present choices. As a consequence post-moderns have problems with commitments and relationships. They are prone to experiment in their relationships in order to resolve some of the tensions that flow from an unwillingness to commit fully to another.
- **Intellectually disengaged** Post moderns are swamped with information, but have difficulty separating the meaningful from the meaningless. Their focus in their studies, to the extent that they have a focus, is on the pragmatic.
- **Able to live with diversity** Post-moderns tend to be more comfortable

with cultural, racial and sexual diversity than any previous generation.
- **Technoliterate** Wired since birth, post-moderns seem to be at ease with the new communication technologies and impatient with those who are not.

Post-modern sensibility can be understood as the stance people assume in adapting to the challenges posed by living in what they perceive to be a fragmented and fragmenting world.

The assumption accepted by advocates of Schema A above is that this state of fragmentation is now *a permanent condition of human existence*. Those who advocate Schema B generally hold that human beings are incapable of living for any length of time in a state of permanent disorientation. A new principle of meaning will develop, one capable of giving coherence to their experience.

Michael Gallagher[120] provides an alternative way of delineating post-modern sensibility, setting out its ten "precepts" as follows:

1. Thou shalt not worship reason.
2. Thou shalt not believe in history.
3. Thou shalt not hope in progress.
4. Thou shalt not tell meta-stories.
5. Thou shalt not focus on the self.
6. Thou shalt not agonise about values.
7. Thou shalt not trust institutions.
8. Thou shalt not bother about God.
9. Thou shalt not live for productivity alone.
10. Thou shalt not seek uniformity.

The picture he paints parallels that of Taylor in many respects. Underpinning these precepts is the notion of almost unlimited choice in constructing a worldview, one not bound by culture, religion or convention.

Post-modern Catholics

Post-modern sensibility has an important impact on how many young Catholics now view religion in general, and their Catholicism in particular. Dean Hoge and his associates identified the impact of post-modern sensibility on the formation of Catholic identity in their study *Young Adult Catholics: Religion in the Culture of Choice*. They found that post-modern Catholics construct their religious identity quite differently from previous generations. Young post-modern Catholics "like being Catholic", have no intention of being anything other than Catholic, but "Catholic" on their own terms. Their religious identity is *self-constructed and selective* in terms of which elements of Catholicism

---

[120] Michael Paul Gallagher *Clashing Symbols: An Introduction to Faith and Culture* Revised Edition (London: Darton, Longman & Todd, 2005), 101–103.

are included. Many young post-modern Catholics in the USA are not alienated from the Church. They are just distant from it.

As Hoge et al.[121] see the situation:

> Although we reject any sense of a Golden Age of dutiful, harmonious, and monolithic pre-Vatican II Catholicism, we believe that Catholicism's outsider status in nineteenth and early twentieth-century America, the general compliance with hierarchical and institutional norms, and the formative power of Catholic culture in its religious and ethnic dimensions powerfully shaped Catholic identity…Today, by contrast, personal choice and religious individualism are dominant. It is this situation – the transformation of Catholicism from a perceived church of obligation and obedience to a church of choice – that has accelerated dramatically in the wake of the 1960s…
>
> Our study shows that this transformation continues today driven in part by exaggerated individualism. Catholic identity construction in America's culture of choice is much less amenable to ecclesiastical control and institutional influence than in the past…Many young Catholics (now) simply construct "being Catholic" on their own terms – which explains in part why many see no compelling reason to leave the Church.

This observation will have many resonances in other Western countries. However, the situation, as Hoge et al. point out, has its positive side since "the shift to individual religious identity construction allows a greater assumption of responsibility within the tradition by many young Catholics for their religious and spiritual life".[122] They suggest that the post-modern experience draws attention to "various legitimate ways of being Catholic in the post-conciliar Church and that diverse Catholics are choosing styles that are relevant to them". These findings point to an important characteristic of post-modernity – *the emergence of diversity and choice as the meta-values of post-modern sensibility.*

The point needs to be made that *not all young people view the world through post-modern eyes.* Many are still attuned to the worldview of modernity. It is the *emergence* of post-modern sensibility as a separate option that characterises the present age.

So far we have endeavoured to bring some precision to the terms post-modernity and post-modern sensibility. Before returning to the main question – why did this new option arise? – we need to develop the conceptual tools necessary to understand and analyse worldviews.

---

[121] Dean Hoge, et al. 225–226.
[122] Ibid., 226..

Developing an Interpretive Map

In order to explore worldviews it is helpful to have a map. Cultural anthropology proves useful here. The important feature of a map is that it provides clarity by simplifying things down to the essentials. In mapping worldviews we need to simplify a complex situation. We do this by concentrating on a small number of key concepts which taken together provide an interpretive framework. These concepts are *worldview, meta-narrative, paradigm, and paradigm shift*. We now treat each in turn.

Worldview Mission anthropologist Paul Hiebert[123] surveys many frameworks used to explore the concept of a worldview before arriving at his own model, which is set out schematically in Figure 8. In his understanding, worldviews *provide a filter through which people pass their experience in attempting to make sense of it and therefore respond appropriately to it*. A worldview brings together what people, individually or collectively, know and believe, feel and value. A worldview has *three interrelated dimensions* – a *cognitive* dimension, an *emotional* dimension and an *evaluative* dimension.

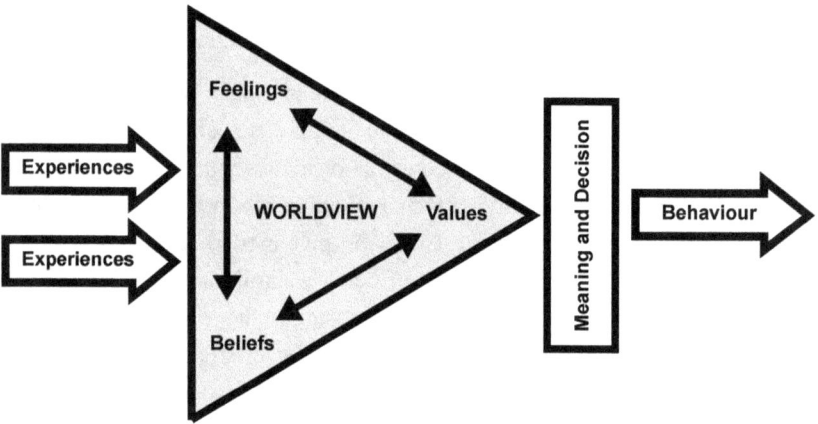

Figure 8. Worldview as an Interpretive Tool (adapted from Hiebert, 2008)[124]

What people value shapes how they think and vice-versa; what they think shapes how they feel and so on. In this context, a Catholic worldview would be a synthesis of what Catholics know and believe, what they feel as Catholics, and what they value as Catholics. To state the matter in this way is to recognise that *there must be multiple legitimate expressions of such a worldview*.

As we have noted previously, the worldview concept, like that of culture,

---

[123] Hiebert, 26.
[124] Ibid.

operates at a number of levels. At the *macro* level we can speak of the worldview of a faith, the worldview of a culture or the worldview of an age. As we understand the situation today faith and culture provide people with a coherent framework within which to interpret their experience. When it comes to interpreting particular experiences, people generally do so by choosing which framework to employ. The worldview of an age refers to a set of understandings shared across cultures at a particular period in history, which is evidenced in shared experiences and shared aspirations. This worldview is growing in importance as the globalisation process advances. It is an important feature of cultural development in the West, as we shall see.

When we speak of worldviews operating at the *micro* level we are alluding to a frame of reference in meaning-making shared within a community or that held by an individual. Worldviews provide individuals and groups with the frames of reference they use to make sense of individual and collective experiences. Worldviews play an important part in how people construct their identity – that is, how they see themselves in the world. This, in turn, shapes their sense of self-worth.

Meta-narrative Cultural worldviews embrace *what a people believes to be true about themselves as a people*, and *how they feel about themselves and their place in the world in which they live*. History clearly indicates that in many societies a dynamic is at play which leads people to pose questions such as – is what we believe about ourselves, "our truth", also true for others; does this make us superior to, equal to or less than others? When the narrative of one group comes to be seen as universal in extension, that is as *something that is true of all people for all time*, then it is called a meta-narrative.

The first eleven chapters of the Book of Genesis are written from just such a universal perspective. After this the biblical account is focused on the story of a particular people. As Rabbi Jonathan Sacks interprets it, in the Jewish meta-narrative the *one* God is the God of all people, but there are *many* paths to salvation. The *unity* of God in heaven is seen as complemented by the *diversity* of God's creation on earth. God's covenant with Israel entails a vocation to be different, so establishing the God-given dignity of difference *for all people*.[125]

Ideologies such as communism and Nazism are proposed by their supporters as meta-narratives. Meta-narratives make claims to truth that are universal.

Paradigm and Paradigm Shift Thomas Kuhn popularised the modern

---

[125] These themes are developed in Jonathan Sacks "Exorcising Plato's Ghost" in *The Dignity of Difference* (London: Continuum Press, 2003), Chapter 3, 45–66.

conception of "paradigm" in his book *The Structure of Scientific Revolutions*.[126] His interest was in how one conception in science comes to replace another. This he called a *paradigm shift*. For Kuhn science advances along two pathways – "normal science" whereby change comes about incrementally, and "revolutionary science" whereby one way of understanding a phenomenon (paradigm) is replaced quite suddenly by an alternative conception that cannot be reconciled with the original.

An example is the behaviour of light. Is the behaviour of light best explained by considering it as a particle or as a wave? In a paradigm shift evidence mounts which contradicts an initial position. Evidence accumulated, for instance, relating to the phenomenon of diffraction that was inconsistent with the particle theory of light. This did not necessarily disprove the existing theory, but led to an alternative theory being proposed – that the behaviour of light is better explained if we understand it as a wave. This alternative theory can be dealt with by the scientific community in a number of ways – challenging the contradictory data, ignoring the data altogether, trying to reconcile it with the original theory, discrediting the methods used to collect the data, discrediting the proponents of the new theory and so on.

However, if repeated experiments indicate that the data on which the new theory is based is sound, then a sense of unease develops within the scientific community about the tenability of the original paradigm, in our example, the particle theory of light. In a paradigm shift, sometimes with amazing rapidity, the scientific ground shifts and thinking that was initially seen as being "outside the square", for example, that light can be considered as a wave, becomes the mainstream explanation, and the wave theory of light replaces the particle theory.

It is important to note that, in the construction of knowledge, it is *what the scientific community comes to accept* that defines what is held to be scientific truth. Science therefore has its own version of the *sensus fidelium* that we noted earlier as providing an important criteria for authoritative Catholic teaching.

Social scientists were quick to recognise the value of Kuhn's conceptions of paradigm and paradigm shift and apply them to their own fields. Within the social sciences, a "paradigm" is understood as a set of related assumptions, concepts, values, and practices that constitutes the way an academic community comes to view some important element in its field of study. These social science paradigms link up to form the "worldview" of the discipline. Any attack on a constitutive paradigm in the discipline can be viewed as an attack on the

---

[126] Thomas Kuhn, *The Structure of Scientific Revolutions*, 3rd Edition (Chicago: University of Chicago Press, 1996).

discipline itself, and is defended accordingly.

The concepts of paradigm and paradigm shift also have currency in theology. Like any other branch of knowledge, theology has its paradigms which are linked together to create the discipline. Theology, like other disciplines, is also subject to paradigm changes. The internal dynamics of many faith communities can be interpreted as the quest for dominance by people holding a particular theological paradigm which is in competition with another. Theological truth, however, unlike science has to deal with not only universal claims to truth, but also absolute claims. This makes the discipline unique.

Following St Anselm, theology is traditionally defined as faith seeking understanding.[127] The theological process is driven by the need to understand God's revelation in the context of changing human experience, to make sense of this, and to communicate meaning to others. In such a process paradigms will be created, be challenged, and will evolve and change. Many of the theological positions found in the documents of the Second Vatican Council have been widely interpreted as setting out new paradigms and initiating some significant paradigm shifts within the authoritative teaching that underpins all expressions of the Catholic worldview.[128] The implications of these shifts have been much debated since the Council. We will return to this matter in Chapter Ten.

Paradigm Shifts within a Worldview – The Case of Galileo

A classic case illustrating the interconnected nature of paradigms within a worldview is that of Galileo (1564–1642), one of the more extraordinary characters in the history of science. Galileo took up the cause of Copernicus (1473–1543), promoting the idea that the motion of the planets could be predicted without the need to have the earth at rest in the centre of the universe, but rather as another planet revolving around the sun.[129] A prominent exponent of the new "science", he was invited by Pope Urban VIII to present "a balanced account" of the pros and cons of the heliocentric paradigm of the cosmos vis-à-vis the geocentric model, "without favoring one position or the other". However, Galileo was temperamentally incapable of doing this and his thinly veiled ridiculing of the geocentric model, including the opinion of his sponsor the Pope, as portrayed in the study he subsequently produced, landed him in serious trouble. His intemperate intervention is thought to have been responsible for the subsequent condemnation of Copernicus' scientific writings as heretical.[130]

---

[127] Richard McBrien *Catholicism* Revised Edition (Harper San Francisco, 1994), 20.
[128] Cf. Gerard Arbuckle *Refounding the Church* (Homebush: St Paul's Publications, 1993), 22.
[129] The model of the cosmos with the earth at the centre and the sun and stars revolving around it – the geocentric model – provided the most obvious explanation of what people saw. The heliocentric model was a more elegant theory because of its wider potential application.

What we can appreciate in hindsight, but was less than obvious at the time, was that the scientific paradigm Galileo attacked was linked to others integral to the pre-modern worldview, including the theological and political paradigms. The Old Testament writers, working with the scientific knowledge of their time, took the geocentric paradigm as axiomatic. In the pre-modern worldview the science of the Bible as well as its theological content were accepted at face value. The heliocentric view of the universe raised serious questions about the science of the Bible. In the pre-modern world disciplines were linked differently from the way they are today. A challenge to Biblical "science" could be viewed as a challenge to the authority of the Bible. It is not surprising, therefore, that the keepers of the old paradigm responded by using all the devices listed above in its defence. It would take considerable time to work out the relationship between the truths of the new "science" and those of faith.

Galileo's critique was also interpreted at a second level. The geocentric universe placed man at the centre of the ordered universe created by God. The idea of living in an ordered universe, one characterised by what Charles Taylor calls "hierarchical complementarity",[131] was central to the social and political structures of pre-modernity. Within the pre-modern worldview people understood that they were born into a position and knew their position and the responsibilities that went with it. The worldview of the time provided not only a political and social framework but also the *moral framework underpinning public order*. The dominant worldview, then as now, determined the *imaginal horizon* within which people lived their lives.

The paradigm Galileo was championing in challenging a paradigm of what we would now recognise as astronomy raised questions about related paradigms – authority of the Bible, the nature of truth, the basis of public order and social organisation. His advocacy of a heliocentric universe was, not surprisingly, interpreted as being politically dangerous. Galileo spent the last eight years of his life under house arrest. His case illustrates the dynamics by which paradigm change occurs and how such changes link up within a worldview.

The Pre-modern Worldview and Constructed Identity

The Galileo case also throws considerable light on the pre-modern worldview. In the pre-modern world the worldviews which we now recognise as those of religion, of culture and of the age, were so closely aligned as to form *a single frame of reference* in which all experiences could be interpreted.

---

[130] The heliocentric paradigm generated little controversy in Copernicus's lifetime, but was condemned by the Church as heretical in 1616, nearly 70 years after his death, largely on the grounds that it contradicted scripture.

[131] Taylor, 164.

As we shall see in the next chapter, the impacts of the Reformation and the Enlightenment were to change this situation dramatically, so that in modernity the worldviews of culture and of the age developed independently from that of religion. In making sense of experience, individuals and communities could now choose elements from each worldview, as well as from the pre-modern worldview, so personal and collective identity, which were taken as givens in pre-modern times, had now to be constructed – that is, they became a matter of choice. This was a major development in human consciousness. The *modern sensibility* that resulted was therefore markedly different from the pre-modern sensibility that preceded it.

In the new sensibility it became possible for an individual or a community to determine what elements of religion or culture they wished to incorporate into their worldview. This became a distinguishing feature of liberal Protestantism in modernity. This spirit of the age became one in which people could choose in areas of life where previously there had been little choice. This was an important factor in the development of Western cultures, which is often present as a "rejection of traditions".

An important argument supporting the case that post-modern sensibility is a later development of modern sensibility is that, in the post-modern period, the situation outlined above had not changed substantially. However, what has changed is the range of choices open to people. This has expanded exponentially. The range is now so broad that when it comes to forming a personal worldview, the basis of self-identity, people become disoriented by the need to make decisions as they face so many alternatives. As a consequence, they feel they are living in a fragmenting and fragmented world and respond by not choosing, or by choosing randomly.

Paradigm shifts, changes in the frame of reference we use to explain things, share common characteristics whether they occur in a culture, in disciplines such as theology or sociology, or in religion. There is a movement from a stable state, *orientation*, to an unstable state or state of chaos, *disorientation*, to a new form of stability, *re-orientation*.[132] We agree with Schreiter that beyond the disorientation of post-modernity lies a period in which people will develop the capacity to form a worldview that is coherent, even given the plethora of choices available to them. The pain of living with a fragmented identity will prove a motivating force in this regard. However, we are still journeying to that more stable state and herein lies the major challenge for educators – how to help young people make sense of their lives in an era of transition.

The mission challenge for Catholic educators is to help students sort though

---

[132] Cf. Arbuckle, 43–55.

the bewildering range of options that are now open to them in constructing a worldview in which they can make sense of their experiences and develop a sense of their own identity and worth. They need to appreciate that culture and religion are resources in this process because both are based on coherent worldviews that have stood the test of time. They also need to learn that God's Spirit is active in the process of identity formation.

CHAPTER SIX

The Narrative of Post-modernity

The Importance of Historical Consciousness

In Chapter Five we posed the question: how did post-modern sensibility arise? Before attempting to address this there is a prior question that needs to addressed: *does history have any intrinsic meaning?*

How people respond to this question has an important bearing on their worldview. In the modern period the answer to the question was an unequivocal "yes". The advent of science and technology had ushered in an era that promised growing prosperity, more opportunity, better health and therefore greater human well-being. In the framework of the humanism that characterised the modern worldview, the goal of history was human progress and the study of Western history demonstrated the reasonableness of such a view.

People with a post-modern mindset, by way of contrast, live almost exclusively in the "now" and in this sensibility the idea of history having meaning is seen as one of many discretionary elements in the formation of a worldview. Choices made in forming their worldview have an important bearing on what people value, how they act, what they believe and what they regard as worth knowing. The Christian worldview, even given its multiple expressions, presents a sharp contrast to both the modern and post-modern views of history.

The Christian contention is that the historical process is meaningful but that its direction is difficult to predict. Whereas the post-modern view is that the direction of history is *random*, Christians hold that it is guided by the mysterious action of God's creative Spirit always at work in the world in pursuit of God's mission. However, as distinct from the modern, the Christian mindset holds that human progress does not follow a *linear* trajectory, because progress is always limited by the impact of human miscalculation and sinfulness. However, Christians remain optimistic that progress can and will be made because the historical process has a goal, the Kingdom proclaimed by Jesus, which will be partially realised within history and reach its fulfilment beyond history.

The central paradigm of Judeo-Christian religion *is a unique and coherent understanding*, conveyed to people through their respective narratives, *of who God is and how God acts within history as it continues to unfold.* In the context of this understanding "frontier time", our time, is charged with meaning. Christian educators play an important role in helping people to discern what this meaning is.

In its various forms, Christianity has built its narrative around a foundational experience, the liberating life, death and resurrection of Jesus. In terms of this narrative, God's mission, the action of God carried on in the world, gives history meaning. The Christian community believes that God is always at work in the world and therefore it has a special responsibility to discern God's presence by reading the signs of the times. However, as recent history readily attests, the Church is not immune from human miscalculation and human sinfulness. Even within the Church there is no guarantee that progress towards the Kingdom comes automatically with the passage of time, as subsequent sections in this chapter will show.

In Chapter Five we considered "post-modernity" as both a period in history and as a sensibility, and noted that there are different ways of categorising recent historical periods and our understanding of them. However, the common reference point is modernity. In making sense of our current age it is necessary to explore *the narrative of how we got to where we are*. In the sections that follow we trace the journey from pre-modern to post-modern times in terms of the changes in worldview that have characterised this movement within Western culture.

The Pre-modern World

In discussing pre-modern times, sociologists often refer to life "under the sacred canopy". By this they mean that the influence of the Catholic Church on the life of ordinary people in Europe at this time was all-pervasive. People lived their lives within a single all-embracing worldview. In pre-modernity the Christian religion lay conspicuously at the heart of most Western cultures and many aspects of life came directly under ecclesiastical control.

For instance, the Church controlled what basic education there was through the licensing of teachers who operated mainly from small cathedral schools. The main function of these schools was to train people for participation in the liturgy, which was celebrated in Latin. What welfare/health care was available was provided as a charitable work of the Church. This was regarded as an important part of the Church's mission and its support was the responsibility of all Catholics. The Church played an integral role in the political system. It provided society with its moral framework and principle of social order. In pre-modern Europe it could be said that *the Church was history*. It is impossible to tell the narrative of pre-modern times without reference to the Catholic Church.

In this period Church leaders had an expansive view of the Church's role within society. It was impossible to see the Church and "the world" as anything but mutually permeable. Christian faith was seen as integral to the cultural worldview and largely defined the "spirit of the age". However, the speed with which this "sacred canopy" fell apart suggests that the first evangelisation of much of Europe did not have very deep cultural roots, particularly in its northern regions.

Life under the sacred canopy began to disintegrate at the time of the Reformation and in the period following it. The dissatisfaction of the reformers with the internal state of the Catholic Church led to the creation of different Christian Churches, many with their own national affiliations. The "catholic" fabric of the Church unravelled quite quickly. Rather than being the source of moral and social order within society, religious tensions exacerbated political tensions and vice-versa, so that religion became a major cause of disorder leading first to years of instability, followed by years of religious wars. The Thirty Years War (1618–1648) devastated most of north-western Europe, bankrupted many of the small states that comprised Europe at the time, and required a lengthy period of recovery. A divided Christianity could no longer provide the basis for social order in Europe and, in the state of disorientation that resulted, a new worldview began to take shape.

Charles Taylor[133] in his impressive study *A Secular Age* demonstrates that the change from a worldview where the primary point of reference was Christianity, pre-modernity, to one where the primary reference point was "appeal to reason", modernity, was gradual. This change ushered in a new understanding of the world.

The European Enlightenment and Early Modernity

Beginning in the sixteenth century, new fields of intellectual endeavour such as economics, science and medicine arose, and older fields such as politics and philosophy adopted new emphases. As science advanced so too did technology. A new outlook began to develop in a transition age, which reached its peak in the European Enlightenment of the eighteenth century. This marked the beginning of what we now call modernity. The period also saw the emergence of the merchant class and mass migration of people from the country into the cities seeking work. The quest for empire, spurred on by the need for raw materials to feed industrial production, was a further feature of modernity. In this cauldron of change *modern sensibility* gradually emerged. People living in the West became much more assertive in recognising the power of human ingenuity driven by "reason".

The European Enlightenment of the eighteenth century was a complex

---

[133] Charles Taylor *A Secular Age* (Cambridge Massachusetts: Belknap/Harvard University Press, 2007).

movement. Even today, its consequences continue to influence the intellectual "countryside" of all Western cultures and the culture of countries colonised by the West. The Enlightenment bequeathed to the West conceptions of democracy, scientific method, industrial production, economic order, the nation state, the secular state, liberalism, and universal education, to mention some of its more notable achievements. It ushered in *an age of optimism* in which human experience became better understood and more highly valued.

Schreiter[134] articulates the "heart of the matter" as this transition unfolded:

> The Western Enlightenment arose…out of an effort to overcome the sectarian feuding of the churches in the seventeenth century. The murderous outcome of holding in uncompromising fashion of each to one's own dogma, thereby not allowing any common ground where all parties could stand, but insisting rather on the irreducibility of one's own position, can lead only to the most powerful winning the day…Only when all accede to the rules of reason, common to all human beings, can such tribalism be overcome.

Such ideas provided the foundation on which a new sensibility could be built, one which would free people from the rivalry of the churches and the power of ecclesiastics, Catholic and Protestant alike. Schreiter goes on to make the point that a growing confidence in rationality, exercised outside the purview of ecclesiastical control, was seen as the *sine qua non* of further technical and political progress.

In France Enlightenment thinking led to the revolutionary destruction of a political system based on "the divine right of kings", a doctrine underwritten by the Catholic Church. The Church's close alignment with the existing political and social order saw it too become the target of revolution. In condemning the excesses and injustices of this revolution, the Church's stance had justification. The advent of Napoleon and his imprisonment of the Pope did little to improve the Church leaders' negative reaction to these new developments, nor did the blatant excesses of the Industrial Revolution.

Put on the defensive by the Reformation and the pressing need for internal renewal, Catholic leaders of the period simply extended their defences and fended off the intellectual challenges of modernity. They chose to cast the Church in the role of victim. The Church withdrew into its own cultural world, a stance which was to prove a serious miscalculation. Catholic cultural anthropologist Gerard Arbuckle[135] sums up the situation with some insight.

> The more the Church's leadership struggled to resist the revolutionary insights and values emerging within the Western world the more the

---

[134] Robert Schreiter, *New Theology Review* Part 3, August, 2007, 58.
[135] Gerard Arbuckle, *Refounding the Church* (Homebush: St Paul's Publications, 1998), 23.

Church withdrew from what was taking place in history and in people's lives. At the same time Rome fostered a form of scholastic philosophy, neo-scholasticism, that provided the Church with a very coherent intellectual framework. Yet this philosophy had one serious disadvantage – namely, it was so self-contained that its supporters saw no need to listen to or even learn from, other philosophies. The Church as a culture became increasingly inward looking, defensive and protective of its members, compelled to live in a world considered to be under the direction of evil or subversive forces.

There is a significant difference in mood between the optimism of the Enlightenment and an underlying pessimism in the Church's attitude to the modern world as the *modern sensibility* took shape. Whereas in pre-modern times the Church was integral to society, as modernity advanced, it was forced to find an alternative place to stand. Within the tenets of neo-scholasticism its leaders came to understand the Church as "a perfect society",[136] one set apart from "the world", and complete in itself. In this period the worldviews of faith and culture, which were synonymous in pre-modern times, began to split from each other, developing according to their own logic. The worldviews of the age and of cultures began to evolve together on a separate trajectory from that of religion, a situation Catholic educators are asked to redress in schools even today.

If the Church had no need of a corrupt world, many in society had no need for a Church turned inward. The Church painted itself into a corner, and was often portrayed both as the enemy of progress and as a bastion of the pre-modern superstition that science sought to overthrow. As modernity developed, so too did a mood in which people became indifferent and even hostile to Christianity viewing it as a religion dominated by the ideology of its clergy.

As Charles Taylor explains, modernity saw the rise within Western culture of a new worldview, that of exclusive humanism.[137] This was a worldview in which the transcendent is either consciously excluded from, or moved to the periphery of, human life. In its more benign form, exclusive humanism sees human life as governed by the laws of nature created by God *and God does not interfere in the working of these laws*. In Taylor's view, exclusive humanism paved the way for the rise of modern atheism.

Pius IX's *Syllabus of Errors,* published in 1864, and Pius X's condemnation of "modernists" in 1907, did little to bridge the growing gap between faith and culture. Both stances were seen outside the Church as attacks on the political

---

[136] By this the Church did not mean "perfect" as in "without fault". "Perfect" is used in a philosophical sense and means a society having at its disposal all the means necessary to achieve its proper ends.
[137] Taylor, 26.

and religious liberalism that characterised life in the emerging nation states of Europe and the USA. They in turn were attacked accordingly, further isolating both the Church and its members from society, and fuelling the sectarianism that characterised early modernity.

The difficulties Church leaders faced in dealing with the Enlightenment and its aftermath were many. They were endeavouring to react to a new worldview still in the process of formation. While the Church acknowledged the injunction to "repay to Caesar what belongs to Caesar and to God what belongs to God" (Luke 20:25), the Catholic Church had in pre-modern societies often sought to play the role of both Caesar and God. The further difficulty the Church faced was that many of those newly arrived to Caesar's role as modern Europe took shape, having wrested control over much of public life from ecclesiastical control, now wanted to take over God's role as well!

The most serious miscalculation on the part of the Church's leaders was to place themselves in the position where they could have little impact in shaping the modern worldview as it emerged. They further failed to recognise or acknowledge the positive values behind the human aspirations embedded in this worldview. The humanism that emerged in early modernity might have been evangelised as it was forming. However, the theological paradigms that would render such a project possible were yet to emerge.

The present understanding that the Spirit is at work in all cultures was missing and people still thought in terms of "civilisation" which in the eyes of Church leaders had clearly taken a turn for the worse. The reigning paradigm held that the Holy Spirit was present and active only in the Catholic Church. Jesus' message of the Kingdom was a further casualty in that the Church was regarded as synonymous with the Kingdom. In the confines of this Catholic worldview, inevitably, mission came to be interpreted quite narrowly. Not surprisingly, the mission of the Catholic school was similarly seen largely in defensive/protective terms.

Early Modernity – Its Aspirations and Development

There are many ways to characterise the early modern period. Lyon[138] sums up the period succinctly.

> Modernity is all about massive changes that took place at many levels from the middle sixteenth century onwards, changes signalled by shifts that uprooted agricultural workers and transformed them into mobile industrial urbanites. Modernity questions all conventional ways of doing things, substituting authorities of its own based in science, economic growth, democracy and law. And it unsettles the self; if identity is given in

---

[138] David Lyon *Postmodernity* (Buckingham: Open University Press, 1994), 21.

traditional society, in modernity it is constructed.

In modernity a person's place in society was no longer determined by the "complementary hierarchy" of pre-modern times, nor was it bound by the moral order that this social structure implied. People now had to make choices about their place in society and for many this situation was highly disorienting. Their experience is insightfully portrayed in the novels of writers such as Anthony Trollope, George Eliot and Thomas Hardy.

Modern society provided *a new moral order*, one based on equality, freedom to choose, and commitment to the well-being of all. This new vision of society was sustained by a growing belief and confidence in humankind's ability to find solutions to problems *through the use of reason*. Modernity promised much and ushered in an era of general optimism. Enlightenment thinking proved the catalyst for the major paradigm shifts associated with modernity.

The Enlightenment's myth of progress was transported around the globe as an accompaniment to European colonisation. The optimism of this era is reflected in the missionary outlook of the time. In the perception of many, the projects of bringing Christianity and "civilisation" (for which read "progress") to new lands were one and the same. In time, the missionaries were to become major critics of the Enlightenment's ideal of "progress", once its exploitative face became more apparent.

While Enlightenment thinking provided the foundations on which the paradigms of modernity were built in areas such as politics, medicine and economics, as modernity advanced new social ideas also began to emerge, some being transformed into the ideologies driving political programs. For example, the concept of evolution, initially posed as a scientific idea in the early modern period, later became the basis for social theories leading to the identification of the *Volk* and the madness of Nazism. The capitalist system that emerged in the modern period was subsequently challenged by the rival communist system with its grand narrative of a workers' utopia. The rivalry between these two ideologies would threaten the world with atomic annihilation.

Crisis in Modernity and the Beginnings of the Post-modern Experience

The optimistic notion that science inevitably leads to progress was in time balanced by the realisation that science contains within itself enormous destructive power. Similarly, the idea that science delivers dispassionate, objective and reliable knowledge has increasingly come under challenge, once knowledge was recognised as an important source of power.

In the light of human experience in the twentieth century, faith in the tenets of the Enlightenment waned. Also, as the study of cultural anthropology advanced, European/Western culture lost its status as the benchmark for human progress. Suspicion grew that the Enlightenment meta-narrative of progress was no longer congruent with human experience. Progress, in the Enlightenment sense, demanded the consumption of virtually limitless resources without any acknowledgement of their true cost, the limited nature of the earth's capacity to provide these resources, the misery wrought in a world divided into developed and under-developed countries, or the deleterious effects of unlimited consumption on the life of the planet.

The optimism of modernity needed to be balanced. The early 1970s saw this occur with the emergence of critical theory and the "hermeneutic of suspicion" – a tendency to examine all claims to power more critically, by considering whose interests they serve. This trend was codified in the work of Habermas and other critical theorists who have been influential in shaping the thinking of educators.[139] Taken to extremes by some of its proponents, this new willingness to question all claims to power soon degenerated into relativism – the belief that there is no such thing as truth *per se*, only "my" truth and "your" truth. This situation became the accepted *modus vivendi* of the modern media which, in order to generate controversy, seeks to relativise almost any claim to the truth of things. One result of this trend has been the emergence of "spin", which seeks to interpret events from a self-serving perspective. "News" became just another product to be attractively packaged and sold.

A new willingness to critically examine truth claims also surfaced in theology, particularly where these were seen as overstated claims to universality. In consequence, a wider recognition developed about the contextual nature of theology along with a suspicion that much of the traditional theology presented as universal was, in fact, Euro-centric in its interests, its formulation and its expression.

The question "what is truth?", famously put to Jesus by Pontius Pilate, emerged as a major concern as modernity entered into a period of crisis. The "crisis of modernity" centres on the question of whether or not the modern worldview is still tenable. A second facet of the crisis centres on the following questions. Can our present experiences still be meaningfully incorporated into the narrative of modernity? Have we reached the limits of exclusive humanism?

The human experience of the twentieth century led to the collapse in many parts of the world of the *ideologies of modernity*, communism and fascism, as

---

[139] A useful discussion can be found in Shirley Grundy *Curriculum: Product or Praxis* (London: Falmer Press, 1987), 7–20.

well as serious questioning of the tenets of capitalism. Belief in the inevitable delivery of progress driven by science was also undermined. This was accompanied by loss of faith both in meta-narratives and the purposefulness of history. Mark Taylor[140] describes the emerging situation well.

> While pre-modern times relied on traditional beliefs and religion to provide these (meta) narratives, the modern era turned to science and (provided) the dominant meta-narrative until the post-modern break in about 1973. Both pre-modernism and modernism viewed history as moving towards social enlightenment and emancipation, with knowledge eventually becoming complete. All would be known either theologically or scientifically. While the modern era saw the scientific model becoming legitimised over unquestioned, untested beliefs, postmodernism is an age of fragmentation and pluralism with no one model offering any dominant, shared meta-narrative. There has been a widespread de-legitimation of previous models and authorities: religion, science, political and economic power, and sources of "knowledge". The modern values of reason and progress and ideas about contributing to a greater good…are taking a sound beating in our post-modern culture.

This de-legitimation process extends the range of options open to people in forming a worldview and in constructing their identity, including that of having no coherent worldview and a confused personal identity.

As some of the major paradigms of the modern worldview were called into question, people living out of the modern worldview experienced a sense of disorientation, of walking on slippery ground. This did not cause them necessarily to abandon their modern worldview. Many people resist what they see as the premise of "post-modern" sensibility – acceptance of a fragmented and plural situation as "normal". Moderns and post-moderns now exist side by side in every Western society, extending the range of choices open to people in constructing a worldview and associated identity. Migrants and refugees coming from pre-modern societies extend the range of perceptible options available to post-moderns even further.

The "Second Modernity"

With a number of other scholars, theologian Robert Schreiter interprets "post-modernity" as a transitional phase in human affairs. In a convincing treatment, he advocates re-evaluating the project of modernity and reformulating it on less heroic assumptions. This reformulation must take into account the phenomena shaping human consciousness in our time – globalisation, migration, the resurgence of religion, and global terrorism.[141] To these could be added

---

[140] Mark Taylor *Generation NeXt Comes to College: Meeting the Post Modern Student* <www.taylorprograms.org/images/Gen_NeXt_article_HLC_06.pdf> (2004).

pluralism, and the need for a more ecologically sustainable mode of living on our planet.

While acknowledging that we live in an environment that is at times fragmented, unstable and obsessed with difference, Schreiter does not see this as a permanent condition of existence because of the human tendency to search for *meaning and coherence*. He argues that mankind's inherent tendency is to seek meaning by constructing paradigms, worldviews and narratives *that mesh together and convey "a sense of the whole"*. Thus he asks:

> Can we find our way forward into a different kind of modernity that will account for what we are experiencing in terms of plurality, difference, contingency and instability without engaging in violence towards one another or creating fortress-like havens of safety where people may survive for a time, but will not flourish?[142]

In answering this question Schreiter rejects the "death of the grand narrative" by suggesting the following:

> If we are able to learn from history and from previous reflection on great human failures, we have a better chance of constructing something that will indeed serve the well-being of the human community.[143]

With this caveat in mind, and also being aware that we can learn from great successes as well, he explores some features of "a new whole", by which he means a worldview capable of making sense of the spirit of our age. He seeks to find a place for faith within this conception. He does this under the banner of the "second modernity". Thus he writes:

> "Second modernity" is an attempt to seek the whole, using the framework of...modernity. It reflects the fact that we have moved beyond the first modernity, but are not mired in a fragmented post-modernity. One of the features of the second modernity is a sense that many of the boundaries that defined the first modernity have shifted...Boundaries that once defined and even protected us are no longer fulfilling these functions.[144]

Schreiter suggests that as we move into the second modernity there is a need to *"rethink boundaries"*. Since boundaries define difference, we need to rethink our attitudes towards difference – in culture, lifestyle, ethnicity and religion. A second area for development is *seeing problems through the lens of "both/and"* rather than "either/or". Analysing life in terms of polar opposites, given the complexity of the contemporary world, is highly problematic. In the more diverse and complex environment in which we now live, he sees

---

[141] Robert Schreiter *New Theology Review*, Part 3, August, 2007.
[142] Schreiter *New Theology Review*, Part 2, May, 2007, 53.
[143] Ibid., 55.
[144] Schreiter Part 3, 61.

two countervailing forces are at work – the *global flow* of communication is homogenising the world, while at the same time there is renewed emphasis on *the importance of the local*. The dynamic interplay between these two trends suggests that the "both/and" options require that the emerging worldview needs to be inclusive rather than exclusive.

Finally, Schreiter believes that in formulating a worldview to underpin the second modernity, we have to *rethink the place of religion* in society as a matter of some necessity. He questions the wisdom of seeing secularisation as the "sole paradigm for dealing with diversity".[145] He also questions the possibility of resolving tensions in a world where many of the issues that create instability relate to religion, when the paradigms accessible to governments in resolving issues around international relations specifically exclude religion.

While many commentators focus on the negative aspects of post-modern sensibility, Gallagher sounds a more optimistic note in helping delineate some aspects of the new worldview:[146]

> …post-modernity is characterised by sensibilities on three fronts: ecology, feminism and the return of spirituality. Indeed the three areas are deeply connected: they are rooted in the realisation that our history has suppressed something precious, which now needs liberation. Modernity was exploitative of the earth and of peoples, forgetful of women and of the feminine in each person, and forced the spiritual dimension of life to retreat to the poetic and the private. If so, post-modernity proposes a series of openings. Already these three horizons, that were not so strongly felt even a generation ago, together represent a major shift in sensibility…

Both Schreiter and Gallagher agree that the emerging worldview must recognise the realities of human suffering and the need for forgiveness and reconciliation. Both seem to envisage a future in which engagement with exclusive humanism through dialogue can lead to the formulation of an *inclusive humanism*.

The picture outlined above is consistent with the argument of the previous chapter that, if it is to be sustainable, the worldview of the second modernity must help people make *coherent choices* when faced with the supermarket of options and ideas now available. Given that this array of options seems likely to continue and may even grow in the future, the pressing need is for *master ideas* that can provide coherence. From an educational perspective, we clearly need to know more about how people construct their identity, seeing this as a developmental process. With such information we will be in a better position for designing our educational programs.

---

[145] Schreiter *New Theology Review*, Part 3, August, 2007, 65.
[146] Michael Gallagher *Clashing Symbols* Revised Edition

Mission in the Second Modernity

Any list of errors, such as those listed in the *Syllabus of Errors*, has embedded within it a corresponding list of truths, and it was on these that the Catholic bishops of the world belatedly, but importantly, focused at the Second Vatican Council. Here they undertook a humbler searching and reconciliation with the past in order to liberate areas of life from which the Church had closed itself off.[147]

The Council's Pastoral Constitution on the Church in the Modern World (*Gaudium et Spes*), addressed not just to Church members but *to the world*, emphasises a changed outlook in its often quoted opening statement:

> The joys and hopes, the grief and anguish of the people of our time, especially of those who are poor or afflicted, are the joys and hopes, the grief and anguish of the followers of Christ as well. Nothing that is genuinely human fails to find an echo in their hearts. For theirs is a community of people united in Christ and guided by the holy Spirit in their pilgrimage towards the Father's kingdom, bearers of a message of salvation for all humanity. That is why they experience a deep feeling of solidarity with the human race and its history.[148]

The text makes it clear that the bishops recognised the need to respond to the aspirations of the times and to influence the shape of new paradigms and worldviews as they form. They did so conscious of the Church's limitations and its own need for renewal,[149] and they sought to engage with all people of good will. Catholic schools carry specific and significant responsibility in carrying this project forward.

At the Council the bishops sought to re-position the Church *within history* again, but in a different manner, and following a somewhat wiser path. As Rivers observes:[150]

> Being open to the world means being open to history. At Vatican II, the church embraced the hazardous task of finding the path of truth in love *amid* the ambiguities of history, rather than *apart* from history. It turned away from the notion that it was possible to build a system of truths free from history. Instead it moved to a theology based on looking at faith experience in the light of history. In theological terms, the Church rejected the theological fundamentalism that gives either a document (the Bible) or a doctrine absolute, ahistorical, self-interpreting authority.

---

[147] Cf. ibid., 108–110.

[148] Austin Flannery (ed.) *Vatican Council II: Constitutions, Decrees, Declarations* (Dublin: Dominican Publications, 1996), 163.

[149] This is recognised forcefully by Pope Paul VI in his 1975 apostolic exhortation *Evangelii Nuntiandi* #15 where he speaks of the Church's need to be constantly evangelised itself.

[150] Robert Rivers *From Maintenance to Mission: Evangelisation and the Revitalisation of the Parish* (New York : Paulist Press, 2005), 7.

Such a stance is not without its challenges in a period of history in which society itself is in crisis and undergoing its own form of renewal. Forging a relationship at a time when both Church and society are exploring the contours of a revised identity can be problematic, but also full of possibilities, hence the need for and importance of, dialogue as a modality of mission.

Educating in a Modern/Post-modern Environment

Educating in a frontier situation is an exciting, albeit a demanding project. Since both society and the Church sponsor the Catholic school, Catholic schooling is one of the prime locations for dialogue between society and the Church. In our "post-modern"/second modernity era the Church seeks to engage with society believing that it is has something important to bring to the shared project of creating a new worldview, one that will enable students to move beyond the dilemmas now inherent in both modern and post-modern sensibility. This represents a considerable challenge and is open to both optimism and miscalculation as paradigms continue to shift in both society and the Church. Catholic education clearly has an important role to play in this dialogue as it continues to unfold. This can occur, however, only if the Church leaders who sponsor schools have sufficient insight into the complexity of the situation which they seek to influence positively.

Early in this chapter we looked at the characteristics of post-moderns and asked the question: why do people see the world the way they now do? In the sections that followed we have endeavoured to respond to this question by outlining two intertwined narratives. These were the narrative of ideas as the West has evolved from pre-modernity to post-modernity and the narrative of the Church's engagement with society as the Western world has moved from the pre-modern times to the situation of post-modernity.

The contention of this chapter has been that our frontier experience is associated with the formation of a new era in history, one that retains many important features of modernity, but extends the range of choices open to people in a significant way. People now have so many ideas and options to choose from that a form of intellectual and emotional paralysis often sets in. In this state people live in the present with no coherent worldview and a confused sense of who they are.

As members of both society and the Church, Christians are seeking to interpret the new co-ordinates of human existence – co-ordinates of time and space and the appropriate ordering of society[151] – and rethink their implications for mission. A new form of human consciousness is in the process of being

---

[151] Paul Lakeland *Postmodernity: Christian Identity in a Fragmented Age* (Minneapolis: Fortress Press, 1997), 2.

formed – one that affects all cultures, but whose shape is yet to crystallise. As Catholic educators we can influence this process, if we understand it. This is part of our mission. Few other generations have had to face such a challenge, such a vocation.

From a faithful mission perspective, a frontier situation means that the Spirit is active and inviting people to respond. Given what we can understand of the situation, we need to consider anew what relevance Jesus' message of the Kingdom of God has for us as individuals and as school communities. We are also challenged to discern the mission direction this message invites us to pursue as a new human sensibility continues to evolve. How best to nurture in staff and students a sense of hope-filled co-operation with the Holy Spirit in taking forward this new human project is a major issue for educational leaders.

The Church is now clearly better placed, both in terms of its self-understanding and sense of mission, to make a more positive contribution to the second modernity as it forms than proved to be the case in the first modernity. One of these contributions was named in the previous chapter. Using the terminology of Pope Paul VI, one of these contributions is *evangelising culture*.[152] Another is affirming the value of historical consciousness and the importance of narrative in an anthropology that eschews the relativism and nihilism that characterises some forms of "post-modern" thought. These are all particularly important mission imperatives for Catholic schools and school leaders at this unique point in history.

A second emphasis in this chapter has been on the importance of narrative in making sense of human experience. Knowing how things got to be the way they are is an important element in understanding our present reality. It is also important in expanding the understanding of others. Narrative has an important bearing on how we see the future and how we understand mission in the light of that future. Leaders need to realise that *the story of the community has a sacred quality and that they hold it in trust for others*. The narrative must be kept alive. It carries within it the unique way in which the Spirit is at work in the life of the community, empowering people to advance God's mission. The effective school leader uses narrative to place current experience in context and make it meaningful for people. Our stories tell us who we are and we neglect them at our peril.

In Part C we will look in some detail at three major factors that are going to be influential in shaping the "second modernity" and therefore the missional frontier. These phenomena are globalisation, secularisation and pluralisation.

---

[152] Pope Paul VI *Evangelii Nuntiandi* #20.

As well as examining the impact these variables have on the developing sensibility associated with the second modernity, we will also attempt to draw out their significance for both mission and leadership in Catholic schools.

PART C

Forces Re-shaping the Frontier of Mission

One of the general theses we have pursued so far is that for the Catholic leader/educator to become a meaning-maker it is necessary for him/her to do grassroots theology. This involves bringing together the worldviews of our faith, of our culture and of our age. These can all make an important contribution because, as we have argued, the Spirit is operative in them all. None of these resources is static; all evolve over time. In our post-modern setting each is changing under the influence of three forces which have their genesis in Western culture, but are global in their impact. These are the forces of globalisation, secularisation, and pluralisation.

All three forces impact on culture and together they are re-shaping the spirit of our times. Each of these phenomena is inherently ambivalent having both positive and negative dimensions. In the post-modern West all three can be viewed positively, although not by everyone. However, people sharing a different narrative and those whose mindset reflects pre-modern or modern sensibilities, view them less sanguinely. In some extreme cases, all three are rejected as new forms of Western colonialism, a rejection which both fosters and sustains stateless terrorism.

Globalisation, secularisation and modern pluralism have proved notoriously difficult to define with any precision. The approach we have taken is to identify only the *principal facets* of each phenomenon. Chapter Seven looks at globalisation and its impact. Chapter Eight explores the various orientations encountered within secularisation. In Chapter Nine we examine empirical and ideological pluralism.

In dealing with each phenomenon we try to establish it *within its own narrative*. Taken together, globalisation, secularisation and pluralisation help create the complex milieu we call the "frontier". For many people it is a situation that presents as a wilderness in which they feel both disoriented, disempowered and isolated. In dealing with each phenomenon we also explore its significance for mission in general, as well as identifying some of the implications for the mission of the Catholic school in particular.

CHAPTER SEVEN

The Many Faces of Globalisation

What is globalisation and what impact does it have on human aspiration and the development of worldviews? In seeking to answer such questions it is important to realise that there is no agreed definition of globalisation. Each of the various social science disciplines has its own perspective on this elusive phenomenon. However, allowing for these differences, there seems broad agreement that the characteristic feature of globalisation is the increasing interconnectedness of the political, economic and social aspects of life across the planet and a consequent blurring or erosion of national, cultural and other boundaries.[153] In dealing with globalisation in his recent encyclical *Caritas in Veritate (Charity in Truth),* Pope Benedict XVI reminds us that

> Underneath the more visible processes (of the phenomenon of globalisation) humanity itself is becoming increasingly interconnected; it is made up of individuals and peoples to whom this process should offer benefits and development…As a human reality, it is the product of diverse cultural tendencies, which need to be subjected to a process of discernment. The truth of globalization as a process and its fundamental ethical criterion are given by the unity of the human family and its development towards what is good. Hence a sustained commitment is needed so as to promote a person-based and community-oriented cultural process of world-wide integration that is open to transcendence.[154]

Globalisation is widely recognised as an ambivalent reality, holding both threat and promise. It is perhaps best delineated by outlining its more commonly acknowledged facets and identifying the threats and promises associated with each.

Globalisation as Complex Connectivity

The first face of globalisation is that of *"complex connectivity"*, [155] multiple levels of global inter-connectedness. Complex connectivity is created by, and expressed through, new communication systems which permit almost instantaneous flow of capital and information, public and private, around the globe, and by the development of transport systems that give increasingly large numbers of people access to relatively cheap means of travel. As a

---
[153] Robert Schreiter *The New Catholicity* (Maryknoll New York: Orbis, 1997), 5.
[154] Pope Benedict XV *Caritatis in Veritate* #43 (*Love in Truth, 2009*).
[155] John Tomlinson *Globalization and Culture* (Chicago: University of Chicago Press, 1999), 1.

consequence, there is an unprecedented capacity to transport finance, news, people and ideas around the world very quickly. These developments have many beneficial consequences, as any international traveller can readily testify. Tickets can be booked, accommodation arranged, and money transferred on the internet almost seamlessly. Similarly, a book not available in one country can be quickly sourced in another, ordered, and arrive a week later. Information on almost any topic can be quickly accessed by entering the topic into an internet search engine. The benefits of complex connectively are now widely shared. Of course to access the "global flow" of information, people must have access to both a computer and the internet.

Complex connectivity, while expanding the scope of what is known, also compresses our sense of time and space. In the process, it is slowly changing human consciousness. As Tomlinson has pointed out, [156] distance is no longer thought of in terms of *miles to be travelled*, but rather as *hours to be flown*! People are more aware than ever of living in what is commonly called "the global village". For some this is a positive experience, but this is by no means the universal outcome of this particular face of globalisation.

The 2008–09 global recession has highlighted the pervasiveness of complex connectivity. A problem with bank lending practices in the USA translates within two years into a global recession that brings many industries to their knees, erodes equity values worldwide, and puts 30 million people out of work in China alone. Complex connectivity has resulted in the creation of a new global market for financial products and services so quickly that governments have been unable to regulate it effectively and in consequence economic prosperity worldwide has now been seriously threatened.

The flow of information around the globe has resulted in the rapid dissemination of knowledge, also with mixed benefits. On the one hand major advances in medicine become quickly known. However, the same connectivity that makes this possible also enables the rapid transmission of diseases such as SARS and swine flu. In dealing with the environment we have access to the latest science, but no country is now immune from the pollution produced by other countries, or the legacy of pollution created by previous generations. Carbon dioxide pollution links all in the present, as well as the present to the past.

Globalisation understood as complex connectivity poses major challenges for educators in Western countries, particularly those concerned with students from disadvantaged backgrounds. It raises the following questions:

- What sort of world are we preparing our students for?

[156] Ibid., 4.

- What sort of skills and understandings will they need to survive and thrive in that world?

Working to a "business as usual" model is hardly responsible as the globalisation phenomenon continues to evolve.

Globalisation as the Knowledge Economy

A second face of globalisation is the advent of the *knowledge economy* [157] in which vast amounts of knowledge and information can be accessed at a speed unimaginable as little as two decades ago. This creates new jobs and new sources of advantage and disadvantage. Ideas and personal data can now be spread with unbelievable rapidity. Social networking has become a new medium of communication. Now, more than ever before, students need to develop the skills necessary to distinguish the meaningful from the meaningless, the good from the bad, and the safe from the unsafe in an information-rich environment.

Another feature of the knowledge economy is the phenomenon of "knowing in real time". Students have access to "the latest" almost instantaneously, whether "the latest" is what is happening in the world of music, sport, fashion, the stock exchange, or international events. They can maintain contact with each other in real time over vast distances at low cost. A new vocabulary has grown up around this phenomenon, that of "texting", "my-spacing", "you-tubing" "skype-ing", "twittering" and so on. The modern technologies that drive globalisation enable people to live in the "now" more so than in any previous generation. There is so much information available about the "now" that any sense of how we got to the "now" seems largely irrelevant. In such a situation, the ability to synthesise information, to build the whole from the parts, becomes an essential survival skill.[158]

Access to the knowledge economy has many positive aspects but, like those flowing from complex connectivity, these are unequally distributed around the globe reinforcing an economic order of privilege of which students in the West are clearly the beneficiaries.

Globalisation as "McDonaldisation"

Globalisation, driven by advertising, is leading to cultural *homogenisation*. Rizer[159] labels this trend "McDonaldisation". The phenomenon of global brands is relatively new. The McDonald's arches now hold the position of

---

[157] See Andy Hargreaves *Teaching in the Knowledge Society: Education in the Age of Insecurity* (New York: Teachers College Press, 2003) for a discussion of the knowledge economy.

[158] For a discussion of "the synthesising mind" see Howard Gardner *Five Minds for the Future* (Boston: Harvard Business Press, 2008), 155.

[159] George Rizer *The McDonaldization of Society* (Los Angeles: Pine Forge Press, 2008).

being the most commonly recognised symbol on the planet – a triumph of modern advertising. Beneath this advertising lies a business strategy to provide a high-status, standardised product of uniform quality and price worldwide. McDonald's is just one company pursuing this aim and in many ways is symbolic of the broader trend of global homogenisation.

Advertising, as marketing strategy, also seeks to establish the obsolescence and irrelevance of what is past. The "new model" is by definition better than the old, and often this is the case. The process of denigrating the past as "old hat" or "irrelevant" undermines the historical consciousness that is an essential building block both in the development of culture and in being human. One possible end-result of globalisation thought of as McDonaldisation is the emergence of a cosmopolitan "world culture".

Opposition to globalisation arises from a number of quarters, but particularly from recognition of the unequal way in which its economic benefits are shared and fear of this homogenising trend. The fear is that the manufactured unity produced by globalisation serves mainly the interests of big business and is produced at the expense of legitimate diversity. Opposition to this trend has resulted in greater interest in, and recovery of, local culture and a nostalgia for the way things used to be. So while globalisation can undermine culture and historical consciousness, this is not its inevitable outcome.

The narrative of globalisation bears many resemblances to the biblical story of Babel, where humankind, united in the thrall of new technology, [160] sought to raise itself to the realm of the gods, an attempt which, in the biblical account, resulted only in division and increased diversity. The search for a balance that respects legitimate diversity in the face of an emerging global culture is an important challenge for all educators.

Osborne, who views globalisation mainly as a social phenomenon, sums up its "sunny and shadow side" as follows:

> Seen *from the sunny-side perspective*, globalization unifies, brings disparate groups together, and provides a oneness in human life that historically has never before been so extensively and profoundly international.
>
> Seen *from the shadow-side perspective*, globalization destroys many individualized and intrinsically positive characteristics of various peoples and countries in the current world. Globalization has destroyed and is destroying valuable aspects of local and regional cultures.

He goes on to observe:

> Unity and diversity are the underlying factors that globalization affects; however, globalization produces unity at the expense of diversity and

---

[160] The technological breakthrough behind the tower of Babel story centred on the new ability to fire clay bricks. See Jonathan Sacks, 52.

creates an unbalanced diversity. One entity in the globalization process becomes richer, while other entities become geometrically poorer.[161]

Globalisation, thought of as homogenisation, has had an impact on the Catholic Church in attempts to rebalance the needs of a centralising Roman curia with those of local churches. One of the negative aspects of globalisation is that, with the advent of modern technology, a central institutional authority is able to micro-manage affairs at the local level in highly selective ways. In such circumstances any search for the ideal of "unity in diversity" can quickly degenerate into an imagination-numbing quest for uniformity in which maintenance takes precedence over mission.[162] Because an institution now has this power, it does not follow that it should use it. In regard to the Church, the Catholic social justice principle of subsidiarity suggests caution needs to be exercised as both the centre and the local churches search for appropriate balance. As Church leaders access the options which globalisation opens up for them, they must seriously address the question: in our search for unity are we trying to corral the Spirit and, if so, for what reason? Inculturation, as the expression of the Gospel in terms of a local culture, is something of a test case of authenticity in this respect.

Globalisation as the New Migration

A fourth face of globalisation is the *new migration*. People are now migrating to developed countries at an unprecedented rate, often drawn by the need for labour in short supply there due to low birth rates.[163] While many come as skilled migrants and become permanent residents, significant numbers come as "guest workers", "illegals", or refugees. Also, as sea levels rise under the impact of climate change, a new class of "environmental refugee" is being created – a scenario now being played out in the Pacific. Increasingly, large numbers of international students move from continent to continent on study programs, and on exchange programs, seeking tertiary qualifications. In "boom" times the migrant presence is generally welcomed, but once the economic climate changes migrants, as minority groups, become easy targets of public hostility through stereotyping and abuse, and are the first victims of changes in government policy.

The *new migrants* often do not share the same attitude to their host country as did those who migrated during the twentieth century. To "migrate" now no longer means to lose contact with one's family at "home" or with one's

---

[161] Kenan Osborne *Orders and Ministry* (Maryknoll New York: Orbis, 2006), 19.
[162] See Robert Rivers *From Maintenance to Mission* (New York: Paulist Press, 2005), 22ff.
[163] Robert Schreiter "A New Modernity: Living and Believing in an Unstable World" *New Theology Review*, February, 2007, 54.

culture. If required, contact can be maintained even on a daily basis through modern communications. "Home" is only a text message away. In this new dispensation, it is now a common expectation that increasingly large numbers of migrants will return home, a situation helped by the fact that funds can be quickly transferred. Often the new migrant is not only in the service of his/her immediate family, but also the agent and source of survival for an extended family in the home country. Due to the relatively low cost of communication and travel, the new migrants can remain oriented to their country of origin, and in many cases this means "living between cultures". The same applies to many refugees. This face of globalisation poses major challenges for social policy makers since a characteristic of the new migration is that, unless a person makes a conscious decision to do so, that person no longer has to re-negotiate his/her cultural identity.

In an excellent study of the social impact of the new migration in the United Kingdom, Jonathan Sacks[164] outlines some of the mechanisms by which new groups have been incorporated into British society. He rejects the project of "multiculturalism" understood as peoples from different cultures living together in toleration of each other, and suggests that community cohesion can come about only when migrants and hosts *both* contribute to the shared projects through which a *cohesive civil society* is built up. We will return to this issue in discussing secularisation.

For Sacks, whose thinking is based firmly in the historical consciousness of Judaism, the challenges of the new migration lie in creating something new together, not in adapting something that already exists for a new purpose. To move in this direction, he claims, requires social *imagination*, that is, developing images capable of giving life and direction to this endeavour. He proposes "the home we build together" is one such image.

An important consequence of globalisation and the new migration is *urbanisation*. Globalisation is essentially an urban phenomenon, the general movement of peoples being from rural to urban areas. The result is an urbanisation in which people, often with limited skills and education, crowd into major cities overtaxing essential services such as housing, transport, welfare and water, thereby changing these urban landscapes. The resulting mixing of peoples leads to a significant "de-territorialisation of culture".[165] All major cultures are now present in most large urban centres.

---

[164] Jonathan Sacks *The Home We Build Together: Recreating Society* (London: Continuum 2007).
[165] Robert Schreiter "A New Modernity: Living and Believing in a Unstable World" *New Theology Review*, November, 2007, 57.

Globalisation – Some Educational Dimensions

A major consequence of globalisation for many people is that *life is now experienced as increasingly fragmented*. Tanner[166] suggests that this is because the principal markers of cultural identity have fragmented in a globalised world that offers competing myths, values systems and social structures. While one can pick and choose elements of an identity in the new cultural supermarket, an identity formed in this way lacks the cohesion provided by culture. The various faces of globalisation outlined above contribute to this sense of fragmentation and provide a sense of the scope of the phenomenon, without being in any way definitive of it. Each facet has its positive and negative features. Each has a corresponding impact on education.

Complex connectivity gives students access to vast amounts of information, but indiscriminately. Valuable knowledge, dangerous knowledge, access to information about ourselves and others, the capacity to destroy reputations anonymously, the capacity to cyber-bully others and so on are all options readily available on-line.

A further by-product of complex connectivity is that many of the sources of employment previously open to a student's parents on leaving school are now closed off to their children so that a growing inter-generational gap is developing in attitudes to employment.

Complex connectivity often means that students from an early age are exposed to a range of value systems and exemplars. There is no privileged place for the Christian value system in a globalised world. Its importance and place can no longer be presumed, but has to be established, often in the face of strong evidence challenging its credibility. On the other hand complex connectivity enables students to engage with students in other countries or in remote areas of their own country, virtually, or by means of exposure visits. Such opportunities are increasingly utilised by Catholic schools as a means not only of developing greater cultural awareness but also of expanding students' imaginal horizons.

The *knowledge economy* presents the challenge of helping students to discern what is meaningful and what is meaningless in the global flow of information in which they find themselves immersed. The key to such discernment is helping them develop what Schreiter has called "a sense of the whole", and Gardner a "synthesising mind" to which earlier reference was made.

The *homogenisation* associated with globalisation is a delicate area in dealing with young people because of the global dimension of youth culture with its

---

[166] Kathryn Tanner *Theories of Culture: A New Agenda for Theology* (Minneapolis: Fortress Press, 1997), 56–58.

pop music, films and TV shows now promoted and shared on a global scale. Since at least the 1950s the music of an era has, for successive generations, become an important marker of personal identity. The capacity to "befriend" contemporary youth culture is almost a *sine qua non* for teachers wishing to create the relational learning environment required for effective education. "Befriending" acknowledges, of course, that like all culture, youth culture both defines and confines. The task of "befriending" youth culture is particularly demanding for those whose identity has been shaped by the music and pop culture of another era.

The homogenisation trend has limits that need to be established within the education process in order to convey to students a strong sense of their *cultural identity as local*. There is need to deconstruct some of the more exaggerated claims for globalisation, including those made by a globalising Church, in order to evangelise globalisation's shadow side. This is an important task in building strong Catholic school cultures. Students need to acquire a sense of both the "local-within-the-global" and the "global-within-the local" so they are well-positioned to critique all excessive claims on them of either the local or the global. This is a new and important goal for Catholic educators, a new task in mission.

Urbanisation and the new migration are related phenomena in most school settings and have an important bearing on the type of community that leaders seek to establish in Catholic schools. Promoting the need to respect "the dignity of difference",[167] not seeing difference as a threat but as an alternative expression of being human, is an integral part of meeting the challenge to see life as a whole. The new migration brings with it a renewed call for Catholic schools to continue to give active expression to the Church's commitment to social justice and to stand in solidarity with the poor and the marginalised.

Drawing on the words of Pope John Paul II in addressing the Pontifical Academy of Social Sciences (27 April, 2001), Pope Benedict reminds us that "globalization, a priori, is neither good nor bad. It will be what people make of it".[168] Interestingly, and by way of demonstration as to what scholars in Catholic education are making of globalisation, in the scope of work of the first ever research centre in Europe dealing with Catholic education, an impressive journal has been launched[169] dealing with Catholic education, not only within Europe, but internationally. The potential of such initiatives to stimulate conversation and studies, and as a consequence quality practice in regard to the mission of Catholic schooling in a globalising world is, we believe, beginning

---

[167] This case is well argued in Jonathan Sacks *The Dignity of Difference* (London: Continuum, 2002), 44ff.

[168] Pope Benedict XV *Caritas in Veritate* #42.

to be realised.

Our students may now be described as "global citizens" more accurately than at any time in history. With the help of visionary educators, they have their best chance of becoming both responsive and responsible global citizens and of making the most of the opportunity that is theirs to develop a world aligned with God's vision for creation, which Jesus described, powerfully, as the "Kingdom of God".

---

[169] Launched in 2009 under the leadership of Professor Gerald Grace, Director of the Centre for Research and Development in Catholic Education, Institute of Education University of London, *International Studies in Catholic Education* is a unique resource for Catholic educators across the globe. Similarly, Gerald Grace and Joseph O'Keefe (eds) ***International Handbook of Catholic Education*** (Springer: Dordrecht/Boston, 2007) is designed to resource international co-operation and collaboration among Catholic educators in meeting challenges worldwide and charting responses.

CHAPTER EIGHT

Secularisation – Friend or Foe?

Secularisation is a second global characteristic of our age. As Charles Taylor points out,[170] this is a term that requires careful clarification. Like the associated adjective "secular", and the nouns "secularity" and "secularism", the term is used in a number of different senses. It is important therefore to differentiate these terms and some of the dynamics associated with the phenomenon of secularisation. As will become evident, secularisation is a significant aspect of the frontier – impossible to ignore in Western societies and important to understand in other cultures.

Since secularisation deals with issues of authority and the place of religion within society, it features in public, academic and theological discourse. Discussion about secularisation is complicated by the fact that there seems no universal language in which dialogue can be conducted. In the discussion that follows the terms "secularism" and "secularity" are used interchangeably to name the *phenomenon*, and "secularisation" the process by which it comes about.[171]

Secularity, Secularisation and Secularism

"Secular" deriving from the Latin word *saeculum* can be translated as "the period of a person's life on earth". Secular refers then to the affairs of "this world" as distinct from those of "the world to come".[172] In scripture the word "world" is used in a number of senses. It can refer to the world as God's creation, something that comes from God and is good, but is not God. This sense is conveyed in the statement in Genesis: "God looked at everything he had made, and he found it very good" (Gen 1:31). In the Gospel of John the theme of God's all-embracing love for "the world" is expanded in Jesus' discourse with Nicodemus: "For God so loved the world that he gave his only Son..."(John 3:16). Another usage is found in the prologue of John's Gospel: "He was in the world, and the world came to be through him, but the *world* did not know him" (John 1:10). Here "*world*" refers to a class of people, those so preoccupied with their own interests and position that they viewed Jesus as

---

[170] Charles Taylor *A Secular Age* (Cambridge Massachusetts: Harvard University Press, 2007), 1.
[171] This is not the precise usage customarily found in Catholic theology but is a common usage in sociology. Church documents use "secularism" to refer to an ideology that excludes all reference to the transcendent (God and religion) from the sphere of public life.
[172] Cf. John Schall SJ <www.ignatiusinsight.com/features2007/schall_secularity_jan07.asp>.

an enemy and sought to destroy him. This group included significant religious leaders of the time. This usage was later generalised to include those outside the Christian community who had not been open to receiving the Gospel. All usages above see "the world" in relation to God. None conveys any sense of "the world" as having nothing to do with God, or being completely separate from God and the things of God. The exclusion of God or the symbols of religion from public life, a common contemporary meaning of secularism, was unthinkable in Jesus' time. The Jewish world of that time lacked a conception of secularity, secularism or secularisation as we use these terms today.

In Medieval times "secular" was associated with the idea of *orders within society*. Distinctions were made between the imperial order, the clerical order whose members were to concern themselves with the affairs of the Church, and the civil or lay order whose members were to concern themselves with the affairs of the world. Secularity referred at this time to one's state within the social order. The *secular state* was one that embraced family life and involvement in civil society in such areas as commerce and politics.

With the break up of Christendom, the imperial order became highly problematic and eventually lost its legitimacy. The nature of the clerical order also evolved. Initially it was understood as an *order of service*. However, when incorporated into Church law by Gratian in Medieval times, a clerical/lay distinction was drawn which separated out, both intellectually and practically, that which fell under Church control, and that which fell under civil control, thus establishing a basis for the distinction between ecclesiastical authority and civil authority, and between canon and civil law. The clerical order was later construed as an *order of authority*.[173] Needless to say, there were many boundary issues that remained in dispute as this distinction was forged.

"Secularity" is used today in a different sense. It refers to sources of *authority* in public life. This usage emerged into the public domain as the notion of the modern state developed. Rolheiser provides a useful descriptive definition of the word used in this sense.

> Secularity is a term coined (ca.1850) to denote a system of interpreting and organising human life on principles taken solely from this world, without recourse to belief in God and a future world.[174]

Defined in this way, "secularity" provides a *principle for organising public life*. Secularity does not necessarily imply denial of the existence of God or lack of appreciation of religious symbols. Nor is it necessarily atheistic.

---

[173] Kenan Osborne *Orders and Ministry* (Maryknoll New York: Orbis, 2006), 62–66.
[174] Ronald Rolheiser *Secularity and the Gospel* (New York: The Crossroad Publishing Company, 2006), 39.

Rolheiser draws a helpful distinction between "secularity" as referring to authority and "secularisation" as referring to the process by which the authority of the state and other global agencies replace ecclesiastical authority in the conduct of public life.

> Secularity is more than just the process of secularization (in which) more and more areas of life and more and more institutions shift from church to non-church control. Ultimately it is a question of authority, namely what is to be the final authority in terms of organising and controlling public life? Divine authority (God, Bible, the churches) or human reason (reason, the democratic process, a rationally agreed upon course of action)? Secularity believes that it is the latter. That, in essence, defines secularity.[175]

The terms "secularity" and "secularism" are used in two senses in the literature:
- as the state of affairs that results from the secularisation process. As we will see this extends somewhat further that just issues of authority
- as an ideology which denies not only the legitimacy of all forms of religious authority, but also the place of the Church in public life.

Sociology tends to use secularism in the first sense. Catholic discourse tends to use the word in the second sense. Kosmin[176] tries to bridge these two usages of the term by referring to secularism as existing on a continuum which runs from "soft" to "hard". Hard secularism is atheistic and anti-religious. This form of secularism is associated with "secularists". Soft secularism is generally tolerant of religion.

In any discussion of secularity/secularism it is important to know which usage of the word is being employed. Kosmin's distinction is helpful, given the general lack of agreement that exists about the usage of terms.

Rolheiser highlights a number of factors that need to be taken into account in formulating a Christian response to secularity/secularism.

1. Secularity is a complex phenomenon, and that complexity needs to be respected.
2. Secularity is multivalent and as such is "mixed" morally and religiously and that also needs to be respected.
3. We are invited to have a certain biblical and Catholic attitude towards secularity, namely, to love the world as God loves it.
4. Secularity is a non-negotiable given in our milieu, and we live in hope knowing that the Gospels are up to the task of engaging secularity.[177]

[175] Ibid., 40.
[176] Barry Kosmin *Contemporary Secularity and Secularism* (Massachuetts, ISSSC, 2007), 5.
[177] Rolheiser, 38–46.

Narrative of Secularisation

Secularisation, like its sister phenomenon globalisation, has its roots in the history and culture of Europe. An important historical point in the emergence of the modern understanding of secular was reached after the Thirty Years War (1618–1648), a religious conflict that began a half-century after the Reformation. Having already been torn apart religiously by the Reformation, Europe was again plunged into turmoil. At the time, rulers of the many states that made up Europe, were able to command the religious allegiance of their people, and Catholic and Protestant rulers battled with one another trying to establish pre-eminence. The religion of the king or prince was the religion of the people. Religion was politics and politics was religion.

The Thirty Years War gave rise to a new breed of mainly Catholic intellectuals, people like Descartes (1596–1650) and Pascal (1623–1662), who were significant figures in the emergence of Enlightenment thinking. As we have noted previously, in pre-modern Europe religion had provided the moral framework for ensuring public order. This was an important contribution providing as it did the social and political conventions of the time. One consequence of the unprecedented devastation caused by the Thirty Years War was that people lost confidence in the moral framework provided by Christian faith as the sole underpinning of public order, and called its authority into question. As the Enlightenment thinkers came to settle the matter, the principles of religion were a *private matter*, since they pertained to an individual's faith. They could not be imposed on society as a whole, as faith on the part of all citizens could not be presumed. The argument developed that, since all people in society shared reason, public order should be built around what people shared, not what now divided them. The authority of reason should therefore replace the authority of faith as the basis for establishing the social and political conventions of civil society.

The principle of secularity, as this position became known, meant that the ultimate legitimation for a course of public action should no longer depend on the authority of traditional leaders – the king, the bishop, or even the Pope, as had previously been the case – but an appeal to the reasonableness of what had been proposed. In other words, the decisions that shaped public life had to be *rationally defensible*, not dependent on authority backed by tradition. From a twenty-first century perspective such a proposal seems unremarkable, but in the seventeenth and eighteenth centuries this proved to be far from the case. Not surprisingly, the Enlightenment proposal was regarded as revolutionary, an attack on legitimate authority and the understanding of order in society that lay behind it.

Adoption of the secularity principle required that the necessary *means* be developed to determine how citizens could decide what was reasonable and, beyond that, how agreed decisions could be implemented. Resolving these issues gave rise to a new political order, one based on secular democratic government. Colonialism saw this new view of order in society exported around the world as normative for good governance. This occurred despite the fact that the new view of order was the result of particular circumstances arising in Europe as the pre-modern world began to be transformed under the influence of Enlightenment thinking.

Secularisation, the process by which this change in the reigning political paradigm came about, is integral to the form of government that replaced both ecclesiastical and royal authority. Like the process of globalisation, secularisation has a number of facets which give the phenomenon the complexity of which Rolheiser speaks.

Secularisation Theory

As the discipline of sociology developed, "secularisation theory" became one of its early paradigms for explaining the relationship between religion and modernity. This theory postulated that in modernity religion, which is based on faith, could not compete in the meaning-making process with "reason", which was based on science, and as a consequence, its decline in the modern period was inevitable. Decline in attendance at religious services as modernity advanced was taken as the key empirical evidence supporting the theory. The narrative of "secularisation theory" was that there had once been a "golden age of faith" in pre-modern times, but with the advent of the "age of reason", faith has been displaced by science rendering religion irrelevant, a stage through which mankind has now passed as human sensibility continues to evolve.

Beginning in the early 1990s a number of sociologists challenged this view. Principal among them was David Martin[178] who pointed to the "fuzzy" construction of the concept of secularisation. He also questioned the appropriateness of church attendance as a measure of decline in religion, particularly as such attendance is voluntary in a number of Christian denominations.[179] Stark,[180] and later Greeley,[181] challenged the view of history on which the narrative of secularisation is based. Secularisation theory is now

---

[178] David Martin *On Secularization: Towards a Revised General Theory* (London: Ashgate, 2005).

[179] By the 1990s the trend for religious identity to be a matter of self-identification, rather than institutional identification via particular religious practices, was growing.

[180] Rodney Stark "Secularization R.I.P – rest in peace" retrieved from
<http://findarticles.com/p/articles/mi_m0SOR/is_3_60?ai_57533381> (1999).

[181] Andrew Greeley *Religion in Europe at the End of the Second Millennium: A Sociological Profile* (Edison N.J.: Transaction Publishers, 2002).

largely discredited and has lost its status as a sociological paradigm. However, as a popular myth, it still enjoys considerable support.

Perspectives on Secularism

There are three broad perspectives which now exist with respect to secularity/secularism. The first perspective is ideological and anti-religious – "hard secularism". People holding this view assume that religion of its very nature is retrogressive, destructive and even delusional. This view finds its radical expression today in the work of secularists such as the biologist Richard Dawkins[182] and the author and reviewer Christopher Hitchens.[183] Hard secularism finds its home in Europe and can be understood as a reaction to the mixed history of the Christian faith on that continent. The view is highly antagonistic to the Catholic Church in particular, which is seen as still tied to the conventions of the pre-modern world, and as a centre of opposition to progress and democracy because of its claims in regard to truth.

Catholic schools are a major target for secularists. They attack their existence from two basic directions. The first is that Catholic schools, being somewhat exclusive in their enrolment policies, do not contribute to the building up of community cohesion and therefore should not qualify for public funding. This is the line of attack in Britain. In Australia a different approach is taken. Here it is argued that, in choosing Catholic teachers to teach in the schools, the employment policies of Catholic schools are discriminatory and contrary to the law. These are attacks against which Catholic system leaders must have a prepared defence. People holding these views often appeal to a false polarity between faith and reason.[184] This form of hard secularism is generally atheistic. According to its tenets human life can have no goal beyond this world.

A second orientation in secularism, one that is tolerant towards religion, developed in Scotland and was later exported to the United States. Here the basic premise of secularity is accepted, but without the need to make pejorative judgments about the worth of religion. The constitution of the United States, for instance, is written from a theistic point of view. Secularity in this perspective does not imply "freedom from religion" as in the case outlined above. It can equally imply "freedom of religion" and "freedom for religion". Its espousal in the United States reflects the strong desire among the founding fathers that

---

[182] Richard Dawkins *The God Delusion* (Earling: Bantam Press, 2006).
[183] Christopher Hitchens *God Is Not Great: The Case Against Religion* (UK: Atlantic Books, 2007).
[184] The Catholic Church, on the contrary, teaches that truths held by faith must be compatible with those reached by right reason. Pope John Paul II argues this case in his encyclical letter *Faith and Reason* (1998) which opens as follows: "Faith and reason are like two wings on which the human spirit rises to the contemplation of truth".

the religious divisions and conflicts that religion had created in Europe, not be imported into the New World.[185] The aim of the founders was to proscribe any form of Christianity becoming the "established" religion of the state.

The third orientation to secularism is pragmatic. Proponents of this form of secularism accept that religion has a proper place in the social order, but that its role needs to be limited. The Australian experience of secularisation illustrates the pragmatic approach. The approach does not proceed on the basis of any clear constitutional principle as is the case in the USA. A uniquely nuanced understanding of secularisation has developed that reflects the pragmatic cast of Australian culture. The approach owes little to ideology which, in Australia, has even less currency than religion.[186] Debate about what should happen in the public square, like so much else in Australian life, is determined by "what works". Commitment to a secular public policy has not, for example, prevented successive Australian governments funding the health care agencies of the churches, and in more recent times, funding faith-based schools. The motivation was, and remains, simple political pragmatism. Pragmatic secularism in this country, however, leaves the Church vulnerable. The freedom to conduct, according to religious principles, such vital expressions of the Church's mission as education and health cannot be taken for granted because it is not enshrined on the basis of principle. The political pragmatism that granted support to Catholic schools in a different political climate could also cause that support to be withdrawn, or to be provided under such restrictive conditions as to achieve the same effect.

Secularisation as a Cultural Phenomenon

Secularity/secularism is a Western cultural phenomenon, a reaction to the experiences generated in what was once a predominantly Christian Europe. Cultures that do not share a common history with Europe, such as those built around Islam, often reject the Enlightenment premise that religion is inherently divisive and therefore should be excluded from the public domain. The Western response to such rejection is to treat it as unenlightened and needing to be changed. The cultural assumptions behind such assertions need to be recognised.

In the sociological literature the term "secularisation" can refer to any one of three distinct processes. The first is the process by which appeal to reason progressively replaces ecclesiastical and other forms of traditional authority. This is called rationalisation. The second is the process by which religion and

---

[185] While the writers of the American constitution were tolerant of religion, they shared with their European colleagues a strong aversion to Catholicism.
[186] The Communist Party in Australia, for instance, dissolved in 1991 for lack of members.

religious symbols are progressively withdrawn from the public square. This is called privatisation. The third refers to the process by which areas of public life are progressively removed from ecclesiastical control as societies become more complex, needs expand and services become more differentiated. This process is called social differentiation. In a modern society the state is the only body with sufficient resources to provide the range of social, welfare and health services expected by citizens, so some form of social differentiation was inevitable.

As we shall see later the Church accepts the principle of secularity. The process of social differentiation becomes problematic only when there are attempts to deny the Church the right to pursue its educational or social mission and in particular its ministries on behalf of the poor and the marginalised. The problematic aspect of secularisation is privatisation. Here the fact that religion is part of culture is often denied as in the case where Christmas carols are no longer allowed to be sung nor cribs to be erected in public spaces. Here ideological secularists often seek to deny children access to the mythology that lies at the root of their culture, in the name of human rights. This form of ideological intolerance is no less objectionable than religious intolerance. It uses human rights as a vehicle to deny freedom of religion in practice.

The Secularisation of Morality

As the West has tried to work out what is appropriate in the public sphere, the idea that the private domain (to which religion is said to belong) has little to offer the public sphere subverts any idea that the public and private sectors can complement each other, nor does it respect the contribution the private sector makes to the creation of civil society. This has particular significance when matters of morality are involved.

Since religion underpins morality, morality is assigned to the private sphere and is consequently excluded from public life. Morality becomes a matter of conscience. However, behaviour in the public sphere presupposes some degree of consensus around what is good and what is right. If religion is excluded from the public sphere, the definition of what is good and right then becomes an open question and public morality becomes a matter of taste or of law. The danger here is that, with no other universal grounding, morality becomes what the state determines for itself. When this happens the state is free to set up its own secular version of morality, and so becomes autonomous.

Autonomous states of various ideological hues were established in the twentieth century and, in many instances, the human cost that resulted was horrific. While the excesses of European communism have largely passed into history, contemporary societies are strongly influenced by an ideology that defines "the good" in terms of self-defined human happiness, and "the right" as free choice exercised within the widest possible discretion. The individualism this produces undermines the concept of committed relationships, whether in the family or in the community, and leaves people feeling isolated and alienated from one another. It runs counter to the biblical understanding of the human person as essentially relational. The export of this ideology around the world, often under the banner of "manifest destiny", has been and continues to be, increasingly resisted by cultures not shaped by Enlightenment thinking. Many of these cultures want access to the technology associated with modernisation, but reject many of the values that go with it, such as secularism.

Nearly three centuries beyond the Enlightenment, and in the face of a religious revival in many societies, particularly outside the West, new questions are being asked about the secularity principle and its translation into various processes of secularisation.

- Which version of secularism is appropriate for the modern state?
- On what foundations should public morality be based?
- What is the proper voice for faith in the public sphere in a multifaith society?

Catholic Discourse on Secularisation

As has been noted above in dealing with the phenomenon of secularism, the theological use of terms is somewhat different from their use in sociology. In Catholic theological discourse about secularity, Jesus' comment that his disciples should "repay to Caesar what belongs to Caesar and to God what belongs to God" (Mark 12:17) is taken as an important reference point. In his ground-breaking work on evangelisation Pope Paul VI defined "secularisation" (in contradistinction to "secularism") as

> the effort, in itself just and legitimate and in no way incompatible with faith or religion to discover in creation, in each thing or each happening in the universe, the laws which regulate them with a certain autonomy, but with the inner conviction that the Creator has placed those laws there. The last Council has in this sense affirmed the legitimate autonomy of culture and particularly of the sciences.[187]

This view suggests that in the human search for truth various academic disciplines have their own proper autonomy. As a definition it raises questions such as: what is meant by the phrase "proper autonomy"; and, more importantly, how is this to be determined? Paul VI's view of secularisation is concerned with the *legitimate autonomy of culture*. This interpretation of secularisation represented a new point of departure in Catholic teaching.

[187] Paul VI *Evangelii Nuntiandi* #55 (Homebush: St Paul Publications, 1976).

"Secularism" as understood in official Catholic teaching is "a concept of the world according to which the latter is self-explanatory, without any need for recourse to God, who thus becomes superfluous and an encumbrance".[188] As already indicated, "secularism" carries a negative connotation in Catholic discourse that it does not have in sociology.

For Pope Benedict XVI "secularity" has become not so much a matter of "authority" but of "exclusion of religion and its symbols from public life by confining them to the private sphere and to the individual conscience".[189]

He is referring here to secularisation in the sense of privatisation discussed above. Defined in this way secularity "finds its public expression in the total separation of Church and state, with the Church not entitled to intervene in areas that concern the life of citizens". The Pope regrets that under the guise of secularity "religious symbols can be proscribed from public places designated for the proper function of the political community – offices, schools, courts, hospitals, prisons, etc.". Secularity interpreted as "exclusion of religion" makes it possible to speak of

> secular thought, secular morals, secular knowledge and secular politics (leading to an) a-religious vision of life, thought and morals…a vision in which there is no room for God, for a mystery that transcends human reason, for a moral law of absolute worth, in force in every time and in every situation.[190]

He therefore challenges all believers to help formulate a concept of "secularity" that

- acknowledges the place that is due to God and God's moral law, and to Christ and his Church in human life, both individual and social
- affirms and respects…man's gradual discovery, exploitation and ordering of the laws and values of matter and society"…(because) material being is endowed with its own stability, truth and excellence, its own order and laws. These man must respect as he recognizes the methods proper to every science and technique.

In his view, balancing these two objectives leads to a "healthy secularity", one which

> involves the effective autonomy of earthly realities, not indeed from the moral order, but from the ecclesiastical sphere. Thus the Church cannot point out the preferred political or social order; it is the people who must freely decide on the

---

[188] Ibid.
[189] Benedict XVI Address to Union of Italian Jurists (9 December 2006) <www.ewtn.com/library/PAPALDOC/b16layjurists.htm>.
[190] Ibid.

best and most suitable ways to organise political life.[191]

"Healthy secularity" seems to acknowledge that the proper "autonomy of culture", which includes the academic disciplines, requires some "exclusion of religion". The minimum condition for this "healthy secularity" is that the state needs to recognise *an objective moral order and the authority of the Church within that order.* The Pope's rationale for this position is that the values of the objective moral order are "human before being Christian".

Benedict XVI's analysis identifies a polarity. On the one side is a moral order pertaining to the individual, prompted by conscience and guided by membership of a Church community, which carries the authority of faith and which seeks the common good. On the other side is a moral order pertaining to the state, which is secular in outlook, guiding the life of its citizens according to the authority of reason and also guided by a notion of the common good. The problem comes when various churches/faiths put forward different moral viewpoints on matters that the state has no option but to address. There is however a basis for dialogue built around a construction of "the common good", which is a key element in both frameworks.

Jonathan Sacks[192] suggests a way forward. He proposes that *civil society – a conglomerate of community groups, social organisations and religious groups – is interposed between the individual and state* and is influential in shaping the conduct of both. This occurs through the "politics of covenant".

> What the great religions understand is that society is larger than the state. Politics depends on pre-political virtues nurtured in non-political environments: the family, the community, the congregation. This is where we first discover the give and take of reciprocity and the healing power of love and forgiveness. They are where we learn to negotiate the tension between independence and inter-dependence…They are where we acquire moral intelligence. Without families, communities and friends, society becomes a mere aggregation of individuals, 'the lonely crowd' without trust or grace or meaning: without hope.

He goes on to argue that the family, the community and the congregation by themselves are not enough if we are to live together free of the various forms of tribalism, which competition for limited resources can provoke. He concludes:

> When we realize this, a particular form of politics is born – the politics that does not see human beings as servants of the state, but the state as the servant of human beings. This is modest politics, politics as non-violent conflict resolution, and as the provider, not of the good life, but of basic

---

[191] Ibid.
[192] Jonathan Sacks *The Home We Build Together* (London: Continuum, 2007), 225–226.

pre-conditions – safety, order, education, health – without which no good life is possible. That is why there is a religious case for liberal democracy, for a politics that does not seek to embody the good, but merely keep the peace between different groups with conflicting views of the good.

In summary, secularity/secularism is a complex matter. It encompasses:
- the loss of the authority of faith as many spheres of life have moved out of the control of Church authorities
- the erosion of Christian religious symbols as public symbols, these being seen as the symbols of a particular group in society
- the loss of the authority of faith in legitimising public policy which now gains its legitimacy from an "appeal to reason"
- the privatising of morality, so that public life is no longer ordered according to the requirements of a universal morality
- a denial of the transcendent as a central reality in interpreting human life and what it means to be human.

In any discussion of "secularisation", "secularity" or "secularism" it is necessary to establish how terms are being used, and what the focus of the discussion actually is. The term secularisation can refer willy-nilly to a number of processes.

Charles Taylor provides a further dimension to the discussion of secularity in his epic study *A Secular Age*.[193] While not disagreeing with the conceptions summarised above, Taylor suggests that the principal issue associated with modern secularism is not that of authority, but of sensibility. He argues that an important consequence of modernity has been the rise of a new worldview, that of "exclusive humanism", which we discussed briefly in the previous chapter. This worldview is now so pervasive in Western societies that it has changed the conditions of belief, rendering it more difficult. If Taylor is correct, then his work has major implications for Catholic educators.

Secularisation – Leadership Issues

The Church community in its various forms, including the Catholic school, exists as an important, Sacks would argue crucial, element in civil society. Its power lies in shaping the common projects and goals that citizens undertake in the form of communal, ecumenical and inter-religious dialogue and action. In this respect the Catholic school can make a contribution to community cohesion not open to public schools because matters of religion can be addressed as a

---

[193] Charles Taylor *A Secular Age* (Cambridge Massachusetts: Belknap/Harvard University Press, 2007).

matter of course.

The authenticity of a Church is demonstrated in the leadership it provides in such an endeavour, by the value of its witness, its solidarity with the other groups that make up civil society, and its commitment to the common good. How thoroughly such an attitude is embedded in the Catholic school or the school's leadership is often far from clear. Commitment to the common good is one of the key principles of Catholic social teaching.[194]

As Rohlheiser's study, referred to earlier, makes clear, secularisation is having a major impact on the faith of young people at a number of levels. Denial of the transcendent, the development of a "culture of choice" guided by a totally secular construction of what is good, and its assertion that faith and reason are incompatible, create a difficult environment in which faith can grow. These are all issues of fundamental importance to Catholic educators seeking to introduce young people to a conception of human life that integrates faith, culture and life (human experience).

In concluding an impressive study of Catholic education in the United Kingdom, Gerald Grace deals with the need for the renewal of spiritual capital in Catholic schools. Not only is this renewal needed for the sake of students and their families, but for the benefit of the whole society. He reminds us that "the very existence of Catholic schools and indeed of all faith-based schools constitutes part of the religious critique of the secular, without which both culture and freedom would be diminished".[195] His rich discussion of Catholic education in the United Kingdom provides a valuable resource for those interested in the dimensions of the Catholic school's mission in today's societies both in western countries and, in varying degrees and manifestations, across the globe.

The challenges which secularisation presents for Christian educators can be posed in the form of questions.

- How effectively does the school promote a sense of the transcendent within the school community?
- What critique of secularism does the school offer in its educational program?
- How effective is the school in establishing the sort of community life in which people are valued as persons existing in relationship to each other and their environment?
- How effective is the school in ensuring that its educational programs

---

[194] John Coleman & William Ryan *Globalisation and Catholic Social Thought: Present Crisis Future Hope* (Maryknoll New York: Orbis, 2005), 16.

[195] Gerald Grace *Catholic Schools: Mission, Markets and Morality* (London: Routledge/Falmer, 2002), 240.

consciously promote "a sense of the whole" consistent with the Christian view of the human person and of history?
- How effectively does the school deal with the issue of personal and public morality and their contested bases?
- How does the school present the need for the Church to be recognised as a credible voice shaping the consensus that gives public policy its moral legitimacy?
- How does the school address the Church's absolute claims when it comes to issues of morality such as its pro-life stance?

It is often difficult for such questions to win space at the contested executive table if school leaders lose sight of their core purpose, its relationship to mission and the Kingdom of God, which is the goal of mission, and for which Jesus taught us to pray.

For Christians this core purpose is, fundamentally, *an encounter with a person, Jesus, and with his message of the Kingdom.* Without some sense of relationship with a personal God, our sense of the transcendent will remain problematic, and with that our capacity to survive the negative impacts of secularisation on our personal, family and community lives. As we cross the frontier, strengthened with this sense of relationship, there comes the confidence that we are part of something bigger than ourselves, and the recognition of the need to reach out to others, assured that the Spirit is at work in the world bringing God's mission to fruition.

CHAPTER NINE

Contemporary Pluralism – The Rise and Rise of Difference

Contemporary pluralism has a number of facets. It is understood as the increased, and increasing, differentiation of people within society because of differences in culture, religion, ideology, and lifestyle. This aspect of pluralism has a special urgency in our age and can be viewed from a number of perspectives as it has both a global and a local face. A second facet of pluralism is the plurality of ideas that arise as a consequence of globalisation. Understood in this sense contemporary pluralism expands the range of options now available to people in all cultures. These two aspects of pluralism can be studied empirically and their impacts analysed.

Pluralism also exists as a philosophic construct dealing with the different ways in which the nature of knowledge, rationality and truth can be construed. Kasper[196] refers to the first two facets of pluralism as empirical pluralism and to the third as ideological pluralism. As empirical pluralism expands, this process highlights issues central to ideological pluralism. We adopt Kasper's distinction in structuring the balance of this chapter which highlights the issues associated with *ideological pluralism* and draws attention to their significance for Catholic educators.

Empirical Pluralism

As an aspect of contemporary human experience empirical pluralism presents under two guises. The first guise focuses on *people*; groups from different cultural and religious backgrounds mix and engage with one another on an ever larger scale, *so that it is simply impossible to ignore each other*. The second guise refers to *ideas;* the rapid dissemination of opinions, ideas and information enabling multiple perspectives to be brought to bear on the consideration of almost any matter.

Empirical pluralism considered in the reference to *people*, raises questions about its value and its limits. How much pluralism can our society cope with before it passes some limit that changes its nature? What conclusion does such a discussion have for the level of migration? On what terms may migrants come or stay? What is the attitude of the government towards refugees? Such questions are now central in the political life of many nations.

When it comes to the rapid *dissemination of ideas*, empirical pluralism raises

---

[196] Cardinal Walter Kasper "The Future of Christianity: The Church and Contemporary Pluralism in the Post-Modern Era" (Official text, *Helder Camara Lecture*, Sydney, July 9, 2003), 1.

somewhat more fundamental value questions. What value do we place on difference and diversity? How much difference and diversity will we permit? Are there limits to tolerance? Such questions are difficult enough to address when applied to culture and religion, but when they are applied to lifestyles, they become socially and politically explosive.

Ideological Pluralism and the Foundations of Knowledge

Ideological pluralism has to do with how different groups within society form their ideas about what constitutes knowledge, reasonableness, and truth, and how they make sense of the plurality of ideas that confront them at every turn. This facet of pluralism is important for school leaders because of the bearing different views of truth, knowledge and reasonableness have on how the task of education is construed and how it is pursued.

Sociologists explore how societies construct knowledge and determine what is reliable knowledge. In doing so, their interest focuses on the basis on which decisions about these matters depend. This basis is called a *plausibility structure*. The plausibility structure determines what is accepted within a given society as being real and true. This plausibility structure is so embedded at the heart of a culture that *it is rarely examined, and even more rarely questioned*. From its position at the centre of things it underpins the worldview of the culture. As Hiebert notes, it provides the logic and epistemological base on which the worldview rests.[197] The concept also features strongly in the sociology of religion because Christians, for example, accept things as real and true, and therefore as reliable knowledge, which others classify as "beliefs". What then, ask the sociologists, is the plausibility structure for knowledge as accepted by Christians?

The highly respected missiologist Lesslie Newbigin,[198] drawing on the work of sociologist Peter Berger, defines plausibility structures as "patterns of belief and practice accepted within a given society which determine which beliefs are plausible to its members and which are not. These vary according to time and place. Newbigin points out that people make judgments about what is "reasonable" according to the *reigning plausibility structure* and the *tradition* associated with the development of this structure. Plausibility structures determine what people accept as "facts", that is what is construed as "public knowledge" and are therefore able to be taught freely within society. It is worth noting at this early stage that plausibility structures are built on axioms which are acts of faith in that they are essentially unprovable. For instance, modern

---

[197] Paul Hiebert *Transforming Worldviews: An Anthropological Understanding of How People Change* (Grand Rapids Michigan: Baker Academic, 2008), 33.
[198] Lesslie Newbigin *The Gospel in a Pluralist Society* (Geneva: WCC Publications, 1989), 6ff.

science takes as axiomatic the belief that nature is intelligible and that causality is reliable and not random, that is, if an experiment is repeated under the same conditions it will yield the same results.

A major achievement of the Enlightenment was to change the reigning plausibility structure of Western culture. If we think of a plausibility structure as a paradigm, then the Enlightenment period saw a paradigm shift in how Western people came to understand the structure of knowledge. A new plausibility structure developed that gave rise to, and legitimimised, the modern worldview. As this modern worldview became dominant in Western societies, many people came to view any re-emergence of religion, which provided the plausibility structure of knowledge in pre-modernity, as a retrograde step, a step back into pre-modernity. Religion, in general, and Christianity, in particular, were seen therefore as the enemies of progress. Such a development raises two important questions: what was the nature of the paradigm shift that occurred, and how did it come about? The answer to the first question lies in the realm of philosophy, while the answer to the second is a matter of history. We trace each of these in turn.

Plausibility Structures in Pre-modernity

As we have noted already, the reigning plausibility structure for knowledge in pre-modern Europe was underwritten by the Catholic faith. This faith, as believed by Christians at the time, provided the touchstone of what was regarded as true and reasonable. The Christian faith of pre-modern times combined traditional Catholic theology and important aspects of Aristotelian philosophy, and therefore placed *a high premium on the use of reason*. This faith was owned by a community which accepted that things were true because that was what Christian faith, as taught by the Church, demanded. However, the limited education available to most people at the time also meant people's practice of this faith could easily, and often did, degenerate into superstition.

Within pre-modern society, therefore, phenomena found their explanation within the framework of the Catholic faith and this was presumed to provide true and reliable knowledge. This knowledge was taken as "public knowledge" and so could readily be taught as "true" within society. The Catholic faith, as understood by the Church *at the time*, defined the imaginal horizon within which people understood the world in which they lived. As a consequence their cultural worldview was inherently religious.

"At the time" is an important qualifier here. Christian faith is capable of development, so how it is understood and expressed at any one time is not fully definitive of the truth it contains. For instance, when dealing with heretics in the third century, a teaching was formulated by theologians such as Origen and Cyprian of Carthage that, as far as heretics were concerned, "outside the Church there was no salvation". This teaching initially targeted those *inside the Church* who were advocating positions not consistent with what was held by most Christians as orthodox teaching. By late pre-modern times this teaching had been extended to include all who were not baptised, or who were Protestants, and were therefore considered to be *outside the Church*. A clear implication was that unless a person was baptised a Catholic, on dying s/he would be damned to hell. Hell and damnation were important realities in the religious consciousness of pre-modern people as the famous painting of Hieronymus Bosch (1450–1516) *The Garden of Earthly Delights* clearly illustrates.

The teaching *Extra ecclesiam nulla salus* provided a special urgency to Christian mission once the New World and its peoples were discovered by Europeans, and when the previously little known regions and peoples of Africa and Asia became better known. The heroic efforts of missionaries such as St Francis Xavier drew their inspiration from this teaching. The meaning given to it in Francis Xavier's time is no longer held today. Theological understanding about the Church's role in the salvation God offers to all people continues to develop.

Modernity and the Principle of Contingency

The alternative plausibility structure formulated in the Enlightenment period was to underpin the development of knowledge in modernity. What was deemed true and reliable knowledge as modernity advanced was shaped by the rapidly growing scientific community and the particular understanding of "reason" that developed within this community. The scientific community came to play in modernity a similar role to that played by the Church in pre-modern times. Within this new paradigm of knowledge things were determined to be true, not because of appeals to Christian faith, but by appeal to the *principle of contingency*.[199]

"Contingency" is used here in the philosophical sense. Something is contingent if its existence depends on the prior existence of something else, that is, it does not contain within itself the explanation of its own existence. Plant life is contingent on water because without water it would not have come into existence. Science invokes contingency in a particular form known as *causality*. Every effect is contingent on its cause. Science studies effects to understand the nature of the causes that bring them about. Once this cause

---

[199] To the modern mindset this principle would be better named the *principle of rationality*. However, rationality is not the preserve of modernity. We have sought, therefore, to avoid the exclusivity of such a claim. Knowledge generated within other plausibility structures is "reasonable" if one accepts the axioms of those structures.

and effect relationship is established, it becomes possible to predict effects based on an understanding of causes. Knowledge translates into power through this process. However, the principle of contingency, as used here, has a wider meaning than simply causality. It means the quest to identify, understand, and explain relationships.

The great achievement of early modern science was to build a store of reliable knowledge using this new paradigm of knowledge. Phenomena were explored and explained in terms of *causal relationship*. It is possible to carry out a thought experiment to see how this works. If you drop a ball, it falls to the earth at a certain rate. This rate can be measured experimentally. If you conduct the same experiment with a ball twice the weight of the first you might predict that it will fall faster than in the first case. Again you can measure the rate at which the larger ball falls experimentally. To a good approximation you will find it falls as the same rate as before. So it seems that the rate at which a body falls does not depend on its weight. This raises the further question: why is this so? Further experimentation will reveal that all bodies fall to earth with more or less the same acceleration. In the course of the investigation we learn to distinguish between weight and mass, to correct our results for air resistance, and eventually we arrive at the concept of gravity. This is the way of science – we explore and explain causal relationships by reference to data that does not depend on any authority other than the data itself.

The scientific community defines knowledge generated in this way as reliable and reasonable. However, it needs also to be acknowledged that the plausibility structure being evoked relies on a small set of axioms that are held to be true, but which are essentially unprovable. Two of these can easily be recognised in the thought experiment outlined above. The first is that the *explanation of all natural phenomena lies within the phenomena themselves* and not by appeal to anything that lies outside nature. The second is that *natural phenomena are intelligible*, and therefore they can be explored through experiment. Both of these axioms are integral to modern science.

While science makes an act of faith in these axioms, it does not require any further acts of faith in the explanation of phenomena, and rejects *a priori* the validity of any explanation of phenomena that runs counter to its own axioms. So, for instance, science rules out the possibility of miracles, since these would imply that there can be a natural effect that is not the result of a natural cause. The success of science in exploring nature within this plausibility structure was taken, then as now, as confirming *the validity of its axiomatic structure*. Other disciplines quickly employed the principle of contingency in the broad sense noted above as the basis for constructing knowledge, but adapted it to suit their own situation.

Within the new knowledge structure of modernity, questions about the purpose of human life became meaningless or unanswerable, if they suggested answers that went beyond the natural realm. From the religious and philosophical perspectives, however, the issues of purpose and mission were, and remain, central.

Faith and the Principle of Purpose

The *principle of purpose*, which is central to religion and philosophy, uses an alternative set of axioms in determining what is reliable and reasonable knowledge. In invoking this principle people seek to create knowledge and establish meaning by determining *the ends for which things come into existence*. The Christian worldview, for instance, takes it as axiomatic that God exists, that God is the creator of nature, and that God has revealed God's purpose in creating human beings and the natural world in which they exist. Truth deemed to be revealed by God is knowledge with an absolute dimension (even allowing for the problem humans have in understanding and articulating it in a meaningful way). In its Catholic construction, "reliable knowledge" is defined *not only* by the principle of contingency, *but also by the principle of purpose*. In the Church's teaching there can be *no irreconcilable differences* between the "truth" of science and that of the Christian religion, properly understood, as ultimately both share a common source, the mind of God.[200]

Religious tradition carried within the Christian, Islamic and Jewish communities cherishes and lives by the story of God's intervention in human history and God's revelation of the purpose of human life in these interventions. While there is disagreement about the nature of this revelation, within all three religious traditions the principle of purpose applies not only to the purpose of human beings and creation, but also to the purpose of history.

Writing from within the Christian version of this plausibility structure, Newbigin[201] observes:

> The gospel gives rise to a new plausibility structure, a radically different vision of things from those that shape all human cultures apart from the gospel. The Church, therefore, as the bearer of the gospel, inhabits a plausibility structure which is at variance with, and calls into question, those that govern all human cultures and religions without exception. The mutual challenge this creates has been present throughout the history of Western civilisation.

Christian faith has a plausibility structure which takes it as axiomatic that all truth is defined in relation to a person, Jesus Christ, and that the question of

---

[200] See for instance John Paul II *Fides et Ratio* #34 (1998).
[201] Newbigin, 9.

purpose finds its ultimate answer in his message and mission.

As happened in pre-modern Europe, however, when the Church is integrally embedded in a particular culture, and its leaders become key players in its political and social institutions, it can easily lose sight of the mission imperative to which Newbigin draws our attention. As the community which holds a reigning plausibility structure in place becomes discredited, so too does the knowledge generated using this structure. In the construction of truth, people then look elsewhere.

Re-definition of "Public Knowledge" in Modernity

Within any culture "public knowledge", that is knowledge that is readily used in public discourse including knowledge taught in schools, is determined by the reigning plausibility structure. In pre-modern Europe statements such as "God exists" or "God is the Creator" or "the Bible is God's word" were accepted as unremarkable, as unquestionable *facts*. In such a world any findings of the new "natural sciences" that challenged such self-evident "facts" were naturally viewed with suspicion, as we saw in the case of Galileo. Within the plausibility structure of the time Galileo's views on astronomy would have been regarded as an *unprovable personal opinion* since they could not be deduced from scripture or philosophy. That there could even be an alternative plausibility structure to that provided by Christian faith lay beyond the imaginal horizon of many Church leaders, even into late pre-modern times.

As modernity advanced, the reigning plausibility structure in Western societies became that of science. Knowledge created by science, or using the methods of science, was now given the status of public knowledge. This is still largely true today. In schools the theory of evolution is taught as "public knowledge". The theory of intelligent design, however, is denied the status of public knowledge.

Knowledge constructed employing the plausibility structure of pre-modernity is now regarded only as an *expression of unprovable personal opinion* and assigned the status of "private values". This was because its truth could not be demonstrated within the knowledge paradigm adopted by modernity. The wheel had turned! The new plausibility structure, once embedded firmly in Western culture, proved to be the genius of modernity, the principal cause of both its benefits and costs to humankind.

The change in the knowledge paradigm that characterised the shift from pre-modern to modern times is often presented as a contest of "faith versus reason". Such an explanation is misleading. As Newbigin's analysis makes clear, what we are dealing with are *two ways of looking at the construction of knowledge* – one that seeks to explain reality primarily from the perspective of *purpose*, and one that seeks to explain it in terms of *contingency*. Both views make use of the faculty of reason – the power of the human mind to think coherently and to sort the data of human experience in such a way that it can be grasped and organised into comprehensive patterns. Faith and science are each "reasonable" within their own axiomatic structures and the traditions to which each gives rise. They are both living traditions; both are capable of further development. However, rather than being viewed as complementary, their proponents are often regarded as being in competition for dominance.

Post-modernity and the Principle of Critique

The post-modern situation we discussed in Chapters Five and Six has arisen partly as a consequence of the plausibility structure of modernity itself coming under challenge. As we have noted above, the reliability and reasonableness of knowledge is determined within a plausibility structure. This has two elements – the community that holds the knowledge and whose credibility validates its worth, and the axiomatic structure which grounds the process of knowing. In the post-modern period both elements of the plausibility structure which underpinned knowledge in modernity came under challenge. Firstly there was a *loss of credibility by the scientific community*. Compromising alliances between science and politics (evident recently in debates about climate change) and between science and big business (where the "objectivity" of the "scientific research" it funds is increasingly called into doubt) have come to light, sometimes in major court cases. In addition doubts have arisen about the value of science as people have seen at first hand its damaging effects. As a consequence, questions have begun to be asked about whether science can still be regarded as a source of reliable and objective truth.

A further challenge came from the post-modern philosophers who have called into question and sought to "deconstruct" the axiomatic structures of *all* plausibility structures. In a world growing increasingly complex, the "objectivity" of science has come to be regarded with growing suspicion, a situation not dissimilar to that faced by Catholic faith in late pre-modernity. As a consequence, the plausibility structure providing the foundation for the modern worldview no longer holds the privileged place it once did in Western society. The post-modern critique of knowledge and its relationship to power has raised the question "what is truth?" with a new level of urgency.

Ideological Pluralism and the Issue of Truth

The main premise of ideological pluralism holds that there is no such thing as "truth", but only truths, and that all truths are relative. As Kasper[202] describes

---

[202] Kasper, 11.

it, "Truth exists only in the plurality of truths". He affirms the need to re-ask the question "what is truth?" and challenges ideological pluralism:

> If the truth question is not raised, we have then a purely aesthetic understanding of the world in which things are judged according to *subjective experience or subjective factors* for deciding what seems to best correspond to one's own idea of happiness. Personal taste becomes the decisive criterion. One helps oneself at the *a la carte* market of possibilities and puts together one's own religion…(emphasis added)

Such a situation is readily open to manipulation.

For Kasper[203] the challenge of ideological pluralism is to reconcile *the claim for truth*, which is essential to Christian faith, with the *claim for freedom*, which confers on each individual the right to choose. He suggests this is possible because we possess the truth only in freedom.

> …though truth is not a merely subjective reality, but something that is given to us, it nonetheless does not exist in itself; it exists…in human subjects…Freedom is oriented towards the truth. For truth liberates us from momentary emotions and interests, from rapidly changing fashions, from the pressure of public opinion: truth widens the horizons of freedom. Truth – as the fourth Gospel says – will set us free (John 8:32). Thus truth and freedom are correlated and they presuppose each other.

The issue is not so much being free to make choices, as being free to make the *right* choices.

Narrative of Ideological Pluralism – The Emerging Worldview of Modernity

We have considered the issue of ideological pluralism so far largely from a philosophic point of view. Further insight can be gained by looking at the phenomenon from a historical perspective that is, by examining its narrative.

At the beginning of the Enlightenment period many of the towering figures such as Bacon, Galileo, Descartes, Pascal and Newton were committed Christians who would have accepted as *fact* that God created the world. Some were theologians in their own right. The belief that God was the source of all truth and had created the "Book of Nature" from which all humankind could learn proved to be a catalyst in the rapid evolution of thinking about science and the scope of science. The task of the scientist was to establish the laws of nature from the "Book of Nature" in much the same way as theologians had attempted to establish the moral law from the "Book of the Bible". The opening stance of science was therefore that *one could learn from nature*. If the laws of nature could be established, then science would be on a par with theology as a

---
[203] Kasper 2003, 16–17.

benefit to humanity. However, this project did not work out as these idealists seem to have intended. Instead a new worldview – that of modernity – emerged as the "spirit of the age".

Shenk[204] captures the development that actually occurred as follows:

> As the notion of natural laws began to permeate European culture, the concept of "nature" began to replace "creation". In the Bible the earth and universe are always referred to as creation, which reveals a worldview convinced that God creates and also sustains what he has created. The biblical worldview also demands human accountability to God for the way we relate to creation. However, by referring to creation as nature, the Enlightenment introduced a subtle yet significant shift in Western culture, for it is possible for nature to function independently of God, governed only by natural laws.

As long as nature is thought of as God's creation, then man has some responsibility to God for it. However, while initially the emerging worldview of modernity held that God created nature and endowed it with its own laws, it also held that the laws were discoverable by the use of human reason alone, so there was no real need for God to be invoked in dealing with nature. God is thus separated from God's creation. The attitude to science quickly evolved from man *learning from nature* to man *controlling nature*. The slide from here to the position that the natural order could be studied without any reference to God could now be made. In modernity science became an autonomous discipline and, as a consequence, so too did all the other academic disciplines as the realm of knowledge quickly expanded.

In the "Book of the Bible" mankind has a destiny *outside of nature*. One of the attractions of Darwin's theory of evolution for the emerging modern worldview was that it placed humankind *within nature* and so governed by the laws of nature. The laws covering human behaviour, like any other laws of nature, were seen as being, at least in principle, discoverable through scientific investigation. With Freud's pioneering work in psychotherapy this understanding appeared to be validated.

In modernity this position was taken further. If scientific investigation could discover the laws governing human nature, such knowledge would provide the basis for a *new vision of what was morally good*. This vision would have its source within nature and would not require any reference point beyond nature. Appealing to the axiom that the explanation of a phenomenon is inherent in the phenomenon itself, moral laws could be uncovered independent of the churches. Such a moral framework would have validity because God

---

[204] David Shenk *Global Gods: Exploring the Role of Religions in Modern Societies* (Waterloo Ontario: Herald Press, 1995), 323.

had built moral principles into the nature of man, and by use of his reason man could discover what these were. Within the modern worldview human sexuality could be studied objectively and came to be seen in an entirely new light, detached from any considerations of human purpose. As Charles Taylor points out, while the modern worldview initially sought to honour God, it also pushed God further to the periphery of human life, paving the way for exclusive humanism.[205] As the place of God in this worldview retreated, it became possible to ask, perhaps for the first time, as does Nietzsche's madman wandering aimlessly in the public square, "Who killed God?" It is hard to deny Taylor's thesis that the exclusive humanism, which developed in modernity, paved the way to modern atheism.

The development of the modern worldview was, however, not yet completed. A morality discovered by studying the laws of nature would be *universal* because it was the product of *universal reason*, something shared by all humankind and therefore accessible to all. This new moral framework would be different from that of religion, which was seen as specific to a *particular faith or denomination*. This morality could become the basis for a new social order, one developed around the universal themes of human happiness and collective well-being. A secular construction of what was "good" and "right" had the potential at least to *overcome the historical divisions created by religion*. It could assist people to live together in order and in peace. Such was the hope![206]

Shenk[207] notes a further development in the modern worldview. Faith and the Church, which had been the "soul of culture" in pre-modern times, were now given the collective label of "religion". Christianity was relativised within the modern worldview by becoming just *one religion among others*. Reduced to being another phenomenon, religion could itself also become the subject of scientific study. When the "Book of the Bible" was studied within the new plausibility structure, one that bracketed out the transcendent and the miraculous, its truth was quickly questioned, found wanting, and seen as in need of revision. In the modern worldview Jesus could not have worked miracles. The claim that he did would mean that God defies God's own laws when it suits. This would make God appear to be capricious. *To the modern mindset miracles represented a contradiction in terms*. This argument was extended further to history. God does not intervene in history, since this would defy the laws governing the normal working of history. This brief outline of the way in which the modern worldview developed has endeavoured to show the

---

[205] Charles Taylor traces this development in considerable detail in *A Secular Age*, 271ff.
[206] This understanding of "universal reason" assumes that "reason" is defined within the limits of the modern worldview as formulated in the West.
[207] Schenk, 325.

coherence of this worldview once its initial premises are accepted.

"Truth" in the Post-modern Worldview

If, as the post-modern philosophers contend, all plausibility structures are problematic, then so too is the "truth" derived by using them. It follows then that all truths are relative since the validity of any claim to truth must be considered within the frame of reference within which it is made. This is the logic of *ideological pluralism*. Ideological pluralism brackets out the possibility of knowing anything absolutely – that is, as true for all people for all time. It therefore calls into question meta-narratives of all kinds both secular and religious.

In modernity truth became that which could be established by reason, first within the axiomatic system developed for science, and later by extension within all the other academic disciplines which, over time, developed variant axiomatic systems of their own. However, as sociology and cultural anthropology developed, it became clear that *all plausibility structures are culturally conditioned*, and in consequence what we view as true and reasonable is culturally conditioned both in its content and in its expression. This raises doubts about modernity's notion of universal reason. This matter has come to the fore in recent discussions about universal human rights. Many developing countries see Western demands on this matter as unreasonable.

As we noted in the previous chapter, when the narrative of a people becomes tied to a particular way of construing truth, a particular view of what is true can easily be projected as universal, that is, true for all people. It then becomes a meta-narrative. The post-modern critique is that *meta-narratives are rarely innocent*; embedded in them are claims to power. This means the plausibility structures on which they depend have within them claims to power.

As the twentieth century progressed, the *principle of contingency* that underpinned the modern worldview was challenged by the *critical principle* of post-modernity. Post-modern philosophy is essentially concerned with the application of the *critical principle* and seeks to "deconstruct" claims to truth, raising doubt about all such claims. It has its own plausibility structure, the axiom of which is "radical doubt" or "the hermeneutic of suspicion". A plausibility structure based on radical doubt is inherently unstable, as it must call into question the notion of radical doubt itself!

In accounting for the fragmentation of culture, as alluded to by Rivers, Schreiter, Gallagher and others above, we now need to include the negative impact that the process of deconstruction has had in unsettling established belief systems of all sorts. The situation can best be interpreted in terms of a growing belief in many cultures that *no truth is totally reliable*. It is always some group's understanding or expression of the truth, open to challenge by another group. The post-modern position is that it is extremely difficult, if not impossible, to know things as they really are, because the process of knowing itself precludes this. We always know conditionally, and the conditions are determined by the worldview implicit in our culture, the plausibility structure embedded in that worldview, and the axioms on which this structure rests. However, if all of these are suspect, then where does one turn to find certainty and coherence? This is the dilemma at the heart of the post-modern worldview.

In contrasting the modern and the post-modern worldviews, Knitter points out that the concern of *modern thinkers* was to move beyond the local to grasp the universal truths of nature applicable to all, and recognised by all. Post-moderns hold a different creed. For them such a project is not only impossible but also dangerous, since people and their cultures are more different than they are alike. The post-modern sensibility is that *universal truths are dangerous and difference is life-giving*. Knitter sums up this post-modern understanding as follows:

> Truth is always truths. It always takes different shapes and assumes different identities – to the point that "it" is no longer one, but many. If there is such a thing as "one absolute truth" we'll never know it, at least not in our present human condition. If any one person or culture thinks they have the one underlying truth that will embrace all the others, it will not be a truth that others can see but a truth that will be forced on them. So truth too is dominated by diversity…Truth is plural not singular because (a) all human experience and all knowledge are filtered, and (b) the filters are incredibly diverse. Just as there is no way we can climb out of our skins and still be who we are, so there is no way we can discard our cultural-historical filters by which we see the world and still be the persons we are.[208]

What does the situation we have painted above hold for Catholic school leaders and educators?

Creating "the New Whole"

In considering the narrative of ideological pluralism we have considered three plausibility structures all with a claim to truth and therefore to authority and power. The plausibility structure of faith faces a peculiar difficulty in that it is linked historically in many people's minds to pre-modern times. People operating from the worldview of modernity often confused the worldview of faith with the worldview of pre-modernity.

The struggle to move from the pre-modern to the modern world came at

---

[208] Paul Knitter *Introducing Theologies of Religions* (Maryknoll New York: Orbis, 2004), 175.

considerable psychic cost in Europe and this cost is still carried in critical memory there, so that today the worldview of faith holds an uncomfortable place in its former home. It cannot entirely escape its historical baggage, a situation that often leads people to view as retrograde, any attempt to consider Christian faith as an option in making sense of life. As Newbigin[209] pointed out some time ago this makes the re-evangelisation of Europe a very difficult and challenging task.

The *principle of purpose*, which is foundational to this worldview has to be included in any attempt to create Schreiter's "new whole" – a coherent worldview capable of taking us past the dilemmas of modernity and post-modernity. As we will show in Part D, the worldview of faith has moved a long way since pre-modernity. However, as a principle taken in isolation, the principle of purpose remains, as post-moderns suggest, dangerous. The resurgence of religious fundamentalist movements supports this view. The Catholic Church has also invoked the principle of purpose erroneously in the past to justify a claim to power based on a belief that, since the moral purpose is the highest purpose in life, the authority of the Church as the God-appointed guardian of moral purpose, is higher than any other, and therefore empowers it to legitimise all other authority. This stance was to prove disastrous. The comments of Pope Benedict XVI on secularity, quoted in the previous chapter, clearly show that such views are disavowed today.

Abuse of power by a set of Church leaders at a point in history no more vitiates the principle of purpose than do abuses of power in the name of science at another point in history vitiate the principle of contingency. Both principles have a claim on truth. This claim is not based on how knowledge is used or misused; the claim is based on the validity of the axiomatic structure on which knowledge and truth are constructed.

The plausibility structure of the post-modern period is linked to the *critical principle*, which stands as a corrective to overstated claims to authority and power particularly in the use of knowledge. This plausibility structure like others is not without its faults in the generation of reliable knowledge since, when no narrative is regarded as definitive, all narratives, including that of post-modernity, can be regarded with suspicion.

In creating "the new whole", a worldview that can bring coherence to the interpretation of complex human experiences and provide direction to people in making the right choices, our contention is that we need a plausibility structure which *acknowledges the value* of all three principles – purpose, contingency

---

[209] Lesslie Newbigin *Foolishness of the Greeks: The Gospel and Western Culture* (Grand Rapids Michigan: Eerdmans Publishing Company, 1986), 20.

and critique –and *holds them in creative tension* since all three have a claim on truth.

In his analysis of the modern worldview Newbigin[210] suggests that plausibility structures are like a set of spectacles through which people look at reality. For him, there are primarily two sets of spectacles, that of faith and that of science. He suggests that which set one wears depends on the situation. Post-modern critical analysis suggests another metaphor. Reality is what we see through our digital camera. The image of this reality we can project on our computer screen and view using various filters. All views offer us something in interpreting the reality we see. The *differences* we note as we change filters are themselves an important part of the reality we must seek to understand. Compressing reality down within the strictures of one particular plausibility structure, as has happened in pre-modernity and modernity, does harm to the nature of reality itself.

As we move beyond post-modernity, into a new or second modernity, the need clearly exists to move off the slippery ground of ideological pluralism onto firmer territory, if this is possible. The suggestion is that in our search for truth we need to develop *a paradigm of knowledge that is capable of holding the three principles outlined above in some form of creative tension*. Whether this will occur, and how this can be done, represents a major challenge facing those seeking to give shape to the second modernity.

Ideological Pluralism – Some Educational Implications

What implications does the above discussion have for Catholic educators? This question can be answered in a number of ways.

The situation in post-modernity raises philosophic issues with practical consequences. Catholic school leaders, for instance, face immense challenges educating young people in circumstances where the plausibility structures that underpin reliable knowledge are called into question. The extent of the problem leaders face is well identified by Rivers.

> The post-modern phenomenon of pluralism holds that there is no right way to do anything. Everything has its claims; no belief is truer than any other belief. We are so accustomed to a plurality of choices that we are reluctant to consider that any one of them might claim to be the truth. Such a claim seems pretentious. Pluralism also tends to make us wary of making commitments to any clear and unambiguous view of reality – although this is exactly what evangelization asks us to do. Yet to do so flies in the face of the dominant thinking today.[211]

---

[210] Newbigin 1989, 36.
[211] Rivers, 40.

Leading in such a situation is bound to be complex as people come to the view that all truth is relative. It is a matter of "my truth" versus "your truth". Educators, particularly those who have to manage students behaving badly, or indeed even teachers behaving badly, face the dilemmas this situation creates on an increasingly regular basis as people lose respect for telling the truth.

As Catholic educators we seek to assist students to integrate the experiences of faith, culture and life.[212] We believe this gives them the freedom they need to make right choices. This is our best aspiration. What we know by faith gains its legitimacy from the principle of purpose. The principle of contingency underpins what we know through culture. As contemporary educators we seek to assist our students to apply the critical principle in the experience of human living. In pursuing the goal of integrating faith, life and culture Catholic educators therefore seek to hold the three principles we have been discussing in tension, at least implicitly.

Ideological pluralism raises important issues about *the nature of reliable knowledge*. How we understand this matter has a bearing on how we understand the curriculum. How the school balances the demands of the principles of *purpose*, *contingency* and *critique* within its various learning programs is clearly an important issue. It is also vitally important to ask how these principles are balanced within the Religious Education program.

If we take Charles Taylor's analysis of our secular age to heart, there is a need to assess the impact of the exclusive humanism that characterises the modern worldview. The logic of this worldview is set out above. We often encounter it as a default condition in the understanding both of teachers and particularly of parents. How do we attempt to acknowledge what is good in this worldview while trying to offset its limitations and challenge people to move beyond them? We will return to this question in Part D.

The emphasis in Part C has been on the nature of the missional frontier, in particular on the over-arching forces of globalisation, secularisation and pluralisation, which are affecting all societies and cultures. It is important that educators feel confident in their knowledge of these forces as they impact on the environment within which they work so as to make sense of their own experience as well as that of their students. *No meaningful theological reflection can take place without some understanding of our contemporary environment and the currents of thought alive within it.*

---

[212] Congregation for Catholic Education *The Catholic School* #37 (Homebush: St Paul Publications, 1977).

PART D

Befriending Our Religious Tradition

So far we have considered in some detail two of the three poles of theological reflection – attending to human experience and attending to culture. The final pole in our model of grassroots theology is "attending to" or "befriending" our religious tradition. Before exploring this pole, it is useful briefly to recall the ground we have covered to date.

As we noted at the outset of the study, for many Catholic educators today there is a perceived gap between the way mission is expressed within the school and what they regard as the challenges of mission revealed in their encounter with students and their parents. An essential task in effective school leadership is to help teachers make sense of this experience in such a way that the school community can move towards a coherent understanding of its own mission. This understanding needs to guide not only decision-making, but also the entire life of the school, and therefore is the concern of all. The alternative to developing coherence in mission is to have only a nominal sense of mission. This results in fragmentation of effort and loss of synergy as teachers pursue their individual or sectional interests. Such a situation detracts from a common witness to the values of the Gospel and reduces the role of the community in demonstrating the plausibility of the faith for students.

To be effective in our modern/post-modern context, the Catholic school leader has to make sense of the often complex experiences of those she/he leads. This requires the capacity to do grassroots theology; the leader needs to engage in theological reflection and, from this vantage point, lead others in the process. Theological reflection brings together the resources of our experience, our culture, and our faith. As Christians we believe that God's Spirit is present in all three, so there is a principle of cohesion deeply embedded in the process itself.

Theological reflection seeks to ground our thinking in something more substantive than the immediate, the utilitarian and the pragmatic. Our analysis of culture (Chapter Four) revealed that the way we make sense of the world around us is shaped by cultural values, and that we are only partly aware of what these are. Culture therefore has both strengths and weaknesses as a resource in theological reflection.

As discussed in Chapter Six, we also interpret our experiences in terms of where we see ourselves in the unfolding narrative of our community. Starting from what we know, we intuit the direction of this narrative and interpret events in terms of this intuition. This process too has its strengths and its weaknesses. Both our cultural and narrative frameworks are being re-shaped by historical movements and global phenomena such as globalisation, secularisation and pluralisation. The impact of such influences is tending to fragment our cultural and narrative frameworks through erosion of the worldviews on which they are based. Such developments can make it very difficult to form a clear or coherent notion of "what should be", that is, of mission, in Catholic education. When the end is not clear, means can easily be given the status of ends as seems to be the case in much of public education today.

The argument of Chapter Nine was that, in a sound Catholic education, the principles of *purpose, contingency and critique* must be kept in balance. This seems an essential element in creating "the new whole" or a worldview that can embrace human experience meaningfully as our "post-modern" era continues to evolve. In actuality, what happens in Catholic schools, under the impact of Government policies, often seems inherently unbalanced.[213] The question then is how can a better balance be achieved? There are no simple answers here.

The Catholic Church is strongly tied to a worldview based on the principle of purpose,[214] a principle vital in exploring *the significance* of what is learned, but one now associated historically with the pre-modern worldview. A major difficulty teachers in Catholic schools face is helping students explore what is "reasonable" in terms of this principle is the danger of giving them the message that "to be Catholic" implies adopting a pre-modern mindset. *There is a need to rescue the principle of purpose from its pre-modern setting.* How can this be done? The first step is to know your own tradition and important currents of thought alive within it.

As Walter Kasper makes clear,[215] the bishops at the Second Vatican Council, together with their large number of advisors, wrestled with the range of issues that this question raises. In doing so, they acknowledged the proper autonomy of academic disciplines as sources of reliable knowledge. This situation was later re-affirmed by Pope John Paul II in his encyclical *Fides et Ratio*. One consequence of these very considerable endeavours has been the development in the Church's self-understanding and in its official teaching.

In the process a new paradigm of mission is emerging, one that stands alongside the more traditional paradigm. The notion of an "emerging paradigm"

---

[213] This issue is often highlighted in discussions about Religious Education in senior classes.
[214] Pope John Paul II makes this clear in his discussion of truth in relation to morality and in relation to faith and reason in his two encyclical letters *Veritatis Splendor* (1993) and *Fides et Ratio* (1998).
[215] Walter Kasper *The Future of Christianity: The Church and Contemporary Pluralism in the Post-Modern Era* (Official text, Helder Camara Lecture, July 9, 2003), 3–5.

implies that a paradigm shift is under way. The new missional vision remains in competition with the traditional missional vision. This tension is obvious in many of the statements of the Second Vatican Council itself, as Arbuckle[216] has pointed out. It is also present in the writings of Pope John Paul II, who often adopted "both/and" rather than "either/or" formulations in dealing with mission. This practice was, in itself, quite "post-modern".

In Part D we now explore in some detail the shape of this emerging vision, which was touched on in Chapter Two, and explore its roots in scripture. Chapter Ten looks at current magisterial teaching of the Church, while Chapter Eleven seeks to detail the scriptural roots of this vision in the life of New Testament communities and in Jesus' teaching about the Kingdom of God. The argument in both chapters is that befriending our religious tradition means *engaging in a meaningful way with a living tradition.*

---

[216] Gerald Arbuckle *Refounding the Church: Dissent for Leadership* (Homebush: St Paul's Publications, 1993), 40.

CHAPTER TEN

Befriending a Living Tradition

For many Catholic educators "befriending their religious tradition" is probably the most difficult aspect of grassroots theology. There are a number of reasons for this, some relating to personal and family narratives, while others derive from living in a secular culture. For some there is a readiness issue, while others simply lack knowledge of their tradition. Whatever the reasons, coming to grips with the tradition is always a "work in progress". The word "tradition" itself causes reluctance in people because they interpret it to mean "something that hardly ever changes". There is often little appreciation that they are part of a *living tradition* and that with life comes challenge and change. In the discussion that follows, we explore the theological bases of the new understanding of mission that has emerged during the last half century, particularly as this has been expressed in the Church's official teaching.

With Life Comes Challenge and Change

In dealing with the narrative of modernity we pointed out that, in the historical circumstances of the time, the leadership of the Church construed its identity as being separate from the world. While there were many reasons to justify this decision, in mission terms it proved a serious miscalculation, which isolated the Church from social and political developments, positive and negative. In adopting this stance, the Church came to be seen by many people of good will as the enemy of all that was progressive. As the optimism that characterised both the Enlightenment and modernity began to wane in the late 1950s, a new mood developed both within the Church and within society.

It was in this situation that Pope John XXIII was elected to the papacy. Within three months of his election the new Pope indicated his intention to call an ecumenical council to deal with issues associated with the nature and mission of the Church and its relationship with the modern world. The Second Vatican Council opened in October 1962 and was conducted in four sessions in the autumns of 1962 to 1965. Over 2000 bishops attended the various sessions. In 1963 after the first session and just before his untimely death, Pope John XXIII took up the theme of re-engagement with the world on a very wide front in his encyclical letter *Pacem in Terris*. His successor Paul VI, in his first encyclical letter *Ecclesiam Suam* published in 1964 before the third session of the Council, also stressed the importance of opening up a "dialogue with the modern world", nominating this as one of three main "policies" of his pontificate.[217]

While not seeking to direct the work of the Council in terms of the specific treatment of issues, the broad direction given by these two popes to the assembled bishops of the world could not have been clearer. It was left to the bishops to chart the way forward in re-engaging with the world, to determine the purpose, shape and scope of this engagement, and to put the enterprise on a sound theological footing. This they did in the various documents of the Council. A major consequence of these endeavours was a reformulation of the Church's understanding of its mission in and to the world and, in turn, a reformulation of its various vehicles for mission, including the Catholic school. The understanding of mission affirmed at the Council created the trajectory of mission on which the Catholic community has travelled ever since.

As the Church began to redefine its mission, it also began to redefine its self-understanding, its identity. It became possible for people to think of themselves as "Catholic" in new ways. This factor is an important aspect of the modern experience of being Catholic, and an unintended consequence of reformulating the mission of the Church.

Mission Theology and Mission Practice – The Connection

A mutuality exists between *how a community thinks about its mission and how it engages in it*, that is, between its theology of mission and its mission practice. The demands of mission practice give impetus to developments in the theology of mission and a renewed understanding of mission, in turn, gives impetus to new forms of missional engagement. This holds true whether one's consideration is focused at the level of official Church theology as set out in authoritative documents and the global mission practice that it informs, or focused on grassroots theology and its relationship to how a school community achieves its mission. In this respect the Catholic experience is not unique, but is mirrored by that of other mainstream Christian denominations.[218] Given that missiology, the study of the theology and practice of mission, is now a highly ecumenical enterprise, this adds to the widely shared sense in the Christian communities that, when it comes to mission, the adage "with life comes change" holds true.

The dramatic development that has occurred in the Church's official

---

[217] Gerald Arbuckle *Refounding the Church: Dissent for Leadership* (Homebush: St Paul's Publications, 1993), 40.

[218] Stephen Bevans and Roger Schroeder cite many of the relevant documents from the evangelical and pentecostal churches in Part 111 of their *Constants in Context: A Theology of Mission for Today* (Maryknoll NewYork: Orbis, 2004). See also James Sherer and Stephen Bevans (eds) *New Directions in Mission and Evangelization* 3 (Maryknoll New York: Orbis, 1999) for some important documentation from the Lutheran World Federation and the World Council of Churches.

expression of its mission theology comes as a surprise to some, particularly given the relatively short time span of less than fifty years in which this has taken place. As has been noted above, leadership has played an important role. Key contributions have also been made by the generous involvement of those working "on the ground". Amid the challenges inherent in a rapidly changing context, an openness to the Spirit in discerning the changing face of mission is clearly in evidence. An important element in this improved discernment has been the establishment of new organisational structures such as synods at the level of the whole Church, as well as various regional and national arrangements for promoting *dialogue within the Church*. These have enabled insights to be developed not only in a region but, with the assistance of new communication technologies, across the globe. It has breathed new life into what Walter Kasper describes as "the oldest global player".[219]

A second level of mutuality exists between *how a community construes its identity and how members understand issues of mission* or purpose. For instance, a teacher construes her identity as teacher in terms of what she thinks a teacher should be doing. As the conception of what she should be doing changes, so too does the way she thinks of herself. This dynamic can work in both positive and negative ways. On the positive side, many teachers seek to create a positive relational learning environment in the classroom as a condition for effective academic learning. For them, this is what teaching is all about – for such teachers learning proceeds on the basis of trust. On the negative side, when the curriculum becomes dominated by the need to achieve high marks on standardised tests in "core" subjects in order to meet predetermined targets, many teachers feel that their profession is undervalued, and that the thrust of educational policy is to make the process of learning "teacher-proof". In such circumstances self-image and morale suffer. Teachers sense that this is not what teaching should be about. *When mission and identity lack alignment, meaning is a casualty.*

In summary, as the demands of mission change, there is an impact on the identity of those engaged in the various ministries through which Christian communities effect mission. Put another way, new mission challenges can initiate a paradigm shift not only in our mission theology but also in the understanding we have of ourselves as disciples committed to mission. This dynamic was at work in the Church during the twentieth century. The mission imperative to engage the modern world and its peoples led to a paradigm shift in mission theology, which in turn led to a re-formulation of identity, a situation with which we are still wrestling today.

[219] Walter Kasper *The Future of Christianity: A Meditation on the Church and Contemporary Pluralism in the Post Modern Era* (Official text, Helder Camara Lecture, July 9, 2003), 14.

The Church as Universal and Local

In discussions about the mission of the Church, the word "church" can be used in a number of ways. It is important, therefore, before considering the Church's mission theology, to take a little time to consider some of the territory mapped by the word "church" so as to better understand the ecclesial context in which a new self-understanding of both identity and mission have come about.

One of the major mission challenges for the Catholic Church in the past half century has been to come to grips with its identity as "a global Church". While the Church has always considered itself as the "universal Church", in the eyes of many people, particularly those in developing countries, it was experienced as a "European Church".[220] Not surprisingly, Church teaching generally took European cultural assumptions as being normative, and tended to disregard other cultures in which the Church had taken root, seeing them as being of lesser significance. In this mindset, mission was seen as an essential element in the process of "civilising" peoples living in non-European cultures, one that carried a moral imperative. This Euro-centric bias derived from the fact that most of the people staffing the central bureaucracy of the Church were European. The Church was global in extent, but European in sensibility.

This state of affairs came under scrutiny during the Second Vatican Council where, for the first time in history, leaders from all the major cultural groups met together. The very nature of the gathering was likely to challenge the Euro-centric nature of the Church, and it did. The seeds of a new consciousness, one which would become more familiar with the idea of Church as a community of communities, were sown.

The Second Vatican Council recognised that the Catholic Church, as a global Church, required an organisational structure that reflected its true identity. As a result, national conferences of bishops were established or, where they already existed, were given more official recognition, thus strengthening their role. Regional assemblies covering the main cultural regions of the world – Europe, Asia, Africa and so on – are held periodically, enabling common aspirations and modes of co-operation to surface and be developed.

In the years following the Council, general synods held in Rome nurtured this development, while at the local level, groups of Catholics began to engage seriously in their own theologising processes. The 1974 Roman synod was particularly important in addressing understandings of mission and evangelisation. In regard to the understanding of "church" we have been discussing, two inter-related issues, human cultures and local church, were particularly pertinent. Coming at the close of the first turbulent decade after the

---

[220] For instance, the vast majority of the 700 bishops attending the First Vatican Council (1869–70) came from Europe and North America.

Council, the work of this synod gave rise to a detailed treatment of evangelisation in Pope Paul VI's apostolic exhortation *Evangelii Nuntiandi* released in 1975. Prior to this synod, the word "evangelisation", while appearing occasionally in Catholic theology, was not widely used.

In *Evangelii Nuntiandi* Paul VI, acting as a spokesperson for the bishops who had convened at the synod, as well as in his own right, taught that the evangelising process includes the culture or way of life of a people, as well as the people themselves – "what matters is to evangelise man's culture and cultures (not in a purely decorative way, as it were, by applying a thin veneer, but in a vital way, in depth and right to their very roots)".[221] Those committed to the Church's missionary work are called to respect a people's culture because culture is the vehicle through which God's word comes to the people and through which they respond to God. The pope also recognises that, as human constructs, cultures have their limitations, and like persons, benefit from salvific encounter with the Gospel carried in genuinely Christian communities. This was a major development in Catholic teaching. It embodied a shift to the modern concept of culture and away from a concept of culture which linked evangelisation with "civilization", and therefore with the dissemination of European values.

One initial consequence was the development of a new language within the Church. The concept of "local church" was now juxtaposed against that of "global church". Theologies of inculturation were developed by theologians[222] which helped formulate the "responsibility of each local church to give shape to the faith it lived".[223] People became more aware of the processes of dialogue, interaction and adaptation that need to occur when the values of the Gospel carried by one community come into a living contact with the culture of another.

Local theology became the term adopted to describe a people's attempts to discern religious meaning in their collective experience. Possibly the most well known example of the emergence of local theology is the development of various "liberation theologies" in South and Central America in the sixties and seventies. Since then there have been developments of local theologies in other cultural regions. Initially, the term local theology referred to attempts to make religious sense of the experiences of "local churches" often understood as those sharing a connected culture and history. At times the idea encompassed

---

[221] Pope Paul VI Evangelii Nuntiandi #20 (Strathfield: Society of St Paul, 1975).

[222] See for instance, Aylward Shorter *Towards a Theology of Inculturation* (London: Geoffrey Chapman, 1988); Peter Schineller A Handbook of Inculturation (New York: Paulist Press, 1990); Diego Irarrazaval *Inculturation* (Maryknoll New York: Orbis, 2000).

[223] Lucien Legrand *The Bible on Culture* (Maryknoll New York: Orbis, 2000), xi.

whole continents or extensive regions.

In more recent developments, however, the term "local church" is used in a more restricted sense, to mean *the Church in a particular diocese*. It is possible therefore to talk of the local church of Sydney, Boston, Bangalore or Dublin. This reflects Paul's usage of the term "church" to indicate the community of believers in a particular place, for instance, when he wrote his letters to the church of Corinth or Rome or Thessalonika.

The conception of the global Church as a *community of communities,* meaning a communion of local churches, is now widespread in Catholic Church discourse. A diocese in turn is seen as the local expression of this community of communities. The Latin word *communio* is now used to reflect this understanding. *Communio* connotes communities working together in unity towards some common purpose.[224]

The diocese under the leadership of the bishop, as "the local church", is the basic unit of mission in the life of the Church. It is possible therefore to talk of the mission of the local church. Local churches are becoming more adept at formulating this mission in relation to the context of the diocese. The leadership given by individual bishops is, however, exercised within general guidelines provided by Rome and directions set by national bishops' conferences. *The global is in the local, and the local in the global.*

The conception of church as both global and local has some bearing on how we understand "the mission of the Church". Clearly if the word "church" is used in a variety of ways, then there are likely to be corresponding ways in which communities understand their proper mission within the Church. Using the one word "evangelisation" to encompass all aspects of the Church's mission can be problematic. Effectiveness in mission generally requires some awareness of the many forms of evangelisation called for by local contexts. On this matter, the magisterial documents of the Church are helpful.

Development of Mission Theology – Magisterial Documents

Developments in Catholic Church thinking about mission have followed a number of trajectories. Foundational to these developments are the documents of the Second Vatican Council. Of particular interest in considering the links between mission and identity are the two documents dealing with the nature and purpose of the Church itself – *Lumen Gentium* (*Dogmatic Constitution on the Church*) and *Gaudium et Spes* (*Pastoral Constitution on the Church in the Modern World*). The first of these deals with the identity of the Church and the second with its relationship to the "world", including the Church's

---

[224] The concept of *communio* is beautifully expressed in Pope John Paul II's post-synodal exhortation *Ecclesia in Oceania* ##10–11 (*The Church in Oceania*).

understanding of its mission in the context of the modern world. The work done at the Council created the platform, as it were, from which further developments in mission theology could be launched.

Official teaching is set out in a range of documents known collectively as *magisterial documents*, that is documents carrying the teaching authority of the church. These address a range of audiences and carry different levels of authority. The documents of a Council of the Church are considered the most authoritative. Popes also promulgate documents addressing a number of subjects, some being directed to the bishops, others to the faithful at large. Roman congregations and pontifical councils also prepare documents which are approved and sent to the universal Church for guidance in important areas of Church life.

Magisterial documents[225] form an enduring record of the Church's official self-understanding across time. They provide a kind of theological "base camp" in the life of a faith community. A document, such as a papal encyclical, generally represents a point that the Church as a whole has reached, and with which most within the local churches can identify. The metaphor of Church as a pilgrim people on a journey is a useful reference point in understanding the role played by these documents. The pilgrims (the baptised, those responsible for mission) are presently working through some very difficult terrain as Christian faith interacts with modernity/post-modernity. In such a situation a major magisterial document might be likened to a sheltered area in which people can gather, check their orientation, rest a little and then move on. The image of a base camp is a useful one. Such documents also function as "places" to which one can return in order to check bearings, if in trekking through complex theological ground beyond the base camp, one realises that the path one is on is not heading in a helpful direction.

Key "Moments" in the Development of the Theology of Mission

In the sections which now follow, we seek to explore elements in the Church's understanding of its theology of mission as these emerged from the Second Vatican Council and have developed to the present. In doing so, we will use as a navigation aid three key "moments" in the Church's developing sense of mission as captured in its authoritative teaching. These three "moments" are: the Second Vatican Council (1962–5), the Synod on Evangelisation (1974), and Pope John Paul II's teaching on mission (1990s). These moments track the emergence of the new paradigm in the Catholic understanding of the Church's

---

[225] Francis Sullivan *Magisterium: Teaching Authority in the Catholic Church* (Dublin: Gill & Macmillan, 1985), 24–34.

mission.

Associated with each "moment" are a number of official documents that frame the discussion:[226]

1. **Documents of Second Vatican Council** – *Lumen Gentium* (*Dogmatic Constitution on the Church*), *Gaudium et Spes* (*Pastoral Constitution on the Church in the Modern World*), *Ad Gentes* (*Decree on the Church's Missionary Activity*), and *Nostra Aetate* (*Decree on the Relation of the Church to Non-Christian Religions*).
2. ***Evangelii Nuntiandi*** (*On the Evangelisation of Peoples*), apostolic exhortation of Pope Paul VI.
3. ***Redemptoris Missio*** (*On the Permanent Validity of the Church's Missionary Mandate*) encyclical of Pope John Paul II. Associated with this document, and in some ways explanatory of it, *Dialogue and Proclamation* (1991) from the Pontifical Council for Inter-religious Dialogue. Also addressing some unresolved issues associated with inter-religious dialogue was the instruction from the Congregation of the Doctrine of the Faith, *Dominus Jesus* (2000).

In the ongoing theologising processes that have helped the Church move forward in the area of mission, we need to recognise not only the importance of local experiences of mission, but the interaction that occurs between what happens locally and its global impact.[227] The Church has a global character which complements the life of local communities. It can, therefore, interpret human experience from both a global and local perspective.

First Moment – "The Church is by Nature Missionary"

In the light of these considerations, then, let us return to our discussion of the key markers along the route of the Church's journey in self-understanding in regard to mission. The insight which paved the way for the new paradigm of mission is to be found most succinctly stated in *Ad Gentes* 2 – "The whole Church is missionary by its very nature…". Since mission is of the very nature of the Church, it is of central importance to *all the faithful*. This key insight was complemented by other important understandings about the Church's relationship with the modern world and its peoples found in *Gaudium et Spes*, *Lumen Gentium*, and *Nostra Aetate*. In *Lumen Gentium* #5 the Kingdom parables from the synoptic gospels set the Church's mission in the context of God's Kingdom. The importance for mission theology of treating the nature

---

[226] Bevans and Schroeder 2004, Part 3, uses a variant of this framework.
[227] Robert Schreiter *The New Catholicity: Theology Between the Global and the Local* (Maryknoll New York: Orbis Books, 1997), 1–27.

and purpose of the Church in this way can scarcely be overestimated.

In order to understand the nature of the paradigm shift which occurred in the Second Vatican Council, we need to set the change within its historical context. Prior to the Council and during the course of it, two schools of thought about the goals of mission had been vying for supremacy. Neither were new approaches. Indeed both are rooted in the experience of the early Church, as recorded in the New Testament. The first held that the priority of mission should be *to proclaim the Gospel* by whatever means are appropriate in a particular context. In terms of New Testament models this approach can be sourced to St Paul who, under the impression that the second coming of Jesus was imminent, sought to proclaim the good news to as many people as possible with all speed. The second held that priority in mission should be *to establish the Church and its structures*, thus ensuring the practice and stability of Church life and the formation of a community to continue the mission of Jesus. In the New Testament period, as time elapsed, it became necessary to structure communities to keep the faith alive, and to provide a means to take it to the ends of the earth.[228] In the *Acts of the Apostles* Luke presents the Spirit as the source of cohesion in this ongoing journey of the Christian communities.

The Council did not choose between these two worthwhile goals, but rather opted for something *more fundamental in nature*. It asked what is the purpose of mission, and from where does it gain its *raison d'etre*? Bypassing the existing schools of thought, the Council returned to an earlier understanding of mission, identifying its nature and source as lying in the very life of God:

> The Church on earth is by its very nature missionary since, according to the plan of the Father, it has its origin in the mission of the Son and the Holy Spirit. This plan flows from "fountain-like love", the love of God the Father.[229]

This statement challenged the older conception of mission in which missionary work was handled largely by Propaganda Fide (popularly known as the Church's "Department of Foreign Affairs") and an elite force of missionaries. Mission was no longer to be the sole responsibility of "experts", it was now a challenge for *all Christians*.[230] This teaching recalls anew that, *in sharing the life of the triune God, each baptised person also shares in God's mission*. Mission lies at

---

[228] Lucien Legrand, 124–130.

[229] *Ad Gentes* #2 in Austin Flannery *Vatican Council II* (Northport New York: Costello Publishing Company, 1996), 444.

[230] This understanding led at first to a "crisis in mission" as people sought to understand its implications. The statement was intended to affirm the role of all Christians in mission but had the unintended consequence of questioning the worth and role of those engaged in specialist missionary work. Pope John Paul II sought to address this issue in *Redemptoris Missio* by affirming the need for mission in the traditional understanding, again opting for a "both/and" solution to the problem.

the centre of each Christian life, and the life of each faith community.

Secondly, the Council Fathers drew the attention of the whole Church to the fact that, since mission is first and foremost God's work, Church communities and individuals are privileged participants in *what God is effecting in the world*. This understanding provides the basis for the Church's dialogue with the world. The bishops of the Council recognised that the understanding of mission that had developed since the sixteenth century was flawed. Mission is not primarily the Church's work, rather it is God's work in which the Christian community is privileged to participate. This change in outlook is often summed up as a change from *God's Church has a mission* to *God's mission has a Church*. Since mission belongs in the first instance to God, it is God who is responsible for mission, not the Church.

In this new understanding, Jesus Christ remains the exemplar for how God's mission is to be carried out in time. His teaching becomes the substance of mission and the Kingdom of God becomes the goal or end of mission. The Church and the world are heading ultimately for the same end, the Kingdom. The Church's role is to be in the service of the world so that it reaches the goal for which it is destined. In this sense the Church's role is an extension of the mission of Jesus; it is engaged in setting up the possibility of the Kingdom coming both in history and beyond history. Far from being in charge of mission, the Church under the guidance of the Spirit, is at the service of God's mission in the world.

During the decades following the Second Vatican Council, faith communities would wrestle with the implications of this paradigm shift. The consciousness that, in terms of Brunner's insightful comment, the "Church exists by mission as a fire exists by burning"[231] would spread unevenly and with a degree of difficulty, but spread it has.

By holding that the whole Church community participates in God's mission, the bishops at the Council were also providing a perspective on a new and broader understanding of salvation. This perspective recognises that God has been at work in the world since the beginning of time among all peoples and cultures. As Bevans and Schroeder point out[232] the Second Vatican Council affirmed an insight that has been present in the Church since patristic times, but lost in the Middle Ages. However the Council went further. In the shortest of its documents, *Nostra Aetate,* the Church is called upon to collaborate with members of other religions "to preserve and encourage the moral truths" found among their adherents.[233] There is acknowledgment in this document

---

[231] Emile Brunner *The Word in the World*, (London: SCM Press, 1931), 11.
[232] Bevans and Schroeder, 25.

that people of other religions can attain salvation through faithful adherence to their own religious traditions. There is also a reaffirmation of the duties that Christians have to witness to their own faith. Two theological principles are finely balanced here: God's universal will that all be saved and the unique role of Jesus as saviour. What are the implications for Christian mission? Exploration of this question continues fruitfully, if at times painfully, to the present.[234]

Second Moment – "Making Present the Kingdom of God"

The 1974 synod on evangelisation wrestled not only with the implications of the Council's teaching on mission, but also with the results of working with the Council's insights on the ground during the decade following the Council. This decade saw an explosion of energy as people "unpacked" the mission theology we have just discussed. It was a time for widespread experimentation in mission thinking and practice. In this period it also became clearer that the traditional paradigm in mission theology was becoming highly problematic. The rollback of the colonial processes added to the confusion. A new understanding of the various forms of mission had to be worked out. Also, if mission was the province of all Christians, then the normal pastoral ministry of the Church had to be considered as an expression of mission. This represented a significant change in outlook for diocesan clergy, in particular, who had been formed in a theological tradition that made a clear distinction between pastoral work and missionary work.[235]

By the end of the first decade after the Second Vatican Council there seemed a clear need to develop greater clarity around the purpose and goals of mission. The 1974 synod on evangelisation was the Church's response to this need. The range of issues covered at the synod was extensive and the bishops left the task of summarising discussions to Pope Paul VI. This he did in his apostolic exhortation, *Evangelii Nuntiandi,* released the following year.

Evangelii Nuntiandi re-affirms the central insight of the Council's mission theology, that mission is a sharing in the life of God. As well, it acknowledged the insights of *Nostra Aetate*. The document also expands the Council's theology of mission by bringing more clearly to the fore the main motif with which Jesus framed his own teaching about his mission, namely the Kingdom or Reign of God.[236]

[233] *Nostra Aetate* #2 in Flannery, 570–571.
[234] John Paul II was to return to the theme of Jesus Christ as universal saviour in his encyclicals *Redemptoris Missio* (1990) and Dominus Jesus (2000).
[235] This is still an issue to be addressed at parish level. It remains difficult to find an answer to the question: what is the mission of the parish? Lack of clarity on this question can make parish–school and parish–diocese relations quite complex.
[236] Cf. *Evangelii Nuntiandi* ##6–12.

Evangelii Nuntiandi proved something of a watershed for those engaged in mission and the study of mission. It clarified key elements in the emerging field of missiology by:

- reclaiming the theology of the Kingdom of God as a basis for mission
- identifying conversion as vital for the evangelising church, as well as those to whom the good news is offered
- recognising that evangelisation applies not only to persons, but also to human institutions and cultures
- recognising that evangelisation is multi-faceted
- identifying the central place of proclamation through word and witness
- accepting the unique way local peoples express their religiosity. "Popular religiosity" is to be not only respected, but valued (#48).

Nearly four decades after its publication, *Evangelii Nuntiandi* continues to be regarded as a seminal document in mission theology. In particular it acknowledges that evangelisation encompasses many *forms*: pastoral ministry, liberation, development of people, work on behalf of justice, evangelisation of cultures and so on. It also recognises that within these forms there is a critical *modality – proclamation of the Gospel* is integral to all forms of evangelisation. Proclamation in Paul VI's teaching requires both *word and witness*. In his view witness that remains unexplained is inadequate as proclamation. *Evangelii Nuntiandi* emphasises the need for Christians to speak to the hope that is in them (1 Peter 3:15) as an integral part of mission. *Witness* (and therefore mission) *must be articulated if it is to be effective.*

Paul VI, in respecting the range of views expressed at the synod, employs two understandings of evangelisation in *Evangelii Nuntiandi*. Used in the "narrow" sense, evangelisation can be understood in terms of its principal modality, proclamation by word and witness. Paul VI, however, also opted for a "broader" understanding, which includes both this basic modality and the many forms through which the modality finds expression. He makes his own preference for this second understanding quite clear. This is a good example of the "both/and" approach adopted in many magisterial documents when popes do not wish to finally settle a disputed matter.[237]. *Evangelii Nuntiandi* stands as the "magna carta" of evangelisation.

---

[237] A Google search of diocesan websites under "evangelisation" reveals that both these constructions of mission still have currency.

Third Moment – "Proclaiming a Person, Jesus Christ"

Pope John Paul II's 1990 encyclical *Redemptoris Missio* offered a rich source of theological reflection on mission. In the decade following the death of Paul VI there was considerable debate about mission theology and the forms of mission not only in Catholic circles but also in Protestant circles as well. For instance, the dictum of Pope Paul VI that "if you want peace then work for justice"[238] was extended to embrace not only people but *creation itself*. Preserving the "integrity of creation" was first identified by missionaries, particularly those dealing with indigenous people whose livelihood was threatened by deforestation as a result of logging, as a form of mission. The concept of human liberation was extended so that advocacy on behalf of dispossessed peoples became a form of mission during the pontificate of John Paul II leading to the Church adopting a "preferential option for the poor"[239] as a central tenet. Peace emerged more specifically as a form of mission in the 1980s, particularly following the fall of the Berlin Wall and the collapse of the apartheid regime in South Africa. It grew in importance with the troubles in Ireland, Rwanda and Bosnia.[240]

Redemptoris Missio was promulgated in 1990 in the context of a new phase of globalisation, and as post-modernity gathered pace. One of its key aims was to remind Catholics of the need to persevere with the task of making the Gospel known and presenting Christ to those who have not yet had an opportunity to know him or his gospel. While the document strongly affirmed the continuing need for mission *ad gentes*, as we understand it from the Acts of the Apostles, it had a wider objective. It also sought to address emerging issues as initiatives in inter-religious dialogue grew in frequency following the example set by the Pope himself. Pope John Paul II was personally committed to inter-faith dialogue, as is demonstrated by his pastoral practice as well as his writing. The great gathering of the leaders of the world religions at Assisi on 27 October 1986, which he initiated, stands as practical testimony to this commitment. His understanding of dialogue and the space given to it in *Redemptoris Missio* entrenched it as a second *modality of mission*, complementing Pope Paul VI's identification of proclamation as the foundational modality.

Dialogue as understood by Pope John Paul II can take place at a number of levels.[241] The Pope's work on inter-religious dialogue was complemented

---

[238] Pope Paul VI Message for Day of Peace, 1 January 1972.
[239] See for example the material provided by the Office of Peace and Justice, Archdiocese of Minneapolis-St Pauls <http://www.osjspm.org/option_for_the_poor.aspx>.
[240] See Robert Schreiter "Globalization and Reconciliation" in Robert Schreiter (ed.) *Mission in the Third Millennium* (Maryknoll New York: Orbis, 2001), 139–143; and Robert Schreiter *The Ministry of Reconciliation: Spirituality and Strategies* (Maryknoll New York: Orbis, 1998).
[241] Cf. *Redemptoris Missio* #57.

and enhanced by the work of the Pontifical Council for Inter-religious Dialogue, which produced in 1991 the important document *Dialogue and Proclamation*. Work on this document had begun prior to the Pope's decision to produce an encyclical and its publication was delayed so that it could serve as a commentary on some parts of it. The document identifies inter-religious dialogue as a form of evangelisation. It provides an extended treatment of both dialogue and proclamation and of the connection between them, identifying four types of dialogue. *Dialogue of life* sees people living together as friends; *dialogue of action* enables people to come together around a common project, for example, justice, peace and reconciliation or, we might add, the education of young people; *dialogue of religious experience*, or what might be described as a dialogue of spiritualities, enables people to understand each other's human experience in being religious, and in some cases this enables them to pray together; and *dialogue of theological exchange* proceeds, both formally and informally, between those with theological expertise. *Dialogue and Proclamation* is an important reference for any student of mission.

As we have indicated, *Nostra Aetate* had opened the way for dialogue with other faith traditions. The multi-faith nature of modern societies has heightened interest in the teaching of *Nostra Aetate* and the document is likely to continue to have an impact over the longer term. Already dialogue with faiths other than Christian is widely recognised as contributing significantly to the mission agendas of the next generation.

Under the impact of the global movement of peoples, significant numbers of adherents of the major faith traditions are to be found across the world especially in cities. Many seek a place in faith-based schools including Catholic schools, which are challenged to respond in appropriate ways. In this dialogue of life and action, we can expect an enrichment of spiritual experience. The evidence is that this is already occurring in schools, colleges and theological institutions in the United Kingdom, the United States and Australia. This is a new frontier for the Church's mission and as educators we find ourselves immersed in its challenges. Moving backwards is simply not an option. The bishops who at the Second Vatican Council accepted that the identity of the Church should be understood in terms of its role as servant, herald and sign of the Kingdom of God, also set a trajectory for a new agenda in mission, although they could not have fully realised this at the time. *Redemptoris Missio* has assisted in the ongoing response of faith communities to the demands of this agenda.

Redemptoris Missio also calls for a "new evangelisation" (#3), that is, a renewed effort in regard to evangelisation, and specifically names three groups to whom the Gospel should be directed – those who have never heard the

Gospel, those in whom the light of faith has grown dim, and the community of the faithful (##31–32). All three of these groups are present in significant numbers in Catholics schools, which by this very fact, become important places as well as vehicles of evangelisation.

Charting the Church's Understanding of Evangelisation

The conception of mission as it has developed over the past four decades can be summed up schematically in the diagram below. Evangelisation has two primary modalities that are implemented through a number of forms. Proclamation involves both witness and word. Witness is provided in a number of forms, as is word. Witness, word and dialogue are integrally related in any form of evangelisation.

The forms of mission will vary with context – both in terms of place and time. For instance, Figure 9 contains certain forms of evangelisation that were not considered in 1975 when *Evangelii Nuntiandi* was written. Not all forms will apply equally in all contexts. New forms, or new variations, are likely to occur in the future because of the needs of people and the demands of their context.

		Modalities of Mission	
		Proclamation by Word and Witness	Dialogue
Forms of Mission	Pastoral Ministry of the Church		
	Human Liberation – Personal and Societal		
	Reconciliation – People and Cultures		
	Justice and Peace		
	Integrity of Creation		
	Inter-religious Dialogue		
	Inculturation		

Figure 9. Evangelisation as the Totality of the Church's Mission

Dialogue as understood in current Church teaching is not seen as a means to get people to change their religion, although it does not preclude that this may occur as a possible outcome. The purpose of dialogue is better understanding, deeper spirituality and more peaceful living, which is seen as progress towards the Kingdom. Dialogue seeks to understand the other *in the other's own frame of reference*, not within one's own frame of reference. Dialogue is seen as an essential aspect of being human, a reflection of the dialogue which is essential to the life of God in whose image we are made and whose life we share through baptism.

All the forms of mission represent ways of carrying on the mission of Jesus and of realising the Kingdom in history, but none of them is an end in itself. They are means to an end. People understand and contribute to mission in different ways. This is how the Spirit works. Mission is always linked to need and to aspiration. It is based on hope – hope for what is not yet but for what can become. This is central to Jesus' understanding of the Kingdom. In this sense mission always has a Kingdom orientation. Being Catholic in this sense is living a life oriented to the Kingdom.

Mission as Local within the Global

The grid in Figure 9 can be used to map mission for a particular faith community, be it a parish, a diocese or a school. It does so by identifying the forms and modalities of the Church's mission and posing the questions where do we fit in and how do we fit in? Every community needs to ask the question which forms of the Church's mission are appropriate for us? They then need to formulate an answer. The answers will reflect the local context and, as a consequence, no two communities will respond in the same manner. It is the collective witness of all communities that most fully effects God's mission. God's mission is carried out by people in Christian communities as well as by people outside these communities. Dialogue helps people see this and work together in a common cause.

When mission is looked at in this way, Catholic schools are rich in opportunity. If, for instance, we focus on the "integrity of creation" as a *form of mission*, the following questions will arise:

- How do we understand this as a mission imperative?
- How do we understand this as related to the coming of God's Kingdom?

In other words, how does "integrity of creation" fit into our school's mission? Switching to the *modalities of mission* we can ask with regard to this form:

- What do we seek to proclaim about this issue? to whom? and how?
- What sort of witness do we seek to provide? to whom? and how?

Going a step further we can ask:

- What types of dialogue do we engage in when pursuing this matter? and with what intention?

The answers to these questions will span the full gamut of what happens in a school. A similar exercise could be carried out on the other forms of mission, for instance, the place reconciliation has in how the school deals with student well-being.

All the forms of mission listed above represent ways in which people can engage in the mission of Jesus. Since identity is tied up with mission, they are all "ways of being Catholic". There are many possible linkage points between the individual and the Church community in contributing to the mission of the Church. As people make one linkage, other possibilities open up for them. This is often how the process of "befriending our religious tradition" unfolds in practice. As Paul VI has pointed out, as we engage in evangelisation we are ourselves evangelised![242]

As the fruits of the Second Vatican Council have unfolded over half a century, the official teaching of the Church under successive popes has facilitated the development of significant insights into the mission of the Church, taking it in directions beyond what could possibly have been imagined at the time. The theological building blocks generated have proved to be of core importance to the task of mission. From bishops' conferences, to dioceses, to small Christian communities, people of faith have been able to identify with the themes of this teaching and work with them because they strike an authentic chord with lived experience. In addition, theologians and those with technical expertise to do so, have also been able to work with these "building blocks" and, secure in the position reached, have been able to move ahead exploring territory beyond these "base camps".

We began this chapter by saying that as Catholics we are part of a living tradition and "with life comes challenge and change". Mission lies at the core of the Catholic worldview and provides an entry point in incorporating the principle of purpose into the life of a school community. The Church's recent teaching on mission contains a full measure of challenge for all those committed to the mission of Jesus and provides a road-map for change.

The official teaching of the Church is at its best when it functions in dynamic relationship to the lived experience of the faithful, with each contributing to the reflective process in a spirit of faith and engagement. The issue for this millennium will be whether this dynamic can be sustained, and whether those engaged on the frontier, such as Catholic educators, have the wisdom and energy to take heart from this authoritative support and do it justice "on the ground".

---

[242] In *Evangelii Nuntiandi* #41 Pope Paul VI quoted his own words to the Council on the Laity as follows: "Modern man (sic) listens more willingly to witnesses than to teachers, and if he does listen to teachers, it is because they are witnesses." These are some of the most-quoted words from *Evangelii Nuntiandi*.

CHAPTER ELEVEN

Gospel Communities Then and Now

The Catholic tradition is a living tradition not only because of the Church's ability to develop in response to new mission challenges and changing contexts, but because it includes a biblical tradition with a trajectory set by God's revelation and a development guided by God's Spirit. If educators are to "befriend" their tradition, then sooner or later they have to befriend this biblical tradition, seeing it as a living resource.

As we have worked with a range of Catholic school educators and leaders, we find that many approach the biblical tradition from a perspective of what might be termed "naïve literalism". Naïve literalism devalues both scripture and the ability to use it as a living resource. It also devalues leadership. To be effective as meaning-makers both educators and leaders need a different approach to the biblical tradition, one that enables them to approach it more confidently and see it for what it is, rather than in narrow, almost instrumental terms.

In this chapter we outline what we mean by "naïve literalism" and then go on to explore an alternative framework and, in the process, draw out the significance of this framework for both meaning-making and leadership today.

Going Beyond Naïve Literalism

Naive literalism is an approach to scripture that takes the text at face value and fails to question it. It is quite a different framework from that of biblical fundamentalism which also takes the text at face value, but which sees it as unquestionable because it is accepted as literally the word of God. Some examples of naive literalism we have encountered in working with leaders are:

- The Gospels are biographies of Jesus, and why there is need for four of them is often unclear.[243]
- The Old Testament is merely a prelude to "the main event", and is therefore of questionable relevance.
- The Acts of the Apostles is a history of the early Church.
- The writings of St Paul and the other New Testament writers are an addendum to the Gospels, written after them.

---

[243] It is interesting to note in this regard that no less a figure than St Augustine thought of the Gospel of Mark as just an abbreviation of the Gospel of Matthew.

- Jesus and the apostles including St Paul were not Jewish.

In the perspective of naïve literalism the *Book of Revelation* is simply incomprehensible.

When viewed from within the framework of naïve literalism scripture is of limited value as a resource. The framework precludes any sense that the New Testament writers were caught up in their time in similar pastoral and missional dynamics as are Christian leaders today – trying, as contexts changed, to make sense of their human experience and that of their community, in the light of their faith, and under the guidance of God's Spirit.

Naïve literalism reduces scripture to the status of a religious product, a source of religious rhetoric. The Gospel message, in particular, becomes reduced to the status of abstract values – "Gospel values" – divorced from the life and mission of the person who gives them meaning. In Catholic schools, naïve literalism translates into "mission statements" that are so universalised they no longer reflect the real mission demands or the hopes of a particular community. God's mission, like God's revelation, is carried out not in the abstract, but in real contexts. Naïve literalism divides the content of revelation from the process of revelation and in disengaging them, devalues the content substantially. It is uncritical in its approach to the truth of the Gospels and other scriptural writings and seems to reflect a lack of confidence in the living power of the text.

Naïve literalism is a far cry from the perspective of biblical scholars Senior and Stuhlmueller[244] who conclude their classic study *The Biblical Foundations of Mission* as follows:

> Equally important for this (dealing with non-Christian peoples) and other pastoral issues facing the Church is the Bible's courageous, inquisitive spirit. Nothing is ruled out: from the exodus to the conquest of the Romans, from the migration of Abraham to the travels of Paul, from the heavenly powers to the depth of Sheol, from God's Son to Balaam's donkey. Every historical event, every layer of the universe, and every human being that shaped the experience of Israel and the early church are part of the biblical story. All are absorbed, scrutinized, interpreted. The biblical writers were not afraid of ultimates, for the God of the Bible is a God who can never be threatened or impoverished by fearless reflection on human experience. The very spirit of the Bible encourages Christians not to cringe before questions posed by the reality of non-Christian religions. Facing such issues is, in fact, fidelity to the Christian mission. It is, after all, the God of the Bible who sent his people out to reveal and to discover his love in places beyond sectarian borders.

[244] Donald Senior and Carroll Stuhlmueller *The Biblical Foundations for Mission* (London: S.C.M. Press, 1983), 346–347.

If school leaders are to "befriend their tradition" and engage in theological reflection that is meaningful, then their understanding of scripture must go beyond naive literalism. There is a need to adopt an alternative framework, one that can hold together both the content and process of revelation in a way that can withstand critical scrutiny.[245] To move in this direction it is necessary to develop a greater understanding of God's revelation and the process by which the various books of the Bible were created, seeing the process itself as revelatory of God and God's purposes. It is to this task that we now turn.

Parameters of Revelation

In terms of the Christian faith, God's revelation was first made to a people (Israel) and then to the community who believed in Jesus and his message (the Church). The understanding of both groups is that they have been given something precious, the receiving of which carries with it obligations. These are understood within somewhat different frameworks in the Jewish and Christian traditions. Central to both traditions, however, is knowledge about God and God's purposes, not only with respect to humankind but also with respect to creation. The bishops at the Second Vatican Council addressed this matter as follows:

> ...the books of scripture firmly, faithfully and without error, teach what is truth which God, for *the sake of our salvation*, wished to confide to the Sacred Scriptures...seeing that God speaks through men in human fashion it follows that the interpreter...if he is to ascertain what God has wished to communicate to us should carefully search out the meaning *which the sacred writers really had in mind.*[246] (emphasis added)

The phrase "truth...for the sake of our salvation" is of critical importance in that it sets an important criterion for reading the text. The fact that the writers have their history wrong, or that their geography is dubious, or that their science is pre-modern is of little consequence, as the Biblical claim to truth does not depend on these areas. The Biblical claim to truth is firmly based on what previously we have called the principle of purpose. But this claim in not made in an uncritical manner.

The Council document goes on to point out that, in determining the intention of the writer, attention needs to be paid to the form of the writing, and to the circumstances of his time and culture, characteristic patterns of perception,

---

[245] Geoffrey Robinson, in *A Change of Mind and Heart: The Good News According to Mark* (Revesby: Parish Ministry Publications, 1994), suggests a four-step process Catholic educators might adopt: constant reading and familiarity with the words of scripture; a study of the insights of other people into the meaning of the words; a personal thinking about this meaning; and the prayer to God that spontaneously flows from this reading.

[246] *Dei Verbum* #11 (*Dogmatic Constitution on Divine Revelation*) in Austin Flannery (ed.) *Vatican Council II* (Northport New York: Costello Publishing Company, 1996), 105.

speech and narrative, as well as to the social conventions of the time. This becomes a second parameter in making sense of the text.

A third parameter is that an individual text needs to be seen *in relation to the whole*. The relationship between the particular and the universal in revelation is complex,[247] but the bottom line is that God is the ultimate source of its coherence. As the *Dogmatic Constitution on Divine Revelation* (*Dei Verbum*) puts it, drawing on St Augustine, "God, the inspirer and author of the books of both Testaments, in his wisdom has so brought it about that the New should be hidden in the Old and the Old should be made manifest in the New".[248]

Content and Process in Revelation

There are two distinct issues to consider in dealing with God's revelation. The first is *the content* of what we know and the second is *the process* by which we know it. Befriending scripture involves attending to both the content and the process of God's revelation. What is known cannot be separated from the process by which it is known without serious misunderstandings occurring. When God communicates, God does so in a concrete manner, with particular people in a particular cultural and historical context. God communicates in a way that is meaningful to them even when God's intention may be more general.

Our knowledge of God and God's purposes is knowledge of a person with its associated mystery. We accept what we know as true because of the trust we place in the person. In this sense our knowledge is relational. As Stephen Bevans points out, our human experience is that we get to know persons only if they allow us to know them, if they choose to reveal themselves to us. He goes on:

> The same dynamic takes place when God reveals Godself to women and men. At certain times in our lives, God's gracious presence becomes manifest in our lives as God communicates God's *subjectivity* through *objectivity*. Through the concrete events of our lives, or concrete persons, or particular words – very ordinary things – God becomes present and palpable to us in all God's incomprehensible, inexpressible, mysterious reality. The third century Syrian–born theologian Irenaeus (circa 130–200) expressed it well when he wrote about the Israelites that "God kept calling them to what is primary by means of what was secondary". This is the pattern of divine revelation: the finite reveals the infinite, *the objective reveals the subjective*, what is ordinary reveals what is Mystery.[249] (emphasis added)

---

[247] Cf. James Okoye's discussion of "canon consciousness" in *Israel and the Nations: A Mission Theology of the Old Testament* (Maryknoll NewYork: Orbis, 2006), xvi.
[248] *Dei Verbum* #16 in Flannery, 108.
[249] Stephen Bevans "The God of Jesus Christ" (Yarra Theological College course notes, 2009), 8

The subject of all personal revelation can be only partially grasped, and on terms decided by the person. This is important when it comes to considering scripture as a personal and communal resource in theological reflection as well as in the development of a spirituality.

In addition, God's communication is made to people living within the imaginal horizon imposed by their time and their culture. This communication is carried out within limitations imposed by thinking styles and communication styles, including language. There are limits imposed by the "objective" things that God uses to convey God's subjective intentions and these have to be taken into consideration in approaching the text.

While God's purpose is to communicate truth about what is necessary for salvation, our human condition is such that the process by which this happens becomes inherently problematic; God's message always comes wrapped in clothes that are culturally and historically-conditioned. Separating the message from the wrapping is not easy. To change metaphors, a people sees God's truth through the lenses of their culture and narrative, giving it a particular hue. When this truth is shared with people of another culture, with a different narrative, they view it through their particular lenses. Both may look at the same truth, but both understand it from within their own frame of reference, and appropriate it accordingly. Neither party ever gets to take off their glasses, so to speak, and view the "pure" truth. This is not only beyond human capability, but outside the process God is using, a process which respects human beings and the ways in which they are human.

It is, therefore, through the dialogue of cultures that greater insight is gained into the meaning of God's truth. However, God's truth ever remains *God's* truth, which will always have an elusive quality about it, because we can always understand it more deeply. Human understanding of this truth is ever partial. To assume that God's truth is fully understood within the confines of a particular culture is to deify that culture.

God's truth is understood more fully through dialogue. This is why dialogue is essential in evangelisation. The Catholic Church has always taught that God's truth is the possession of *the whole believing community* and, for this reason, the "the sense of the faithful" provides an important condition in the reception of any doctrine. A post-modern critique of this teaching is that, throughout much of Christian history, "the faithful" has generally been understood to be the "European faithful". Such an interpretation of "the faithful" is coming increasingly under pressure from outside Europe.[250]

As Catholics we face a new and challenging situation, a "frontier" in human history, which is not entirely different from that faced by the writers of the sub-apostolic age,[251] whose experience in dealing with God's truth bears similarities to our own. They were caught up in the same traditioning process as we are, with the same guiding Spirit, and sharing the same hope. It is this line of thought we wish to explore in the balance of this chapter.

Backgrounding the New Testament Texts

Each of the New Testament texts was prepared to meet the needs of a particular Christian community that had come into being as a result of missionary work which had occurred in the decades following Jesus' death and resurrection.[252] The Gospel writers, following the example set by the writer of the Gospel of Mark, communicate using the form of *narrative theology*. While the narratives cover roughly the same ground, the theologies are quite different in their emphases, reflecting the situation of different contexts and cultures. These written narratives were produced between approximately forty and seventy years after Jesus' death and resurrection, by which time communities of the new faith were established in a variety of socio-cultural milieus within the Roman empire.

The contexts in which the Gospels were written were very different from that in which Jesus lived. In Judea the political tensions, very much alive in Jesus' time and which he sought to sidestep during his ministry, resurfaced in AD 67. A general uprising occurred that saw the revolutionaries take control of Jerusalem. This uprising was crushed by the Romans under Titus three years later. In reprisal, the city and the temple were totally destroyed as was the social fabric of Judea when the bulk of the city's inhabitants were dispersed. The Jewish people lost not only the key symbols of their identity, Jerusalem and the temple, but also their cultic leadership as well. Jamnia became the new centre of the Jewish faith and a revised form of the Jewish religion developed under the leadership of the Pharisees. It was in this new dispensation that the break between Christians and Jews became formalised.[253] The Christian community in Jerusalem, which had retained its Jewish identity, was caught up in these events, and soon faded from the scene. It was against this background

---

[250] See, for instance, Peter Phan in *In Our Own Tongues: Perspectives from Asia on Mission and Inculturation* (Maryknoll New York: Orbis, 2003); or Thomas Malipurathu and L Stanislaus (eds) *The Church in Mission: Universal Mandate and Local Concerns* (Gujarat: Gujarat Sahitya Prakask, 2002).

[251] The sub-apostolic age is the time from about AD 70–110. It is during this period that the texts of the Gospels were written.

[252] See Raymond Brown *The Churches the Apostles Left Behind* (Ramsey New York: Paulist Press, 1984) in which he traces the development of the text in relation to seven early Christian communities.

[253] The exclusion of the followers of Jesus from synagogues was quite a recent event at the time the Gospels were written and explains the negative presentation of the Pharisees and "the Jews", meaning the Jewish leaders, found in the Gospels.

that the Gospel writers, in particular, sought to make sense of God's action in the world.

In telling the story of Jesus, the Gospel writers tried to maintain a balance between two elements – one was to proclaim who Jesus is, seen in the light of their post-resurrection faith, and the other was to proclaim what Jesus said and did during his ministry. The choices the writers made in relation to this balance give each of the Gospels its unique orientation. For the writer of Mark, "who Jesus is" is something of a secret to be revealed through the record of what he says and does. For the writer of John, "who Jesus is" is the central feature of the narrative. Each writer made his own choice in the light of the situation of the communities for whom he wrote. The writers were not writing for a universal audience; they wrote to anchor their own communities in the narrative of Jesus.

Doing Narrative Mission Theology – The Gospel Process

The New Testament writers were faced with a situation with which many Christian parents and educators today can deeply sympathise. By the sub-apostolic age two problems had arisen. People coming new into the Christian community could no longer interact with members who had known Jesus directly. Also, a younger generation was growing up within the Jewish Christian community who had not been born when Jesus was alive, and who needed to be introduced to Jesus and his message. A new model of passing on the "good news" had to be developed, *one open to the young*. As well, the story of Jesus had to be formulated in a way that made sense to people who were not Jewish by culture. In many ways school leaders face a similar situation today. With the Gospels' authors they often ask how can we pass on what we have come to know and love in a new and challenging context? In effect they are asking *how they can see their community's narrative as a continuation of the Gospel narrative.*

The leaders of the New Testament communities sensed a pressing responsibility. Some concluded that the story of Jesus, till then carried by means of communal and individual memory, and with the aid of some short collections of written material, needed to be retold systematically and in writing. Others focused on practical issues facing the early communities or problems of interpreting Jesus' message or applying it in new situations. As the years extended out well beyond Jesus' lifetime, the Spirit stirred *a process of theological storytelling.*

Mission was put on a firm theological footing through this endeavour, because all New Testament writing was formulated in the context of mission. In their classic work *The Biblical Foundations of Mission*, Senior and Stuhlmueller

make this point forcefully:
> The communities from which and for which the Gospel originated were communities freshly formed by the missionary efforts of the church. There is every reason to believe that they were "mixed", that is, made up of both Jewish Christians and a swelling majority of Gentile Christians. Such a mix was bound to cause problems of adjustment. It seems likely that the Gospels were meant to give these same communities fresh perspective in difficult times as they struggled with basic questions about Christian responsibility to the world.
>
> ...the Gospels are mission literature in the fullest sense of the term. They are not propaganda, not equipment designed for proclamation to nonbelievers. There are mission documents for the church itself, meant to justify, renew, and motivate the church's claim on the heritage of Jesus' own boundary-breaking ministry.[254]

There were many accounts of Jesus' life extant by the end of the first century and some continued to be written into the second century. However, the early Church communities came ultimately to accept only those written under the names of Mark, Matthew, Luke and John as being absolutely trustworthy, albeit unique, accounts of Jesus' life and message. In their judgment, each expressed authentically, the memory of Jesus carried within the Church community. These four accounts were included in the canon of scripture. In this sense it can be said that *it is the Church community that has given us the gift of the Gospels*. The texts were authenticated by the authority that held these loosely federated communities together as a believing Church. This is ultimately the authority of God's Spirit.

It is important for today's educators to realise that Christian communities continue to be called to engage in the work of theology, and that this is a serious obligation of mission. The responsibility exists for each community to tell its own story and write its own "good news", from the perspective of its faith. This is an important way of expressing its identity, stating its purpose, and saying what its life is about. It is a way of discerning and celebrating the action of the Spirit in the life of the community and the special witness *this community* presents to the world in carrying on the mission of Jesus as part of the wider Church community, and of communicating this to succeeding generations of teachers, parents and students. It is a way of affirming the "local within the global" as well as making "the global present within the local". Unfortunately, it is too often the case that the narrative of "local churches", and the "local communities" within them such as schools, has been lost, or remains

---

[254] Donald Senior and Carroll Stuhlmueller *The Biblical Foundations for Mission* (London: S.C.M. Press, 1983), 211.

untold and so rarely celebrated. *This is to ignore the "objective" through which God communicates.* It happens to the detriment both of the community and of God's mission.

The idea that all engagement in practical ministry, such as education or leadership, brings with it a responsibility to continue the same kind of endeavour that resulted in the Gospels, might seem not only novel, but even fanciful to some. Yet few would doubt the impact this strategy has had in forming Christian identity down through the ages. The reality is that, unless the memory of Jesus is reinterpreted for, and within each faithful community, both informally and at important times formally, it remains a distant memory. If, on the other hand, it is appropriately reinterpreted, then Christianity becomes a living tradition in which Jesus' life and teaching take root afresh in every age and circumstance. Without this theological work, the chances of the Gospel capturing the imagination of parents, students and teachers in a life-transforming way is even more remote than would have been the case had the authors of the original Gospels shirked their leadership task.

The Gospels came out of very different communities, in different time frames and geographical and cultural settings. Each is marked by its own particular emphases. Ours is a living tradition and the Gospels speak as living voices.[255] The Gospels are about content and process. As content they speak to perennial human issues and questions and therefore provide the richest of resources for our theologising. In engaging in our own grassroots theological work, we engage in *the Gospel process*, the work of striving to interpret the needs and circumstances of our own individual communities in the light of Jesus' life and teaching. Our insight into the Christian tradition as a living tradition grows as the Gospel content and process come together in our lives and in the life of our communities.

It is important that Catholic educators and leaders are convinced of the need to continue this vital understanding in the process of developing and sustaining Gospel communities. For this to occur, leaders need to acquire both the understandings and skills necessary to make it happen. Furthermore, this is a serious obligation of mission. In terms of the theological formation of school leaders, therefore, much more is at stake than simply becoming familiar with theological interpretations produced by quality scholars, valuable as this is.

The Gospels as Narratives

If Catholic educators are to be successful in locating the narrative of their communities within the Gospel tradition, they need to be very familiar with the nature and content of the canonical Gospels themselves. The Gospels

---

[255] Cf. Francis Moloney *The Living Voice of the Gospels* (Mulgrave: John Garratt, 2006).

of Mark, Matthew, Luke and John were written in narrative form for good reasons. Narrative is a dynamic form of writing, which invites the reader to enter into the story and to make a response. Among the New Testament writers, the authors of the Gospels are unique in using this form. For example, Paul, who ministered in the early years not long after Jesus' death, never resorted to writing a narrative.

The decision on the part of the Gospel writers to adopt the narrative mode in telling the story of Jesus for their communities was an inspired one. Firstly, it was inspired in the broad meaning of the term, in that the narrative mode was particularly effective in terms of the purpose for which it was chosen. Secondly, the decision was taken under the inspiration of the Spirit who was guiding the life and mission of the communities. Naïve literalism occurs when, in reading the text, people enter into the narrative accepting the accounts solely as *narrative*, rather than as *narrative theology*, that is, as *theology couched in narrative form*.

The narrative mode was particularly suited to the reshaping and reinterpreting of the Christian message for new audiences in new times and places. There are few people who do not love a story, especially when it speaks so tellingly to what they are experiencing. Stories are an excellent form of cross-generational and cross-cultural communication. They carry meaning at different levels, the factual and the symbolic, for instance, which gives them emotional depth. They appeal to the whole person.

The four different narratives that have been accepted in the Christian tradition as authentic retellings of the story of Jesus leave us with the task of interpreting the meaning that lies beyond their narrative form. In this task we are well placed through the excellent work that has been done by scripture scholars across the last half century. We now have access to insights not previously available. This is an area where our tradition is very much alive at the present time.

Naïve literalism, which tends to see all the texts as representing eternal verities that can be understood independent of the context in which they were written and the intention of the writer in writing them, stands outside this developing aspect of the Christian tradition. Often this is through ignorance of the Gospel process.

Gospel Narratives as Pastoral and Missional

The Gospels were written for particular communities. In the first instance their purpose was pastoral, but all were written from the perspective of carrying forward the mission of Jesus under the guidance of God's Spirit. Only secondarily did they represent a story to be taken *to others*. Another way of saying this is that there was a strong pastoral element in the decision to write the Gospels which gives each its focus. If the early communities could be secure in their faith, in their own understanding of the message of Jesus and the sharpness of its relevance to them, then they would be in a position to continue with the kind of mission endeavours which had brought the Gospel to them. In this context Senior and Stuhlmueller comment that

> The evangelists drew their material from the traditions of their communities, traditions forged in the dynamic missionary era of the Church. At the same time they wanted to respond to the pastoral needs of their communities. Many of the needs were the result of the mission of the church. In this process the evangelists shaped a re-interpretation of the Christian message. The gospel was preached again, in a new time, a new place, and, we might add, in a new way, by means of narrative.[256]

The Gospels of Mark and Matthew illustrate this point. It is now fairly widely accepted that the Gospel of Mark was produced for the benefit of the Christian community in Rome, a community that had recently been savaged by an atrocious persecution under the emperor Nero. This situation had produced mixed reactions within the community. For some the response had been heroic testimony to faith in Jesus and his Gospel; for others the response had been betrayal and cowardice. This was the pastoral situation that Mark sought to address. Jesus' disciples, as depicted in the Gospel, represent not only Jesus' disciples at the time of his ministry, but also this shattered community for whom the Gospel was written. Jesus' disciples appear in a great many of the Gospel's scenes, and are as similarly prone to failure as Mark's community, yet called again and again to renew their discipleship by Jesus, who had himself triumphed over terrible suffering and death. Mark's account is movingly pastoral not least because in Mark's Gospel failure does not have the last word.

Matthew's pastoral concern was different, but equally a driving force in shaping his Gospel. The issue for the author of Matthew was the appropriate development and emerging shape of the community itself.[257] His was a complex pastoral situation embracing both Jews and gentiles. Scholars are of the opinion that Matthew's community, originally Jewish, had established itself in Syria as a result of the upheaval of the Jewish revolt and its subsequent crushing by the Romans. They were a community in exile. As with the community addressed in the Gospel of Mark, the writer of Matthew is dealing with disorientation; he is also dealing with significant numbers of gentiles wanting to be involved

---

[256] Senior and Stuhlmueller, 112.

[257] Helpful discussions on the situation of the Matthean community are found in David Bosch *Transforming Mission* (Maryknoll New York: 1991), Chapter Two; and Senior and Stuhlmueller, Chapter Ten.

in the spiritual project in which the community was engaged. These were not particularly interested, and certainly not to the same degree as its Jewish members, with the significance of Jesus as the fulfilment of Israel's hopes, Jesus as a Jewish Messiah, the new Moses. They were, however, attracted by his religious teaching, which they saw as very good news, and which answered so many of their human yearnings and aspirations.

On the other hand, the original members had their own pressing pastoral needs. They needed to be able to see that, in Jesus, the old unresolved tension involving Israel and the nations, had finally been resolved. Jesus was the new Moses, the great teacher, and the fulfilment of Israel's hopes. In the light of his resurrection, however, the logic of Jesus' life and ministry became clearer. They would become convinced that the good news that it encapsulated must be taken to the ends of the earth.

As in the life of the Church today, in the original Gospel communities meeting pastoral needs and carrying forward the mission of Jesus *were two sides of the one coin,* not two different coins. The Gospels provided them with a much needed resource, shoring up their meaning systems in times of difficulty, persecution, unforeseen demands, and the ongoing challenge to understand and be at peace with their faith in new circumstances.

Another vital ingredient in the theologising processes of the New Testament communities, and one with which we can readily identify from our own experience, was the engagement of the communities with their broader societies and the impact these societies and cultures had on the communities, raising questions for their life and mission.

The community out of which Matthew's Gospel came provides an example. We have seen that this community seems to have been significantly affected by the Jewish revolt of AD 66–70 and its consequences. The shape of the community was certainly affected by the strict interpretation of Judaism that its re-founders adopted as they re-shaped their tradition after the destruction of the temple. For Matthew's community, dilemmas arose when gentiles sought membership into a predominantly Jewish community. The issues surfaced around such questions as what shape should a Jewish/gentile community take, given that Jews were forbidden to eat with gentiles; what should be expected of gentile members; and did they need to become Jews? The issue of who is in and who is out and what should be expected in terms of the faith community continues to confront the Church today at many levels. We experience this in the Catholic school as a clientele, wide-ranging in its faith background, seeks to share in the school's educational project.

The Lens of the Resurrection

A vital factor in understanding the Gospels is the lens of the resurrection. All four Gospels were written in the light of faith in Jesus having been raised from the dead, and they seek to throw light on the significance of this extraordinary event. For the Gospel writers the resurrection brought the significance of Jesus' ministry into new focus, and helped the communities understand the importance of continuing his mission. The risen Jesus provides a point of departure for each of the Gospel writers when it comes to dealing with the issue of mission. We have already made the point that the Gospels need to be approached with an awareness of the perspective the authors brought to their task. These are accounts of the risen Jesus, alive and at work still within the particular community through the agency of the Spirit. Even the material dealing with Jesus' earthly ministry is, in a sense, presented as if it were occurring in the present. The point the writers seek to convey is that Jesus continues to do what he had done in his earthly ministry, but now through his Spirit guiding the community in the here and now. His ministry is now their ministry, but with the "nations" as its canvas.

This is an insight in danger of being lost for many Catholic educators due to a shortcoming in their professional development which often results in failure to make the connection between *the values* Jesus taught (his "ethic") and *the person* whose witness to these values gives them their significance. Overcoming this division between ethic and person is a major challenge for the leadership of Catholic school systems. The core of this issue seems to lie in developing a spirituality appropriate to the present context of Catholic education, one capable of *integrating* both its secular and religious purposes. Too often Catholic educators are content to acknowledge and fiercely defend their Christian values, such as the dignity of the human person or the importance of justice, peace and reconciliation, but are less clear or less able to acknowledge *the living person* who continues to embody these values. In terms of our earlier discussion, it might be said that the "objectivity" of such endeavours can easily become a barrier to the revealing "subjectivity of God" central to the purpose of all mission.

As indicated earlier, all the mission theologies of the Gospels focus on the person of Jesus, and each demonstrates in its own way that, foundationally, *the person is the message*. Jesus' message is utterly transparent because of the deeds, choices, and modes of living of the person delivering the message. Another way of saying this is that in the Gospels, Christology, theology and missiology are inextricably connected.[258] This means that each of the Gospels

---

[258] Senior and Stuhlmueller, 283.

presents Jesus in a way that is true to the historical Jesus, but also underpins *the mission theology that the author is developing for his community.*

Let us consider Mark's portrait of Jesus. The writer of Mark, like each of the evangelists, presents Jesus as a prototype of mission.[259] His emphasis is on Jesus as the proclaimer or herald of the good news that God's promises to Israel are about to be fulfilled. Mark's Gospel focuses on the essentials. The writer places Jesus centre stage and as the Gospel develops, it becomes clear that he is the good news and that the whole of his life, death and resurrection authenticates this proclamation.

We need to be clear about the distinction between gospel as an announcement of good news, gospel with a small "g", and Gospel as the theological retelling of Jesus' life, teaching, death and resurrection, Gospel as we now have it in the four Gospels.

> It is the history of Jesus, from his baptism by John to his death and resurrection, that forms the beginning and the foundation for the Gospel… Manifestly, Mark is asserting here that the proclamation of Jesus Christ in primitive Christianity…comes down historically as well as actually, from Jesus of Nazareth himself, who came to Galilee as a messenger of the gospel of God (1:14) and called for faith in the gospel (1:15). From Jesus' gospel, Mark is telling us, the Gospel of Jesus Christ emerges: the message of his life, death and resurrection.[260]

Missionary Commission in the Gospels

The living quality of our tradition comes from the challenge to make the good news known to people in every age, of every age, and to every culture. Since narratives unfold and cultures constantly evolve, this is a challenge with a beginning and no end in history. All four Gospels contain a mission commission, and in each case it is associated with the resurrection of Jesus. It is the impact of the resurrection and their understanding that God's Spirit was with them, that propels them to "the ends of the earth".

Catholics, when asked about mission in the Gospels, usually identify what has become known as the "great mission command" in Matthew 28. Most would struggle to identify similar accounts in any of the other Gospels. This is understandable, given that most Catholics do not have a close and exact acquaintance with the texts. Also it is Matthew's account that is generally the subject of homilies in church, as it is this text that underpinned the modern missionary movement. This has had some unfortunate consequences. Not the least of these is a perception of mission that lacks the richness and complexity necessary to deal with the mission situations with which we are confronted in

---
[259] Legrand, 41.
[260] R. Pesch quoted in Legrand, 41.

our globalised, secularised and pluralised societies.

The fact is that missionary mandates are found *in all four Gospels*. In each case the accounts of *the resurrection and of the missioning of the disciples go together*. Mission is, as Legrand puts it,[261] unintelligible without the resurrection. While there are examples within the Gospels of earlier local commissionings of disciples (for example Mark 10), none has the solemnity or significance of the post-resurrection accounts. Mission, understood as engagement with the world, is presented in the Gospels as a consequence of Jesus' resurrection. Legrand has furnished us with a thorough discussion of the missionary mandates given within the context of the resurrection.[262] He points out that there is a good deal of convergence among the accounts despite the variations in those to whom the message is addressed and the locations in which the message is given.

Despite widely varying circumstances, the early communities were very clear about the significance of both the resurrection and mission, and the connection between the two. The mission commissionings always occur in a post-resurrection setting, albeit varied. They always reflect the mission theologies that have been developed within the individual Gospels themselves. This enables the reader to see that the mission, as carried out by Jesus and depicted in the main body of the Gospel, is in fact that which Jesus is depicted as handing on to his disciples. The key references here are to be found in Matthew 28:19–20, Mark 16:15, Luke 24:47–49 and John 20:21–23.

Matthew depicts Jesus as the new Moses with all the authority such status would carry. Appropriately, then, the commissioning in Matthew occurs on a mountain. The disciples are commanded to form disciples, and to teach. Both Luke and John, being particularly concerned about the developing shape of the Church within the Roman empire, emphasise in their accounts the role of the Spirit in both shaping the Church and in mission strategy. In Mark's Gospel the commissioning takes place when Jesus joins the disciples who are having a meal. Jesus first of all chides the disciples for not believing those who had seen him after the resurrection, and then commands them to go to the whole world, to every creature, and to baptise. He promises that the power of God will go with them and that they will be able to do wonderful things.

In regard to this point, some further remarks need to be made about the Gospel of Mark. Mark's Gospel has two endings, the original and, as indicated by the change in language usage, a later addition that is the work of an editor. Both need to be considered in terms of the mission theology of the Gospel, as each has theological significance in terms of mission. The original ending

[261] Legrand, 70.
[262] Ibid., 68–84.

features the empty tomb and the exchange between the young man (angel) and the women. This exchange, like the rest of the Gospel, is a very direct proclamation. "He has been raised. He is not here." (Mark 16:6) It is the longer ending however, the work of later editor(s), that best fits the pattern described above. It continues Mark's depiction of frightened disciples failing when asked to do difficult things. The women, for example, go away and do not carry the good news to the other disciples. Yet as the early communities knew from the evidence of their own experience, God's word has power. It continued to be proclaimed and to form disciples despite human inadequacy.

Jesus' Teaching on the Kingdom – Gospel Content

In discussing the living nature of our tradition, the focus has been on what we call the Gospel process. The living nature of the tradition is also evident *in the content of the Gospel message itself*. Across the past half-century biblical scholars have mounted three major efforts to uncover what can be said about the "historical Jesus". The complexity of this undertaking is reflected in the work of John Meier particularly in his multi-volume study *A Marginal Jew*.[263] What seems clear from this endeavour is that everything Jesus said and did, his preaching and teaching, his choice of relationships and the way he handled those relationships, speaks to us of how he understood his mission. When Jesus put this understanding into words he used metaphors, symbols and parables.

The metaphor of the Kingdom of God is the centrepiece of his teaching. As Senior and Stuhlmueller point out, the symbol of the Kingdom was not new to the religious consciousness of Israel. It had a fluid character, capable of many interpretations.[264] Jesus, keenly aware of the political climate in which his mission was carried out, provided his own interpretation to the symbol of the Kingdom, without ever defining it precisely. He did this through parables and various analogies. We are probably not surprised by this. Any good teacher knows how effective analogies can be in helping people to access new and/or complex ideas. The politics of the situation aside, in Jesus' case there was an added reason for using metaphor and analogy. The language that he spoke, Aramaic, did not easily handle abstract concepts, except through analogies and symbols. Therefore, Jesus built up his hearers' understandings by a range of metaphors woven into parables, stories which added a depth of meaning to his hearers' understanding of "the Kingdom of God".

John Fuellenbach has devoted a large portion of his academic career as a theologian to the study of the Kingdom of God, exploring both its Old

---

[263] Cf. John Meier *A Marginal Jew* (New York: Doubleday). In the first volume of four published to date (1991, 1994, 2001, 2009) Meier focuses on criteria for judging the historicity of the various sayings and deeds of Jesus as recorded in the Gospels.

[264] Senior and Stuhlmueller, 144.

Testament roots and its New Testament expressions. Drawing on the work of Cabello, he summarises Jesus' approach as follows:

> Although Jesus' use of the phrase *Kingdom of God* as the central image of his proclamation and mission was unique, it was based on the religious experience of his people. The God of the Old Testament is a God who cares, loves and forgives – a compassionate God. Every parable that Jesus offered is a vivid witness to this God. His audience could at least sense and in some way participate in the "new experience" Jesus offered, because the parables he employed constantly referred to Israel's experience with Yahweh in the past. For us, it is important not to forget that the Old Testament God-experience expressed in the symbol of the Kingdom of God remains present in the New Testament.[265]

People heard the phrase "Kingdom of God" according to their own mindset and interests. It was not surprising, given the political overlordship of the Romans, following hard on that of the Greeks, that for many hearers the phrase had national-political overtones.

In his teaching about the Kingdom of God, Jesus was endeavouring to reshape the expectations of his people, starting from their understanding of God. It is therefore important to identify the main contours of these expectations. Israel was very familiar with the notion of God as king of creation and celebrated God's kingship in its liturgy, for example Psalms 74 and 93–97. Israel also recognised God's sovereignty when recalling Yahweh's liberating interventions on Israel's behalf (e.g. Deuteronomy 26:5–9; Exodus 15:1–8). When Israel became disillusioned with its own kings and priesthood, particularly after the Babylonian exile, Israel's theologians began to express more clearly a future hope of further intervention by Yahweh in the form of a Messiah.

For some, Yahweh's intervention on behalf of Israel could be hastened by human effort, the scrupulous adherence to the law. Others, influenced by the prophetic stream of religious consciousness within Israel, saw Yahweh as reigning over all the nations with Israel's construction of social realities, based on the terms of God's covenant with them, offering a clear alternative to the social understandings of the time. We need to be aware that, in the case of the prophets, there was no understanding of a future life, and this gave an added sharpness to their prophetic utterances on behalf of the poor and marginalised. It was only in the latter part of Jewish history that a sense of afterlife developed, and this was not universally held even at the time of Jesus, which is why the fact that Jesus died ruled out the possibility of his being the Messiah for many devout Jews. A dead Messiah would have been viewed by

---

[265] John Fuellenbach *The Kingdom of God* (Maryknoll New York: Orbis, 1995), 77–78. Unless otherwise stated, much of the following discussion is indebted to the work of Fuellenbach.

many as a contradiction in terms.

In the light of Israel's long experience of political oppression, and the views held in regard to the afterlife, we can see why Fuellenbach can claim that

> No Jew could ever envisage a purely spiritual kingdom without expecting as well a complementary historical and political realization on behalf of Israel. Jesus went beyond these physical and material aspects of God's kingdom, but he definitely did not abandon them.[266]

In what is known as the inter-testamental period (roughly the two hundred years prior to Jesus' birth), other related ideas took root in Israel and shaped the understandings that would act as the filter through which Jesus' teaching on the Kingdom passed to his listeners. One stream of belief was that Yahweh's intervention would involve a new reality beyond present experience; another that Israel would be delivered from foreign rule and, in the process, all the nations would be called into Yahweh's liberation. Depending on the school of thought to which one subscribed, the Messiah was envisaged either as a national-political figure who would lead the people of Israel once Israel's oppressors had been vanquished, or as a more transcendental figure calling both living and dead to account in the inauguration of God's Kingdom. As we shall see, Jesus rejected these views, seeing the Kingdom as the gift of a compassionate and loving God with one dimension of its reality being within history and another beyond history.

The task of steering creation in the direction of this Kingdom Jesus entrusted to his disciples as their mission. The Kingdom therefore remains both a gift and a responsibility.[267] It is both eschatological (oriented beyond history) and apocalyptic (breaking into history), political and religious, offering salvation to individuals and also the possibility of transformation for societies and cultures. It is impossible to talk of the Kingdom as presented by Jesus in "either/or" language; it is a supreme example of "both/and".

The Kingdom in History and Beyond History

The synoptic writers have the Kingdom as a central motif in their narratives – the "good news" is Jesus' message about the Kingdom of God. By the time the Gospel of John came to be written, almost half a century of Christian living had taken place. The realisation had grown that Jesus was the Good News incarnate, the embodiment of the Kingdom. John follows the example of Paul in placing the main focus of his teaching on the person of Jesus rather than his Kingdom message. For John, Jesus was the embodiment of the Kingdom message.

---

[266] Ibid., 33.
[267] Thomas Groome *Christian Religious Education* (Melbourne: Dove Communications, 1980), 45.

Paul, who wrote some thirty or so years earlier, had a similar focus to the writer of John. He makes the link between the Kingdom and the Old Testament understanding of "righteousness" or "justice". Paul is credited with the only "definition" of the Kingdom in the New Testament – "for the kingdom of God is not a matter of food and drink, but of righteousness, peace and joy in the Holy Spirit" (Rom 14:17).[268] This interpretation is consistent with Jesus' usage. For both, righteousness has to do with *living in right relationship*. The Kingdom is characterised in his teaching by living in right relationship, with God, with each other, within society and with all of creation.

Jesus' way of imaging God was unique and provided the foundation for his teaching about right relationships. His teaching about who is to be construed as "the neighbour" whom we must love was also different from that prevailing at the time. As his parables illustrate, Jesus was clearly at home in the natural environment. He acknowledged the rights of civil authorities and his parables make it clear that he is very much at home in nature. Reconciliation and forgiveness are central to the presence of God's Kingdom. At the same time the quality of these "horizontal" relationships needs to be continually reviewed and renewed in the light of our "vertical" relationship with God. Jesus' commitment to prayer is witness to this.

The new order preached by Jesus has a binding quality on his followers which includes accountability. To believe in Jesus is to participate in the cosmic battle with evil and we are gifted by God to do this. This engagement will not occur without suffering as the early Christian communities were soon to experience, and which has been the pattern of Christian life ever since. In Jesus' ministry words and actions reinforce each other. Jesus epitomises the Kingdom in that he proclaimed good news and was good news. He was both a teacher and a healer of bodies, psyches and spirits. He embodied what "righteousness" means.

The Kingdom of God in its fullness exists beyond time, but it is also present in time. The words of the Our Father remind us of this: "Thy kingdom come, thy will be done on earth as it is in heaven." Furthermore, proclaiming and working for the Kingdom of God in history will produce a variety of effects and induce a variety of responses – many of which will be surprising. Paul, who wrote before the Gospels were composed, takes things even further. For Paul the whole of creation is heading for the Kingdom. This is the goal of history. God's mission is to assist all of God's creation to reach this goal.

---

[268] Scholars emphasise that the phrase "in the Holy Spirit" applies to each element in the definition. See for example Fuellenbach, 172. Fuellenbach is drawing on the work of Leon Morris *The Epistle to the Romans* (Grand Rapids Michigan: Eerdmans Publishing Company, 1988), 488–489.

The Gospel writers make it clear that in Jesus' teaching the Kingdom of God is open to all, but can be received only by the poor in spirit, those who know they are dependent on God and whose relationship with God and others is such that they are open to the empowering influence of God's Spirit. Affluence is seen as an obstacle to this openness as it makes people self-sufficient, blinds then to the needs of others, and cramps their imagination in thinking about real alternatives to the status quo. Irrespective of social or economic background, it is those who recognise Jesus in the poor, the oppressed and the disadvantaged who receive the gift of the Kingdom. Throughout history, it has often been the "poor" and "sinners" who have played an effective role in bringing about the Kingdom of God. This is because they know at first hand the consequence of its absence, and therefore are sensitively attuned to the need for the help of God's empowering Spirit if things are going to change. The rich and the powerful often stand in the way of the Kingdom being realised. For instance, the underlying belief of modernity was that it could formulate its own version of the Kingdom, constructed by science, that would benefit all humankind. This belief was embedded in all the great ideologies of the twentieth century. It empowered some at the expense of many, and its consequences now threaten the whole of creation, not with nuclear conflagration as was a clear threat until recently, but by slowly strangling the planet through the pollution brought about by its excesses.

The Church and the Kingdom

Jesus' message of the Kingdom has disappeared in the course of history whenever Church leaders have equated the Kingdom of God with the Church. As we saw in Chapter Ten, since the Second Vatican Council this equation has been decisively abandoned. The Church is journeying towards the Kingdom, so too is creation. The mission of the Church is, therefore, not only to provide a practical demonstration of the Kingdom "on the ground" as it were, but also to be at the service of all of God's creation. This means recognising the contribution of others beyond the Church, supporting them and, where appropriate, joining them to effect a renewed creation across the entire globe. Working in partnership can be a humble ministry at times. Being effective on behalf of the Kingdom requires that profound conversion process demonstrated officially in recent times in the directions taken by Church leaders at the Second Vatican Council, and embraced in subsequent years by a myriad of local communities across the globe.

The credibility of the Church depends on the cumulative witness provided by the local communities that comprise the Church and their ongoing dialogue with the world about them. This witness provides the foundation for proclaiming

Jesus and his Kingdom message and for engaging others in common projects that point towards the Kingdom. Such witness, and the engagement with others that it entails, provides a basis for dialogue that challenges people beyond the Church to see the Kingdom as the fulfilment of their hopes. As we saw in Chapter Ten this dialogue lies not principally in words, but in the human experience of sharing life together across boundaries of culture and belief that can so easily divide. Central to such an endeavour is working together on common projects that address recognised needs and that build the common good. The unity of the Kingdom beyond history is built on the diverse expressions of the Kingdom within history.

For young people and their parents the Catholic school community is a laboratory of the Kingdom. In the language of Chapter Nine it forms part of the plausibility structure, which gives faith its credibility. If the leadership in Catholic schools cannot provide the circumstances in which the Christian belief in the Kingdom comes alive and provides the type of witness that mission demands, then they have failed. For mission to happen they have to be able to lead their communities in the dialogue of life and action that make it possible for the Kingdom to come alive. They also need to be able to *articulate* what is happening and why it is happening. The Christian narrative as it is presented in the Gospels is one resource, *but so also is the good news of the local community.*

The thrust of Part D has been to explore what "befriending the tradition" can mean as an element in meaning-making for those living and working on the "frontier". The major point made in Chapters Ten and Eleven is that, as Catholic educators and leaders, we are heirs to *a living tradition*. Because it is a living tradition, the Catholic tradition has the potential to enable a community, such as a school, to preserve its sense of mission and therefore its identity as an authentic faith community, even in the most demanding of circumstances.

CONCLUSION

CHAPTER TWELVE

Catholic Educators as Explorers and Meaning-makers

Making Sense of the Frontier Experience

We began this book by observing that many Catholic educators today experience a gap between community expectations of the mission of the school and what they find they can achieve in practice. A number of the assumptions on which the Catholic school has traditionally operated appear to have lost much of their salience. These relate principally to the nature of the contemporary Catholic community and how people construct their Catholic identity. These create changes in the pastoral situation that seem to call for renewal in the understanding of the school's mission.

As we have seen, issues of mission and identity are inter-connected and have cultural, historical and religious dimensions with their sources in changing worldviews. The educating role of the school is to mediate meaning as it is encountered in these worldviews in such a way that students can begin to make a personal synthesis capable of giving their lives a purpose and a direction. The position is summed up in Figure 10.

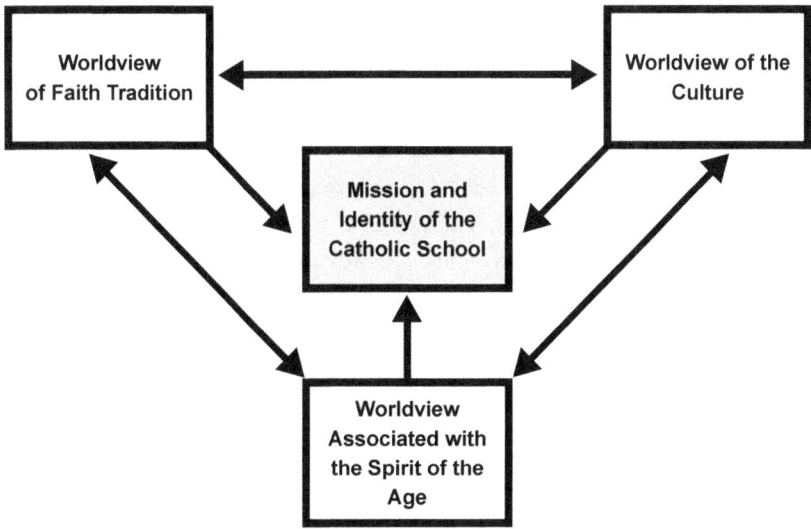

Figure 10. Catholic Education at the Nexus of Worldviews

The task of Catholic school educators and leaders as mediators of meaning is made particularly complex by the fact that all three worldviews are in the process of rapid development. This creates tensions within the communities which sustain the plausibility of each worldview. It is not only in the world of religion that one encounters fundamentalists and radicals!

The "spirit of the age" is split between two worldviews with fundamentally different pre-suppositions – the modern and the post-modern. Mission anthropologist Paul Hiebert demonstrates clearly that the spirit of the age of modernity is qualitatively different from that of post-modernity, even given that the latter can be understood in a number of ways.[269] Each of these epochs has its characteristic worldview which persists in the present. In many communities people holding one or other of these outlooks live side by side. Their outlooks certainly converge in Catholic school communities. This split between the two worldviews also has its impact within cultures as people endeavour to adapt their "plan for living" to accommodate these competing outlooks.

As changes in all three worldviews proceed, the "old" and the "new" are often left sitting side by side, competing for our attention and allegiance, a situation that creates further tensions, generally associated with the struggle for dominance. These transformations, all occurring at the same time although at different rates, create what we have called the "frontier experience", which educators and school leaders encounter today. They have a significant bearing on how we now understand and articulate the challenges of mission and religious identity.

It is perhaps not surprising then that, given our present context, new questions are being asked about the meaning of Catholic identity and the mission of the Catholic school. It would be more surprising in the circumstances if such questions were not raised. Nor is it surprising that this new situation poses major challenges for Catholic educators working at the interface between the official Church and a Catholic community that seems somewhat inattentive and disengaged when judged against more traditional criteria of Church membership. While it is important to make sense of the situation, educators and school leaders, being practical people, also want to do something about it! What seems needed is a framework within which to understand the situation and to respond so they can firstly *shape*, and then *tap* local aspiration in the service of the students they educate. In this final chapter we propose such a framework of understanding, and in the process explore some of the implications for the mission and identity of Catholic school systems and Catholic educating

---

[269] For a full discussion of the changing worldviews of modernity and post-modernity see Paul Hiebert *Transforming Worldviews: An Anthropological Understanding of How People Change* (Grand Rapids Michigan: Baker Academic, 2008), 144–264.

communities. We view this as the starting point of what needs to be an ongoing dialogue.

The Ecology of Human Growth

The organising idea in this task comes from Pope John Paul II who proposed that there is an "ecology" at work in education.[270] He articulates the idea as follows:

> An all-round education seeks to develop every aspect of the individual: social, intellectual, emotional, moral and spiritual. For there is an *ecology of human growth* which means that if any one of these elements is overlooked, all the others suffer.[271] (emphasis added)

The two major characteristics of an ecology are that it is comprised of interacting sub-systems and that the health of the entire system depends on the status of each sub-system. If one sub-system becomes problematic then all the rest suffer. This is a useful metaphor in making sense of our mission in the context of the Catholic school. It suggests the question *what are the sub-systems that must work together so that the Catholic school provides the environment in which all members of the community can learn and, in the process, grow?*

We suggest that there are three *essential* sub-systems at work here – an ecology of *knowledge*, an ecology of *relationships*, and an ecology of *community*. The school's contribution to the human growth of its students, parents and staff depends on the vitality of these three interacting sub-systems. Taken together they constitute the ecology of human growth.

An Ecology of Knowledge

The argument of Chapter Nine, addressing the issue of ideological pluralism, was that the worldviews identified in Figure 10 above proceed on the basis of different understandings of what constitutes reasonable and reliable knowledge. All three appeal to reason and so all three lay claim to rationality. In Chapter Six we traced their historical development. Here we focus on their contribution to an ecology of knowledge.

Religious worldviews operate from the *principle of purpose*. In the oft-quoted words of Stephen Covey, those working from the principle of purpose "begin with the end in mind".[272] In the Christian worldview, our relationship to God and God's relationship to us are pivotal to all sense of purpose and,

---

[270] The bishops of England and Wales also employ this metaphor in addressing issues associated with the education of children of other faiths in Catholic schools (see later).

[271] John Paul II's address to the ambassador of the Republic of Malawi, 14 December 2000, quoted in the statement by the Catholic Bishops of England and Wales *Catholic Schools, Children of other Faiths and Community Cohesion: Cherishing Education for Human Growth* (Westminster: Catholic Education Service, 2008), 8.

[272] Stephen Covey *Principle-Centered Leadership* (New York: Simon & Schuster, 1992), 42.

because of this, faith is foundational to human growth. A religious worldview provides a particular, but by no means exclusive, way to approach the issue of purpose. Questions associated with purpose are also perennial in philosophy.

The dominant cultural worldview in the West sees the world as essentially self-contained. It is constructed around the *principle of contingency* often expressed as an "appeal to reason". In this structuring of knowledge, reliable knowledge depends on the discovery of relationships and the integration of such relationships into systems of thought. The "appeal to reason" that characterises Western thought and Western constructions of knowledge contains within it an implied assumption – "reasonable as defined by us in the West". The globalisation process, in mixing together people from different cultures, brings people raised in a western milieu into contact with other systems of logic – ways of construing what is reasonable and reliable knowledge – which they need to understand if they are to live peacefully with other peoples. The imaginal horizon within which Western people customarily think makes this difficult to comprehend, let alone address.

The Western paradigm of education is based largely on the modern worldview. The anthropology associated with this worldview sees humans as part of nature. Natural laws, accessible by reason, provide the basis for morality. The modern worldview eschews questions about the transcendent and about ultimate purpose, seeing them as essentially unanswerable. Most modern academic disciplines operate under the assumptions of this worldview. Approaching knowledge in this way has generated great human capability that has been used to create both good and evil. Those holding the modern worldview deal with questions of purpose by privatising them, denying them any public significance. This was done initially to "keep the peace" in societies faced with divisions over religion, but has resulted in the rise of secularist ideologies which deny religion any public standing as societies have become more complex. To raise questions of purpose in the contemporary world, Christians have to be able to make their case within the constraints imposed by Western rationality. This situation has important implications for all Christian education, not only for Catholic schools.

Post-modernity provides a third approach to the construction of knowledge, one based on the *principle of critique*. This principle questions all accepted answers and makes a concerted attempt to "deconstruct" them and to show their hidden biases, the self-interests they favour, and the claims to power that underpin them. This orientation to knowledge is an integral component of contemporary educational theory and practice.

All three principles – purpose, contingency and critique – view what is "reliable knowledge" and "what is reasonable" from within their own frame of reference. All three have a claim on our allegiance, as all are necessary principles in the pursuit of knowledge, but in an ecology of human growth none, taken by itself, is sufficient. The three principles exist in relation to one another. The value we place on one determines in large part the value we place on the others. How we think about purpose, for instance, determines what we value, and this in turn provides the basis for critique. If we think questions of ultimate purpose are beyond our comprehension, then issues of meaning and value become open-ended. In the creation of a school learning environment, an ecology of knowledge requires that all three principles – those of purpose, contingency and critique – *be held in tension.* The learning environment is compromised if one dominates at the expense of the others.

This form of ecology is particularly important in the context of a faith-based school. Public curricula as specified by governments are constructed on a secular basis. This usually means that "public knowledge" is constructed on the basis of the principles of contingency and critique, with questions of purpose assigned to the "private" sphere. As societies, including those in the West, become more diverse in terms of the religious commitments of their citizens, this way of construing knowledge is becoming more and more problematic. It is certainly inadequate from the perspective of an "ecology of human growth". Figure 11 conveys the relationship between the principles and their impact on education. All three principles must find a place in a sound Catholic education.

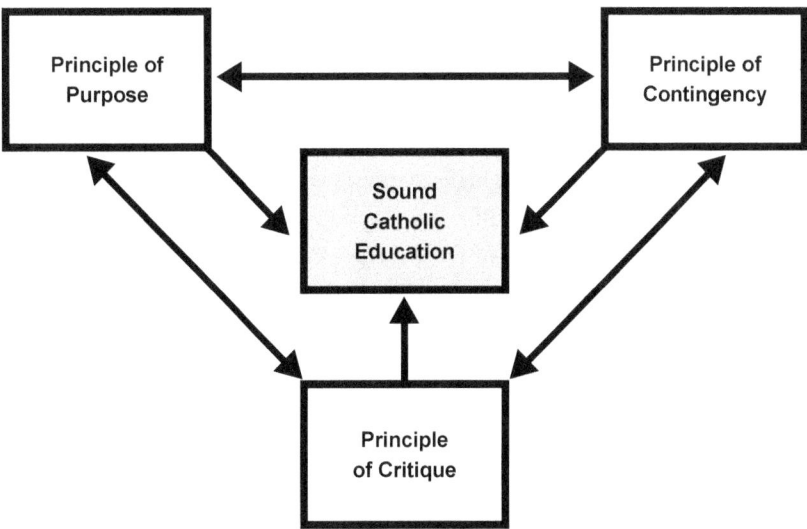

Figure 11. The Ecology of Knowledge

Purpose is critical in the process of meaning-making. The difficulty faced in Catholic schools is that, increasingly, teachers come to their task with a professional preparation that is essentially secular in its orientation. This impacts on how they construe knowledge and the place they assign to religion in education. The assumption is often made by school leaders that teachers will see it as important because they are Catholic or because they have their teaching qualifications from Catholic tertiary institutions. Experience in a number of Western countries would seem to suggest that this assumption is now problematic. Without major initiatives on behalf of Catholic school systems and Catholic tertiary providers to re-balance this situation, the ecology of knowledge in the schools readily becomes distorted. Students emerging from those Catholic schools where this distortion exists go on to tertiary education which is likely to have a strong secular orientation. They then return to Catholic schools as teachers. A self-defeating cycle can easily be created if the problem is not identified and addressed. For this reason, much more time and resourcing needs to be invested in addressing thoroughly the issues of mission and identity than was previously the case.

The way in which the principles of purpose, contingency and critique are *balanced* in structuring the curriculum of the Catholic school shapes its *academic learning environment*. If the academic learning environment is to remain healthy and a means of student growth, then all three principles need to be embedded as elements of the total curriculum. The principle of purpose cannot be carried by the Religious Education program alone. It needs to be present within the total curriculum because it opens people to the challenges of mission which relate to the whole of human life. The principle of critique is often present in the curriculum in its *post-modern form* – deconstructing. It also needs to be present in its *pastoral form*, questioning how the school deals with the issue of difference in capacity and capability in terms of curriculum provision, particularly for marginalised groups within the community, that is, it needs to provide the basis for affirmative action within the school community.

The appropriate integration of the three principles of purpose, contingency and critique in the curriculum needs to be identified as a primary goal of school improvement. How school communities construe knowledge and how this understanding is translated into the curriculum defines a primary direction in their understanding of and commitment to mission.

Ecology of Knowledge and the "Catholic Curriculum"

Over the past three decades many efforts have been made to explore the concept of a "Catholic curriculum" and those responsible for such efforts often report a lukewarm response from teachers.[273] Secondary school teachers in particular pose questions such as – can there be such a thing as "Catholic" science or "Catholic" mathematics? Stated in this way, the answer is clearly "no", since all academic disciplines have their own methods and autonomy and this is readily acknowledged in Catholic teaching. The question needs to be posed differently.

An alternative approach might ask – how can subjects like science and mathematics address issues of purpose and how open are they to critique? Taking such an approach further we might ask the following questions. How can science (or topics dealt with in science) be best harnessed to serve the common good?[274] How is scientific knowledge really created? Who decides what is true in science? What beliefs underpin all science? What does science value? Are there limits to what scientists should do? Who decides these matters? How? For whose benefit? What is being attempted here is to bring a *philosophic as well as a religious* perspective to bear in dealing with the issue of purpose. At a more general level these questions seek to explore the value of what students learn in science, the forms of rationality that underpin the learning, the place of critique, and how the subject promotes what is true and good.

Balancing education in this way places demands on the knowledge of teachers, the worldview from which they approach the subjects they teach, and their willingness to engage in the form of critique that an ecology of knowledge demands of them. If the ecology of human growth perspective is to have meaning, the balancing of principles by which knowledge is constructed must be looked at *systematically*. This generally requires *system support*. It is quite labour-intensive, and is only rarely addressed adequately by individual Catholic school authorities.

A Sense of the Sacred, a project developed and supported by the Catholic Education Office in Sydney over the past fifteen years, provides an important illustration of what is possible in creating an ecology of knowledge for a Catholic education system. This project was inspired by earlier projects sourced from a number of countries and began using standard values-integration practice. The program translates the three principles that are integral to an ecology of knowledge into a set of five Catholic meta-values. These are

- the sacramentality of creation
- the dignity of the human person
- communion – past, present and future

---

[273] For a summary of various approaches see Therese D'Orsa "In the Second Modernity it takes the whole curriculum to teach the whole Gospel" *Journal of Catholic School Studies* (Vol. 80: Issue 1, May/June 2008), 36–52.

[274] This approach in used by the Radical Maths movement in the US which seeks to integrate principles of social justice into the teaching of mathematics. See <www.radicalmath.org> for details.

- cultural transformation
- reconciliation and hope.

Each meta-value was broken down into more specific values relevant to the Australian cultural context of the school system. Collectively, these values also incorporate the broad understanding of evangelisation discussed in Chapter Ten, with particular emphasis given to the values enshrined in Catholic social teaching.

The development team worked with curriculum leaders from secondary schools covering the seven academic learning areas as defined in the state's curriculum. Over a period of several years these groups worked together to develop two sets of resources to support the initiative:

- a *Foundations* document setting out the rationale for the approach and its methodology
- *practical resource kits* that all teachers could use in dealing with particular topics in each key learning area.

The resource documents were mapped to the curriculum in each learning area taking into account the developmental stage of students. For each learning area stage-specific links were made between the curriculum area and the Religious Education program for that stage. The resources developed to support teaching practice were printed and made available to all schools in the system. In a subsequent and important development at the system level, the role description for curriculum co-ordinators in all schools was extended to include responsibility for the implementation of the program. Professional development was provided to enable them to meet this responsibility.

In a second phase of the program, the materials supporting *A Sense of the Sacred* were made available on-line.[275] Responsibility for the implementation of the program at school level now rests with the academic department heads. How they meet this responsibility forms part of their annual performance appraisal. *A Sense of the Sacred* is now seen as integral to the culture of the school system.

This project provides a good illustration of how an ecology of knowledge can be delineated and embedded in the culture of a Catholic school system. It also indicates the degree of commitment as well as the time needed to mount such a venture. The *Foundations* document sets out the broad parameters of the project.

A Sense of the Sacred is a values integration project across all subjects in the school curriculum drawing on Gospel values, Church tradition and

---

[275] This greatly extends the school system's capacity to support the program by updating materials and adding new materials, thereby ensuring that the project remains current.

Catholic social teaching in order to enable students to think reflectively and critically, to enter the process of values clarification, analysis, acquisition and judgement, and to appreciate the integration between faith and life & faith and learning.[276]

An Ecology of Relationships

A second component in the ecology of human growth in a school community is the *relational learning environment*. Students learn in relationship to others – their family, their peers and their teachers.

In *Fides et Ratio*, Pope John Paul II, writing as a philosopher and religious leader, points out that in the human condition most of us *learn first by believing*. He observes, for instance, that it is simply not possible to critically assess all the findings upon which modern life is based. We learn in the first instance by taking what our parents and teachers tell us largely on faith. It is only later that we submit this to critical examination. Developing this theme he continues:

> In believing we entrust ourselves to the knowledge acquired by other people. This suggests an important tension. On the one hand the knowledge acquired through belief can seem an imperfect form of knowledge, to be perfected gradually through personal accumulation of evidence; on the other hand, belief is often humanly richer than mere evidence, because it involves an interpersonal relationship and brings into play not only a person's capacity to know, but also the deeper capacity to entrust oneself to others, to enter into a relationship with them which is intimate and enduring. It should be stressed that the truths sought in this interpersonal relationship are not primarily empirical or philosophical. Rather what is sought is *the truth of the person* – what the person is and what the person reveals from deep within. Human perfection, then, consists not simply in acquiring an abstract knowledge of the truth, but in a dynamic relationship of faithful self-giving with others. It is in this faithful self-giving that a person finds fullness of certainty and security. At the same time, however, knowledge through belief, grounded as it is in the trust between persons, is linked to truth; in the act of believing, men and women entrust themselves to the truth which the other declares to them.[277]

The act of knowing and the teaching–learning relationship within which this occurs are therefore important to the ecology of human growth.

The quality of the relationship, which includes the pedagogy used in teaching, is not something that can be left to chance, but is something that must be developed.[278] Just as it is possible to ask can there be such a thing as a Catholic curriculum? It is also not only possible, but very important, to ask can there be such a thing as Catholic pedagogy? Australian educator Dan White

---

[276] Catholic Education Office, Archdiocese of Sydney. The full set of resources available on-line can be accessed at <http://senseofthesacred.ceosyd.catholic.edu.au>.

[277] Pope John Paul II Fides et Ratio #32 (Faith and Reason) (Strathfield: St Paul's Publications, 1998).

suggests that there is.[279] White's argument is that approaches to pedagogy have much to learn from the way in which God deals with humankind, in particular what we know of the pedagogical method used by Jesus – this he refers to as "divine pedagogy". His interpretation of "Catholic" in the context of "Catholic pedagogy" takes its direction from the *Catechism of the Catholic Church*:

> The Church is catholic in a double sense: first she is catholic because Christ is present in her. "Where there is Jesus Christ there is the Catholic Church" (St Ignatius of Antioch, *Ad Smyrn.* 8,2). Secondly, the church is catholic because she is sent out by Christ on a mission to the whole of the human race.[280]

A Catholic pedagogy is a mission pedagogy, one which carries on what we have called "the Gospel process". White goes on to explore four characteristics of such a pedagogy:

- a willingness to suspend disbelief and engage with mystery
- searching for the truth as well as celebrating the truth that we hold
- asking God's questions as well as asking man's (sic) questions
- making Jesus real through fostering relationships.

He then poses the question:

> How does an educator in a Catholic school develop an authentic approach to pedagogy, across all curriculum areas, that is hope-filled and challenges students to meaningfully answer God's questions?

He suggests the need for a "Framework for Catholic pedagogy" and builds an answer to the question above around four methodological questions to be used in planning for teaching:

- does the strategy allow for meaning-making?   (**D**iscernment)
- does it individualise the learning ?   (**E**nrichment)
- will it engage each learner?   (**E**ngagement)
- does it actively encourage collaborative learning?   (**P**articipation)

White's DEEP model[281] provides a good starting point in developing both an understanding of how a Catholic pedagogy might be conceived and what it might look like in operation. Like *A Sense of the Sacred* noted above, White's work makes a promising contribution in addressing the challenges of mission

---

[278] Australian researcher Marcellin Flynn, for instance, in a ten-year study of senior students in Catholic secondary schools was able to show that the relational environment of the school (what he called climate and ethos) was by far the best predictor of academic success for students. See Marcellin Flynn *The Effectiveness of Catholic Schools* (Homebush: St Paul Publication, 1988), 315.

[279] Dan White "Catholic Pedagogy: Nurturing Pilgrims or Educating Tourists?" *Journal of Catholic School Studies* (Vol. 80: No. 1, 2008), 53–65.

[280] Libreria Editrice Vaticana *The Catechism of the Catholic Church* (1997), 830–831.

[281] White, 61.

as they currently present in Catholic schools.

The relational learning environment of the school is shaped by the quality of its pedagogy. Commenting on this the Congregation for Catholic Education notes, reflecting the emphasis of Pope John Paul II:

> A variety of pedagogical theories exist; the choice of the Catholic educator, based on the Christian concept of the human person, should be the practice of a pedagogy which gives special emphasis to the *direct and personal contact with the students*.[282] (emphasis added)

This contact happens both within and outside the classroom. Therefore the DEEP principles outlined above apply to "teaching" often in the forms of witness and dialogue. They cover the range of "teachable moments" in which learning can be directly related to life. This broader view of teaching has implications for how leaders work with both teachers and students.

Teachers are now called on to develop the skills necessary to relate to a wide range of students, not only in terms of their cultural background, but also in terms of their ability, their capacity to learn, and their capacity to behave in what are considered appropriate ways. This is a very challenging area in the modern school, where increasingly staff find themselves dealing with students whose behaviour evidences limited capacity for self-control. The concept of what might be considered a "normal classroom" is being rapidly reshaped by our post-modern/modern situation as it continues to unfold. This impacts importantly on how teachers construe their sense of personal mission.

Within school improvement processes, the current focus on developing the relational learning environment provides an important point of entry in highlighting the vital part relationships play in the ecology of human growth as this is pursued within a Catholic school community. Many schools have adopted, as a major strategic direction in their mission, the need to improve this aspect of school life.

An Ecology of Community

The third sub-system in the ecology of human growth in a Catholic school is *the life of the school community itself*. Catholic school communities vary considerably in their nature and composition depending on how the mission of the school is construed. At one end of the spectrum is the Catholic school for the children whose parents attend Sunday Eucharist on a regular basis. At the other end is the Catholic school in a rural area where education is seen as a service the Church offers to rural families whatever their faith background, or the Catholic school in an inner urban setting where the school is open to all

---

[282] Congregation of Catholic Education *Lay Catholics in Schools: Witnesses to Faith* #21 (Homebush: St Paul Publications, 1992).

and seen as a symbol of the Church's commitment to be in solidarity with the poor. Most Catholic school communities lie somewhere between these two poles. They have a core clientele of Catholics balanced by students of other denominations, other faiths and no apparent faith.

The credibility of what students learn, and thus what they see as its relevance, is underpinned by the perceived strength of the community which sponsors the knowledge gained through learning. Students accept what they are taught in science because they accept the scientific community and the knowledge it sponsors as credible. They learn the framework in which this knowledge is developed and so are eventually able to make their own judgments about scientific claims. The scientific community occupies a key place in the plausibility structure of science, as does its axiomatic structure.

The Catholic school plays a similar role for an increasing number of its students when it comes to the integrated view of life that lies at the heart of its learning program. The life of the community becomes both the medium and the message by which students judge the worth of Kingdom values and the value of further participation in the life of the believing community. This happens often in the face of counter-witness from within their own families. *The capacity of the school community to work together in mission becomes a touchstone of the value of mission itself.* Our own experience and that of the Catholic teachers with whom we work is that the school community, through the witness it provides to transcendent values, plays a key role in highlighting for students of all faiths and no faith, the place of the transcendent in human life. This is a precursor to growth in faith.

At another level the school community provides Catholic students with a form of enculturation into a broader Catholic culture itself in the process of regeneration. For many students, this is a formal step on the path to the Kingdom, something on which God can build. Its importance in the development of the student's faith is often underestimated and unrecognised. However, if Fowler's stages of faith are accepted as providing insight into the matter of faith development,[283] it becomes clearer that students need to pass through the stage of cultural faith on their way to developing a personal faith. If there is no culture of faith in the home, then the Catholic school, often by default, becomes the cultural context in which faith develops.

As a community with its own Catholic culture, the school becomes not only a means of evangelisation, but in accepting this role, opens itself to be further evangelised. This process, which involves ongoing conversion and renewal, builds the quality of the local faith community. Cumulatively, such growth

---

[283] James Fowler *Stages of Faith: The Psychology of Human Development and the Quest for Meaning* (Blackburn Victoria: Dove Communications, 1981).

across a system of schools contributes much to the regeneration of the wider Church. The community and the health of the community's culture, those of the school and of the broader Church, are essential elements in the ecology of human growth.

The bishops of England and Wales adopt the ecology of community explicitly in dealing with the issue of "community cohesion" in Catholic schools. In 1997 they commissioned a study *Catholic Schools and Children of Other Faiths*[284] which set out to examine the principles that apply when children of other faiths are accepted for enrolment into Catholic schools, and how these principles should be translated into practice.[285] In more recent times it has become a requirement of public policy in England that schools supported by public funds demonstrate their contribution to the building of community cohesion. The bishops' 2009 statement *Catholic Schools, Children of Other Faiths and Community Cohesion*[286] seeks to address both sets of issues. Their paper applies the conception of "an ecology of community" to a major issue facing Catholic education in Britain – dealing with the multi-faith nature of the society and its implications for Catholic schools. In introducing the document Archbishop Vincent Nichols points out that "integral human development" lies at the heart of Catholic education and continues:

> In this thinking education for human growth can be spoken of as the development of the environment or ecologies in which the human person flourishes and prospers. All can contribute to the promotion and protection of these ecologies.[287]

The document expands on this theme suggesting that the ecology of community itself is made up of three sub-systems: *the ecology of daily living, the ecology of justice,* and the *ecology of faith and religious experience.* The text goes on to outline how these ecologies can be lived out in practice within the context of the Catholic school. It matches the three sub-ecologies to three forms of dialogue mentioned previously in our discussion of evangelisation – the dialogue of life, the dialogue of action and the dialogue of religious experience.

In the bishops' understanding of the ecology of community, the multi-faith,

---

[284] Catholic Bishops of England and Wales *Catholic Schools and Children of Other Faiths* (Westminster: Catholic Education Service, 1997).

[285] The practice of enrolling students other-than-Catholic in Catholic schools is quite common and in some cases necessary in countries in which governments co-sponsor Catholic schools as a form of public education.

[286] Catholic Bishops of England and Wales *Catholic Schools, Children of Other Faiths and Community Cohesion: Cherishing Education for Human Growth* (Westminster: Catholic Education Service, 2009).

[287] Vincent Nichols "Foreword" in ibid., 4.

multi-cultural nature of many Catholic schools in the United Kingdom is seen as an important opportunity for evangelisation in the rich and full sense of that term as explored in Chapter Ten.

Community as Holder of Identity

There is a further dimension to the ecology of community and that is the role community plays as the *holder of identity*, in particular as the holder of Catholic identity. Noted Old Testament scholar Walter Brueggemann explores how identity and education are related in the life of Israel and in the Old Testament literature. In dealing with the issues of mission and identity in Catholic schools, we find his treatment compelling.

Brueggemann proposes that there is a traditioning process that underpins the Old Testament similar to what we have called the "Gospel process", and that this process is in many ways as revelatory as the content these scriptures contain.[288] His contention is that, when the text is analysed, it reveals the existence and interaction within the community of Israel of three distinct forms of religious awareness or consciousness. *Torah consciousness* underpins the Pentateuch and is concerned with God's purpose and disclosure; it is *the important element* in "what Israel knows".[289] The Torah has a central place in Israel's identity because the Torah is "what God has promised". The covenant relationship represents the highpoint in this development.

Prophetic consciousness came to prominence in the life of the community from a very early stage. The prophets consistently highlighted the gap that existed in the life of Israel between what God had promised and what the rulers, political and religious, had delivered. Failure to live up to God's covenant became the basis for the prophets' critique which took to heart God's concern for the poor, the weak and the strangers. The prophetic tradition, which was a conservative tradition calling people back to the heart of God's relationship as expressed in the covenant, provided the framework within which Jesus understood his mission and, as set out in the Gospels, presented himself to his people.

Wisdom consciousness emerged as an integral part of the tradition that was concerned with *practical wisdom* in living and sought to relate "what Israel

---

[288] Walter Brueggemann *The Creative Word: Canon as Model of Biblical Education* (Philadelphia: Fortress Press, 1982). See Chapter 2 "Canon and the Educational Repertoire", 1–13.

[289] Torah is often translated as "law". This is a quite limiting view. A better understanding arises when it is translated as "teaching". In the narrative style of the scriptures, Torah as the first five books of the Bible, cannot be equated to law even though it does set out the Law as understood in the theology of Israel. The teaching in the Torah is the result of over 700 years of reflection on, and imaginative reconstruction of, the basic narratives of Judah and Israel. Modern biblical studies indicate that the teaching was developed in primitive form some time after the time of David (ca. 1000 BC) and was edited into its final form around 400 BC.

knows" to what other cultures of the time knew.[290] As Old Testament scholar Dianne Bergant observes of this strand of literature:

> The corpus of books that we know as the wisdom literature…asks the question, what kind of role does God play in everyday life?…these books provide a kind of guide to successful living. Since every person in every culture must struggle with the questions of life, there is a universal character to this literature.[291]

Bergant goes on to note that this form of religious awareness is essentially humanistic and pragmatic in its orientation, concerned with what works – "whatever benefited humanity was a good to be pursued". Its major concern was not so much with means and ends, a characteristic of Greek wisdom, but with the practical wisdom that holds a community together.

Brueggemann's contention is that the interaction of these three forms of religious consciousness – Torah, Prophetic and Wisdom – played a key role in sustaining Israel's sense of its own identity and the vitality of life within the community. Taken together, and held in tension, they sustained identity across a tumultuous history. When one or other awareness gained the ascendency at the expense of the others, either through the exercise of power or through force of circumstances, then the confidence and vitality of the community waned.

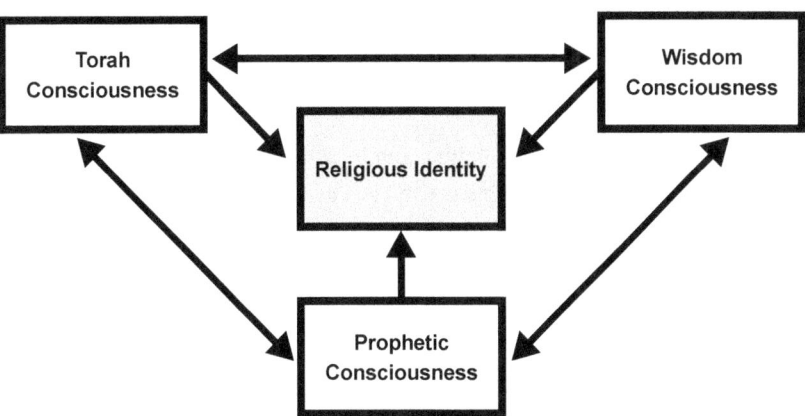

Figure 12. Dynamics Shaping Israel's Identity

The relationships at work in the dynamics of this community are set out in Figure 12. They parallel closely the relationship between the three principles

---

[290] This tradition is evident in the Books of Genesis where "what Israel knows" is set out in part as a re-interpretation of the myths and laws of other cultures. It takes on a more definitive form in the wisdom literature created much later in the development of its written tradition.
[291] Dianne Bergant "The Wisdom Books" in *The Catholic Study Bible* 2nd Edition (Oxford: Oxford University Press, 2006), 234.

of purpose, contingency and critique as discussed in the ecology of knowledge above. Each form of awareness reflects commitment to one of the three principles and interprets life primarily from the perspective to which this gives rise. It is through the interaction of these three perspectives in the life of Israel that community identity and life is sustained. These, in turn, underpin the credibility of its beliefs.

These forms of awareness did not exist in a pure form. Individuals operated from a mix of positions, and generally had a preference for one rather than another. However, the key to maintaining Israel's identity lay in the community's placing a high value *on all three*. The interactions, which began long before the text was created, stand behind the text and help determine its final form. Hence Brueggemann's assertion that the process by which the text is created is in itself revelatory.

An ecology of community, understood in this way, implies that *pluralism is an inherent part of the Judeo-Christian tradition*, particularly as this relates to the identity and vitality of the faith community. Conversely, if there are questions arising about the vitality or identity of the faith community, it may be helpful to look at what value it places on each form of consciousness. Brueggemann argues that to maintain the identity of a faith community, its education program needs to nurture all three forms of consciousness, not seeking to promote one at the expense of the other, because the health of the faith community, as well as the security of its identity, depends on the presence and interaction of all three.

The factors that give life to a faith community, as set out by Brueggemann in relation to the Old Testament, have also been in evidence throughout Christian history. Their presence continues to stabilise the identity of the Church today, at both global and local levels, including particular communities such as Catholic schools. The case is still convincingly made that, when all three forms of religious consciousness are held in creative tension, the optimal conditions exist for the flourishing of Christian life. In matters pertaining to the life of the faith community, there must be a place for the authoritative voice, for the prophetic voice, and for the voice which brings practical wisdom to discussions. However, having a mix of voices has its benefits only if there is a *willingness to dialogue* about what is important, and a corresponding willingness to work towards consensus on issues that divide. The dialogue envisaged here can take multiple forms reflecting its richness as a fundamental modality of evangelisation.

Brueggemann reminds us of an important fact. The three principles – purpose, critique, and wisdom – must be held in tension *by the conscious choices that communities make.* This understanding lies behind the Catholic teaching on the "sense of the faithful" mentioned in Chapter Two. There was a time in Catholic education when a strong Catholic culture could hold the three principles together, but only because the culture was owned by the community. That time has passed and in most places choices about how to "hold things together" now need to be the result of conscious effort. This occurs when communities seriously consider their mission and plan on the basis of mission. Holding the elements of an ecology of human growth together is something the community must now strive to do *intentionally.*

How the ecology of community is understood and how it is developed are important matters in the life of the school and the life of the Church. In the new space educators occupy on the frontier, it is important to bear in mind that, not only is the school an ecclesial place, it is often the only experience of Church for many, if not most, of its students. If we accept that this is the reality, then we need to ask the question what consequences does this situation have for us? The answer given to this question will have an important bearing on how we understand the mission of the school and the mission of the local church.

Life inevitably projects students beyond the school community and the program of the school has to take this into account in any realistic ecology committed to their growth. In this respect the development in many schools of forms of youth ministry that link students to a broader Christian experience is very promising. This is clearly a major area for discussion as the community begins to move clear of the present frontier and gain some sharper perspective on its future direction.

The Place of Grassroots Theology in an Ecology of Human Growth

Grassroots theology as undertaken by leaders in schools and school systems is currently done on a basis of "need" as challenges in management, curriculum, community development, policy settings or school improvement arise. It is often episodic. However, as currently practised, it provides a good starting point and a sound methodology for more systematic reflection. If teachers and leaders wish to make sense of their work, then acquiring the understandings and skills of theological reflection is essential. The notion of "befriending", that is "feeling at home with", is central to the model we have suggested. It is important to remind ourselves that the alternatives to "feeling at home" are "feeling alienated from" or "feeling indifferent about".

As we work with teachers and leaders we find that few appreciate the plural or living nature of their religious tradition. That school communities actually need people with different understandings relating positively together in order to sustain identity, as Brueggemann suggests, is both a new insight and a freeing one. In many cases, as teachers come to realise that evangelisation can take many forms, some of which they are already engaged in, an opening arises in which revisiting their religious tradition takes on new meaning. At the same time, many teachers seem quite ignorant about culture and its potential as a resource in the development of an ecology of human growth. This extends even to those responsible for the development of Religious Education courses.

The idea of bringing culture, human experience and the religious tradition together in the structured conversation we have called "grassroots theology" is relatively new in educational discourse. As with all beginnings, doing it is not easy initially. However, the proof comes in the doing, in reaching better-informed decisions and in the human development processes that take place when people engage in this form of reflection and dialogue. Meaning-making is of the essence in leadership.

Because so many teachers in contemporary Catholic schools have been trained in secular tertiary institutions, the almost inevitable result is to interpret human experience predominantly within secular mindsets. This remains a major hurdle to be negotiated as people have to redevelop the intuitive base from which they customarily look at the world, and in White's words, to ask "God's questions" with more facility.

We have endeavoured to explore "doing grassroots theology" in the light of the insights of contemporary missiologists who provide much of the intellectual scaffolding used in this book. The two projects, those of the bishops of England and Wales and of the Catholic Education Office in Sydney, cited in this chapter have been included for two reasons. As we have come to understand them, each applies sound missiological principles to education, and, secondly, each is illustrative of the "long haul" involved in bringing about the kind of substantial change which both drives and is driven by an expanded imaginal horizon.

"The Heart of the Matter"

Many of the chapters in this book have been developed by engaging in grassroots theology ourselves as we have reflected on the mission challenges in Catholic schools today. There is no simple solution to the complexity which characterises the present situation in which educators find themselves. Making sense of life on the frontier in a comprehensive way is difficult. However, we believe that this is the heart of the leadership task facing educators today. Doing grassroots theology, approaching the broad objective of meaning-making on an issue-by-issue basis is, in our view at least, a most promising option. Cumulatively, taking the opportunities which present themselves in dealing with policies, curricula, school reviews and many others, educators build meaning for and with staff and, through the staff, for and with all in the school community.

We believe that "Catholic curriculum", "Catholic pedagogy" and "Catholic community" have the potential to become master ideas through which a worldview that is Catholic can be inculturated into the local theology of mission. Such a theology provides the foundation and gives purpose to all that happens in a particular Catholic school or other educational institution. Theological reflection is the process by which this goal is achieved. It is the age-old process for getting to the "heart of the matter".

Grassroots theology is important because it is a practical means by which teachers and leaders can bring together the principles of purpose, contingency and critique in relation to particular issues. It becomes a way of exploring how the three worldviews that impact on education today – those of the local culture, the spirit of the age, and the Catholic faith – influence decisions about particular issues. It provides a basis for negotiating the dilemmas posed in living between the competing worldviews that define the spirit of our age, and in assisting teachers and students to make the journey to the second modernity. As a methodology it places great store on the interpretation of our experience. It is only by monitoring experience and making sense of it that we discover our own worth and the worth of what we do as teachers and leaders. It is in prayerful reflection that we develop sensitivity to the Spirit at work in our communities.

The greatest challenge posed by living on the frontier is not knowing more or doing more; *it lies in imagining more.* In our view, the ministry of imagination is the most important ministry of our time. Too often, without even being aware of it, we are trapped within the limitations which our culture, our understanding of religion, and the spirit of our age impose upon us. So much of what we know and do is limited by what we can imagine. We need a way of shifting our individual and collective imaginal horizons in order to meet the challenges of the present and future with hope.

We believe missiology, the study of mission and culture, has much to offer Catholic education in this regard. God's dream for humankind, the mission for which Jesus worked and prayed and which he described as the Kingdom of God, is the grandest vision of all. As we enter into the processes demanded by commitment to that vision, we not only "befriend" a living tradition, but our educating communities genuinely enrich that tradition in unique ways, further endowing it with the energy and capacity to continue to both enlighten and enliven.

INDEX

References with "fn" refer to a footnote on that page.

A
A Secular Age 81, 115
academic theology 4–7
acculturation 47–8, 52
achievement through sustained effort 69
Ad Gentes 18, 144, 149
adapting to situations 69
afterlife 170–1
anthropological exploration 16
Arbuckle, Gerald 54, 82–3, 136
Aristotelian philosophy 120
The Art of Theological Reflection 29–32
aspiration
   human 12, 14, 42, 57, 65–6, 84, 90, 152
   local 23–4
assertiveness 69, 81
astronomy 75–6
atheism 83, 109, 128
attitude
   of certitude 30
   of exploration 30
   of self-assurance 30
Australia
   bush 3
   Catholic schools in 6, 109, 110
   pragmatic secularism in 110
autonomous states 111
axioms, unprovable 119, 122

B
Babel 98
Bacon, Francis 126
befriending terminology 39–40
beliefs 119, 172
believing 183
Bergant, Dianne 189
Berger, Peter 119
Berlin Wall, fall of the 149

Bevans, Stephen 10, 12, 14, 24, 35, 146, 157
The Biblical Foundations of Mission 160–1
Bonaparte, Napoleon 82
Bosch, Hieronymus 121
Bosnia 149
both/and 88, 89, 136, 148, 171
boundaries 88, 105
Brueggemann, Walter 188–91, 192
Brunner, Emile 146
bush 3

C
Canada 6
canon law 105
capitalism 85, 86
Cardijn, Cardinal 29
caring for others 69
Caritas in Veritate 17, 95
Catechism of the Catholic Church 184
Catholic community 193
Catholic culture
   Catholic "on their own terms" 70, 71, 175
   change in 1
   defined 41–2
   disappearing 21
   enculturation into a broader 186
Catholic curriculum 180–3, 193
Catholic discourse 106, 112–15, 142
Catholic education 42 *see also* Catholic schools; school education
Catholic educators, as explorers' guides and meaning-makers 175–93
Catholic imaginary, reclaiming the 14–15
Catholic imagination 14
Catholic meta-values 181–3
Catholic pedagogy for mission 184–5, 193
Catholic schools *see also* school education
   in Australia 6, 109, 110
   in Canada 6
   composition of students 185–6
   division between the person and ethic of

Jesus 166
evangelising in 150–1
  and ongoing renewal 186–7
and globalisation 101–3
in Ireland 6
lay and religious staff 20
mission in 186–7
mission statements 155
as the only experience of Church for many 191
orientation 23
pastoral form of critique principle 180
pressure for compliance 23–4
in a second modernity environment 91–3
and the Second Vatican Council (1962–65) 20, 90
socialising role 20
system support 181
as a target for secularists 109
in the UK 6, 109, 116, 187–8
in the USA 6
values integration project 181–3
and worldviews 66
Catholic Schools, Children of Other Faiths and Community Cohesion 187
Catholic Schools and Children of Other Faiths 187
Catholic Schools on the Threshold of the New Millennium 17
The Catholic School 20
causality 121–2
change, rate of 12
China 96
choice 68–9, 71, 77–8, 79, 85, 87, 89, 91, 126, 191
Christian living 59, 62
  living in right relationship 172
Christian Religious Education
  balancing the three principles 133, 180
  and dialogue 60
  and local culture 61–2, 192
  and purpose 180
  and shared Christian praxis 25
Christian Religious Education 27
Christian tradition see religious tradition
Church

and choice 71
as a community of communities 142
and the divine right of kings 82
as European 140
as global 140, 141, 142
and the Kingdom 84, 146, 150, 173–4
as local 140, 141, 142
place 113
and the pre-modern world 80–1, 83
re-positioning itself within history 90
role 10, 65, 80–1, 82–3, 105, 106, 107, 120–1, 146
as universal 140
and young post-modern Catholics 71
The Church and Cultures 46
civil authority 105
civil law 105
civilisation 44–5, 84, 85, 141
civility 69
clerical order 105
climate change 99, 125
colonialism 45, 47, 85, 94, 108
Columban Fathers 6
commitment 69
common good 114, 116, 174, 181
communism 47, 73, 85, 86, 111
communities in exile 164
community
  an ecology of 185–8
  cohesion 187
  as a holder of identity 188–91
complex connectivity 95–7, 101
Congregation for Catholic Education 17, 185
consensus, a willingness to work towards 190
consumerism 68–9, 86
context
  changing 8–9
  and culture 8, 59
  human experience 42
contingency, principle of 121–3, 125, 129, 133, 178, 179
Copernicus, Nicolaus 75
Cote, Richard 48, 49, 53–6
Covey, Stephen 177
creation, God's 127, 149, 152, 172, 173
critical reflection *see also* theological

reflection
    in education 25–7
    on mission issues 24
critique, principle of 125, 129, 131, 133, 178, 179, 180
crossroads, image 7
cultural homogenisation 89, 97–9, 101–2
cultural information and the Whiteheads 28–9
culture
    befriending 41–2
    changing frameworks of understanding within 8
    classicist view 41, 44–5, 46
    and context 8, 59
    de-territorialisation 100
    definitions and meanings 14fn15, 40, 41, 42, 43–4
    dynamism of 50, 58, 59
    empirical 44, 45fn77
    enculturation and acculturation 47–8
    evangelising 42, 61–2, 92
    and faith 44
    global youth 101–2
    and God's truth 158
    and the Gospel 59–63, 141
    and human existence 14
    and the imagination 13, 14
    inculturation 59–61, 99
    insiders and outsiders 52, 54, 57
    as the learning place of the faith community 43–63
    legitimate autonomy of 112
    local 37, 61–2, 98, 99, 102, 192
    and meaning-making 42
    models 48–58
        iceberg 53–8
        society's design/plan for living 49–53
    modern view 45–7
        understanding 41, 48–58
    and narrative 13, 53–8
        and religion 44
        as a resource 8, 43
        respecting a people's culture 141
        and social identity 47–8
        and theological reflection 36–8, 43, 62–3
        and worldview see worldview

cultures, living between 100
cynicism 69
Cyprian 121

D
damnation 121
Darwinism 47, 127
Dawkins, Richard 109
de Beer, John 24, 29–32
De Mesa, Joe 24
deconstruction, process 129, 180
DEEP model 184–5
Dei Verbum 157
delayed gratification 69
Descartes, René 107, 126
dialogue see also proclamation
    of action 150, 187
    in Christian Religious Education 60
    in evangelisation 150, 151, 158, 190
    and God's truth 158
    inter-faith 39, 149, 150
    inter-religious 19, 39, 62, 149–50
    and Kingdom of God 151
    of life 150, 187
    between missiology and education 2
    and mission 60, 91, 141, 149–50, 152
    purpose of 151–2
    of religious experience 150, 187–8
    in teaching 185
    of theological exchange 150
    willingness to 190
Dialogue and Proclamation 150
diocese 142
disadvantaged, the 173
discernment process 16–17, 184
diseases 96
disorientation 77, 81, 85, 94, 164
distrust 69, 131
diversity 69–70, 71, 73, 89, 98–9
divine revelation 156–9
Divini Illius Magistri 20
Doing Ecclesiology 31
dynamic myth 54–6, 57

E
early modernity see modernity

Ecclesiam Suam 137
ecclesiastical authority 105, 106, 108, 110–11
ecology 89
  of community 185–8
  of daily living 187
  of faith and religious experience 187
  of human growth 177–88
  of justice 187
  of knowledge 177–80
    and the Catholic curriculum 180–3
  of relationships 183–5
ecumenism 19
education *see* Catholic schools; school education
educational theory and practice, contemporary 178
Egan, Gerard 48
either/or 88, 136, 171
employment opportunities 101
enculturation 47, 66
engagement with the modern world 19
Enlightenment
  and early modernity 81–5
  foundation for modernity paradigms 85
  impact on the pre-modern worldview 77
  and Islam 110
  myth of progress 85, 86
  and nature 126–7
  and a paradigm shift in the structure of knowledge 120, 121
  and religion as a private matter 107–8
  thinking, resistance to 112
  towering figures of 126
entertainment 69
environmental refugee 99
environmental sustainability 88
Evangelii Nuntiandi 61, 112, 141, 144, 147, 148, 151
evangelisation
  and Catholic meta-values 181–2
  charting the Church's understanding of 151–3
  and culture 42, 61–2, 92
  and evangelising the evangelisers 60, 153
  and globalisation 102
  and magisterial documents 142

and Pope Paul VI 112, 141, 147–8
re-evangelising of Europe 131
and renewal in Catholic schools 150–1, 186–7
and role of dialogue 150, 151, 158, 190
superficial 56, 61, 81
Synod on Evangelisation 140–1, 143, 147–8
in UK Catholic schools 188
evolution, theory of 85, 124, 127
Extra ecclesiam nulla salus 121

F
failure 164
faith
  authority of 107
  axioms as acts of 119, 122
  cultural and personal 186
  and culture 44
  and imagination 15
  and learning 183
  and the principle of purpose 123–4
  and religion 44
  and science 108
  as superstition 120
faith community, culture as the learning place of the 43–63
faith versus reason debate 124–5
fascism 86
feminism 89
Fides et Ratio 135, 183
floors 43
forgiveness 89, 172
Fowler James 186
fragmented and fragmenting world 70, 77, 87, 101, 129
France 82
freedom
  to choose 68–9
  to make the right choices 126
Freire, Paulo 25
frontier
  coping with the 4
  experience, making sense of 175–7
  of hope, living on 7
  image 1, 2–4, 7

of mission
    forces reshaping 94
    Spirit is active 92
moving beyond the 39
time 79
Fuellenbach, John 169–70
fundamentalism 90, 131, 154

G

Galileo, Galilei 75–6, 124, 126
Gallagher, Michael Paul 48, 53, 70, 89, 129
The Garden of Earthly Delights 121
Gardner, Howard 23, 101
Gaudium et Spes 16, 42, 90, 142, 144–5
Genesis, Book of 73
global recession of 2008–09 96
globalisation
    and acculturation 47–8
    characteristic feature 95
    as complex connectivity 95–7
    educational dimensions 101–3
    and evangelisation 102
    and homogenisation 89, 97–9, 101–2
    as the knowledge economy 97
    and the local 89, 102
    many faces of 95–117
    as "McDonaldisation" 97–9
    and mission 94
    and narrative 8
    narrative of 98
    as the new migration 99–100
    and the new wilderness 3
    and the second modernity 87
    and the worldview of an age 73
God's creation 127, 149, 152
God's mission 18–19, 21–1, 39, 80, 92, 146, 152, 155, 162, 172
God's revelation in scripture 156–9
good news
    each community to tell its own 161
    Jesus is the 167, 171
    as Jesus' message about the Kingdom 171
    of the local community as a resource 174
    making it known to others 167, 169
    passing on the 160
Gospel, the *see also* Gospels, the; New Testament texts; scripture
    and church building 18
    complexity 15
    and culture 59–63, 141
    and grassroots theology 35–6, 37, 162
    of John, the word "world" in 104–5
    and local culture 99
    making it known to others 149, 167
    message 155
    and a new plausibility structure 123
    proclamation of 148
    and the signs of the times 16
    truth and freedom 126
    written for local contexts 38
Gospel communities
    carrying forward the mission of Jesus 164, 165
    engagement with the broader societies 165
    and Jesus' expected return 64
    pastoral needs 164, 165
    then and now 154–74
Gospel values 155
Gospels, the *see also* John; Luke; Mark; Matthew
    choices made by the writers of 160
    Christian narratives as a resource 174
    as content and process 160, 162, 163, 169–71, 184
    context in which they were written 159–60, 162
    gift from the early Church communities 161
    as mission literature 160–1
    missionary commission 167–9
    as narratives 162–3
    as pastoral and missional 163–5
Grace, Gerald 116
grassroots missiology
    authors' experience 6–7
    conversations 2
    driven by 5
    goal 17
    practitioners 5
    and professional missiology 5–6, 7
grassroots theological reflection 8
grassroots theology *see also* local theology

and academic theology 4–7
characteristics 5
doing 22, 23–40
  model for 36–8
educational discourse 192
and engaging in the Gospel process 162
and meaning-making 35
from a mission perspective 10
systematic 10–11
terminology 2, 25
Gratian 105
Gravissimum Educationis 21
gravity experiment 122
Greeley, Andrew 14, 108
Groome, Thomas 24, 25–7
guilt 69

H
Habermas, Jürgen 25, 86
Hall, Edward T. 48
heart of the matter 31–2, 37–8
heliocentric universe 75–6
hell 121
heretics, dealing with 120–1
Hiebert, Paul 43, 48, 53–4, 57–8, 72, 119, 176
historical consciousness 79–80, 87, 90, 92, 98, 100
Hitchens, Christopher 109
Hoge, Dean 70–1
homogenisation 89, 97–9, 101–2
hope
  and energy 22
  lifeblood of mission 7, 38–9, 152
  moving with 10, 39, 92
  for a new moral framework 128
  sustaining 9
human consciousness
  new 91–2, 96
  of pre-modern people 121
human development, integral 187
human experience
  aspiration 12, 14, 42, 57, 65–6, 84, 90, 152
  befriending 41–2
  context 42
  and culture 14
  and the Enlightenment 82

and fragmentation 70, 77, 87, 101, 129
getting to know others 157
and narrative 92
and official Church teaching 153
as a pole in theological reflection 28, 29, 30, 36–8
as a resource 8
human growth, ecology of 177–88
human rights, universal 129
human sensibility, new 92
human sexuality, study of 128
human suffering 89
humanism
  exclusive 83, 84, 86, 89, 115, 128, 133
  inclusive 89

I
iceberg model of culture 53–8
ideas, rapid dissemination of 118–19
ideational environment 50
identity
  and choices 77–8, 87
  community as a holder of 188–91
  local cultural 102
  and mission 139, 142, 153, 180
  and modernity 85
  and music of an era 102
  and the pre-modern worldview 76–8, 85
  re-negotiating one's cultural 100
  social 47–8
  and worldview 73, 76, 77
ideological intolerance 111
imaginal capacity 10
imaginal horizons
  and complex connectivity 101
  culture creates 14, 52–3, 158
  and dominant worldview 76
  and insight 23
  and limited options 10, 21
  in pre-modernity 120, 124
  reflective practice on our 14
  shifting our individual and collective 193
  transcending 13, 22
  Western people 178
imagination *see also* missiological imagination

Catholic 14
and culture 13, 14
defined 12–13
and faith 15
ministry of the 193
missional 13
social 53, 56
imperial order 105
inculturation 59–61, 99, 141
individualism 71, 112
Industrial Revolution 82
insight
  flow 60
  search for 23–5
intellectual disengagement 69
intelligent design, theory of 124
inter-faith dialogue 39, 149, 150
inter-religious dialogue 19, 39, 62, 149–50
inter-testamental period 171
Ireland
  Catholic education in 6
  peace in 149
Islam 110
Israel's identity as a community 188–91

J
Jamnia 159
Jerusalem 159
Jesus
  an encounter with a personal God 117
  commitment to prayer 172
  expected return of 64
  as the grassroots theologian 35–6
  historical 169
  at home in nature 172
  is the good news 167, 171
  as a Jewish Messiah 165, 169–70
  life, death and resurrection of 59, 80, 160, 161, 165, 166–7
  making him known to others 149, 161–2, 164, 165, 167
  and miracles 128
  and mission 169, 188
  the person and ethic of 166–7, 171, 172
  proclaiming the person of Christ 149–51, 166–7
  as saviour 147
  teaching of 146, 147, 152, 169–73
  and the truth 123–4
  in the world 104–5
John, Gospel of 104–5, 160, 161, 163, 168
Judea 159
Judeo-Christian religion, central paradigm 79
justice 19, 172, 187
Justice in the World 17

K
Kasper, Cardinal Walter 118, 125–6, 135, 139
Killen, Patricia O'Connell 24, 29–32
Kingdom of God
  within and beyond history 79, 171–3
  and the Church 84, 146, 150, 173–4
  and dialogue 151
  in *Evangelii Nuntiandi* 147–8
  as Jesus' life and mission 21, 38, 146
  Jesus' teaching on 169–73
  and mission 152
  and other faiths 39
  and the passage of time 80
  and school communities 92, 103, 117
  steps on the path to the 186
Kingdom parables 144
Kingdom values 62
Knitter, Paul 130
"knowing in real time" 97
knowledge
  from academic disciplines 135
  construction 74, 119
  ecology of 177–83
  economy 97, 101
  foundations of 119–20
  plausibility structures as 120–5
  and the principle of contingency 121–3
  and the principle of purpose 123–4
  public *see* public knowledge
Kosmin, Barry 106
Kuhn, Thomas 73–4

L
land 51
learning
  by believing 183

and culture 43–63
and faith 183
and mission 10
relational 183–5
and theological reflection 29, 193
Legrand, Lucien 168
liberation
of humans 149
theologies 62, 141
light 74
local theology *see also* grassroots theology
defined 7, 141–2
doing 35–6
importance 11, 60, 89
mission theology as 38–9, 193
Luke, Gospel of 161, 163, 168
Lumen Gentium 142, 144
Luzbetak, Louis 46, 48, 49, 52, 59
Lyon, David 84–5

M
magisterial documents 142–3
A Marginal Jew 169
Mark, Gospel of 159, 160, 161, 163, 164, 167, 168–9
marriage 69
Martin, David 108
Martyr, Justin 60
Matthew, Gospel of 161, 163, 164–5, 167, 168
meaning
creating 13
and history 79–80
meaning-making
and culture 42
and grassroots theology 35
and the missiological imagination 21–2
and narrative 42
and purpose 180
time and its significance in 64–5
medicine 96
Meier, John 169
merchant class, emergence of 81
meta-narrative
as a concept 72–3
and embedded claims to power 129

loss of faith in 87
and truth 129
Method in Ministry 27–9
migrants 87, 118
migration
debates 58
level of different groups of people 118
mass 81
new 99–100
and the second modernity 87
miracles 122, 128
missiological imagination
defined 10, 12
developing a 7–8, 12–22, 15, 39
and meaning-making 21–2
and new perspectives on mission 22
and reclaiming the Catholic imaginary 14–15
and theological reflection 8, 12
missiology *see also* grassroots theology
anchors theology 19–20
defined 2fn4
and education, dialogue 2
professional 5–6, 7
as a study 19–20, 39, 138, 148
mission
as an integrating force 4
anthropology 45–6
basic unit of 142
in Catholic schools 186–7
as "civilising" peoples 140
communal sense of 4
conversations 2, 5
and critical reflection 24
defined 10, 84
and dialogue 60, 91, 141, 149–50, 152
as engagement with the world 168
forces reshaping the frontier of 94
as global within the local 102, 142, 161
and globalisation 94
God's 18–19, 21–1, 39
grid, for use in schools 151–3
hope as lifeblood of 7, 38–9, 152
and identity 139, 142, 153, 180
and the Kingdom 152 *see also* Kingdom of God

and learning 10
as local within the global 102, 142, 152–3, 161
meaning of 18
and missiological imagination 22
modalities of 149, 151
new understanding 18–19, 137
nominal sense of 134
of the parish 21
pedagogy 184–5, 193
perspective and grassroots theology 10
in the pre-modern world 80–1
reconceptualising 9
in school education, new perspectives on 20–1, 102
in the second modernity 90–1
and secularisation 94
and St Paul 64, 145
and theological reflection 19
and theological storytelling 160–1
traditional understandings 18
mission theology
　and a communal sense of mission 4
　development 142–3
　　key moments 143–51
　as local theology 38–9, 193
　and mission practice 138–9
　and the person of Jesus 166–7
　missional imagination, developing a 13
modern
　age 66
　world 42
modern pluralism 3, 88
modern sensibility 77, 81, 83
modernisation 112
modernity
　crisis 85–7
　decline in attendance at religious services 108
　early 81–5
　hope for a new moral framework in 128
　and indifference and hostility to Christianity 83
　a Kingdom constructed by science 173
　and the narrative of ideological pluralism 126–9

and plausibility structures 124–5
and the principle of contingency 121–3
and public knowledge 124–5
and school education 91–3
second 87–93, 132, 193
and sectarianism 84
study of human sexuality in 128
truth in 129
and universal reason 129
worldviews 68, 77, 79, 83, 84
moral laws 127–8
morality
　in modernity, hope for 128
　and natural laws 178
　secularisation of 111–12
multi-faith nature of society 187
multiculturalism 48, 100
music of an era 102
myth 54–6, 57, 65, 85, 109

N
naïve literalism 154–6, 163
narrative
　and culture 13, 53–8
　defined 40, 42, 56–7
　form of the Gospels 162–3
　of globalisation 98
　and God's truth 158
　and human experience 92
　of ideological pluralism 126–9
　importance 92
　and meaning-making 42
　and post-modernism 8
　of secularisation 107–8
　shaped by global processes 8
　and worldview 65, 73
narrative mission theology, doing 160–2
narrative theology 159, 163
nature 126–7, 172
Nazism 73, 85
needs 49–51
neo-scholasticism 83
Nero 164
New Testament texts *see also* Gospels, the; scripture
　background 159–60

New Zealand, Catholic education in 6
Newbigin, Lesslie 119, 123, 124, 131, 132
Newton, Isaac 126
Nichols, Archbishop Vincent 187
nihilism 92
Nostra Aetate 144, 146–7, 150

O
obsolescence 98
Old Testament literature 53, 62, 73, 76, 154, 157, 169–70, 172, 188–90
oppressed, the 173
optimism
  age of 82, 83, 85–6
  in post-modern world 89
orientation 77
Origen 120
Osborne, Kenan 44, 98–9
Our Father (prayer) 172

P
Pacem in Terris 137
Palmer, Parker 12
paradigm
  causal relationship 122
  as a concept 73–5
  emerging 136
  of Judeo-Christian religion 79
  plausibility structure as a 120
paradigm shift
  as a concept 73–5
  Enlightenment as a 120, 121
paralysis, intellectual and emotional 91
parents, "Catholic" commitment 1
Pascal, Blaise 107, 126
peace 19, 149
Pharisees 159
physical environment 49
plausibility structures 119–25, 129, 130–2
pluralism
  contemporary 118–33
  empirical 118–119
  ideological 118, 119–20, 125–9, 129, 132–3
  in the Judeo-Christian tradition 190
  and mission 94

modern 3, 88
post-modern 3
pollution 96, 173
poor, the
  God's concern for the poor 188
  the preferential option for 149
  in spirit and the Kingdom 173
  those who recognise Jesus in 173
Pope Benedict XVI 17, 62, 95, 102, 113–14, 131
Pope John Paul II 39, 102, 135, 136, 143, 149, 177, 183, 185
Pope John XXIII 137
Pope Paul VI 17, 61, 92, 112, 137–8, 141, 147–8, 149, 153
Pope Pius IX 83
Pope Pius X 83
Pope Pius XI 20
Pope Urban VIII 75
popular religiosity 148
Populorum Progessio 17
post-modern age *see* post-modernity
post-modern Catholics 70–1
post-modern experience, exploring 42, 64–78
post-modern pluralism 3
post-modern sensibility 68–70, 77, 79, 87, 89, 92, 130
post-modern students, characteristics 68–70
post-modernity *see also entries which begin with* "post-modern"
  characteristics 89
  defined 68
  early 85–7
  narrative 8, 79–93
  period in history 64, 65, 67–8
  place of religion in 89
  and the principle of critique 125, 129, 131
  and school education 91–3
  and truth 129–30
  understanding 66–7, 77, 79, 87, 130
powerful, the 173
pragmatism 69
prayer 172, 193
pre-modern world
  and the Church 80–1, 83
  human consciousness 121

identity 76–8, 85
imaginal horizons of 120, 124
impact of the Enlightenment 77
and migrants and refugees 87
mission in the 80–1
plausibility structures 120–1, 124
public knowledge in 120
in relation to the modern world 42
school education 80
and a single worldview 76–8, 85
superstition 83, 120
and truth 120
pre-modernity *see* pre-modern world
privatisation 111
process
    and Killen and de Beer 30–2
    and the Whiteheads 29
proclamation *see also* Jesus
    of a person, Jesus Christ 149–51, 166–7
    by witness 148, 151
    by word 148, 151
progress 10, 79, 80, 83, 85, 86, 87, 109, 120
Propaganda Fide 145
prophetic consciousness 188, 189
Protestantism 77
Protestants as heretics 121
public knowledge
    in modernity 124–5
    and plausibility structures 119
    in pre-modern society 120
    in the school curricula 179
purpose
    in Catholic curriculum 180–1
    principle of 123–4, 125, 131, 133, 135, 156, 177
    ultimate 178, 179

R
rationalisation 110
re-orientation 77
readiness 30, 137
reason
    appeal to 81, 85, 107, 108, 110, 120, 121
    faith versus reason debate 125
    and moral laws 128
    reasonableness 107, 108, 119, 122, 125, 178
    universal 129
reconciliation 19, 89, 172
Redemptoris Missio 144, 149, 150
Reformation 77, 81, 82, 107
refugees 87, 99, 100, 118
relationships
    an ecology of 183–5
    living in right relationship 172
    reluctance to commit 69, 112
relativism 86, 92, 129
religion
    and culture 44
    and faith 44
    and hard secularism 109
    as a label 128
    place in post-modern society 89
    and politics 107
    as a private matter 107–8
    as a product 66
    resurgence of 87
    symbols in public places 111, 113, 159
    and tolerant secularism 109–10
    and wars 81, 107
Religious Education *see* Christian Religious Education
religious tradition
    befriending our 28, 39–40, 134–6
    contributions 8
    as living 8, 28, 37, 137–53, 154
    as a pole for theological reflection 36–8
    and the Whiteheads 28
resurrection
    lens 166–7
    life and death of Jesus 59, 80, 160, 161, 165, 166–7
    and missioning of the disciples 168
rich, the 173
right relationship 172
right to choose 69
righteousness 172
Rivers, Robert 90, 129, 132
Rizer, George 97
Rolheiser, Ronald 5, 105–6, 108
Roman empire 159, 168
Rome 164

royal authority 108
Rwanda 149

S
Sacks, Jonathan 73, 100, 114–15
salvation 146, 147, 156, 171
scepticism 69
school education *see also* Catholic schools
   an ecology at work in 177
   and balancing a number of areas 190
   critical reflection in 25–7
   and enculturation 47
   means and ends 135
   and missiology, dialogue 2
   and modernity/post-modernity 91–3
   new perspectives on mission in 20–1
   and pre-modernity 80
   as a product 66
   and public knowledge 124
Schreiter, Robert 24, 35, 77, 82, 87–9, 101, 129
Schroeder, Roger 146
science
   as an autonomous discipline 127
   axioms 120
   and faith 108
   and the Kingdom 173
   objectivity of 125
   and public knowledge 124–5
scientific community 121, 122, 125
Scotland 109
scripture *see also* Gospels, the; St Paul
   content and process in 157–9, 160, 162, 163, 169–71
   and goals of mission 145
   God's revelation in 156–9
   God's truth wrapped in a culture and a narrative 158
   inter-testamental period 171
   living power of the text 155
   naïve literalism 154–6
   and tradition pole 30
   understanding 156–7
   the word "world" in 104–5
second modernity see modernity, second
Second Vatican Council (1962–65)
   and autonomy of academic disciplines 135
   and the Catholic school 20
   and culture 46
   discernment process 16–17
   documents 144–7 see also specific documents
   and paradigm shifts 75, 135–6
   and reading the signs of the times 15–16
   understanding of scripture 156–7
   understanding the Church's mission 8, 18–19, 90, 137–8, 140–2
sectarianism 84
secular state 105
secularisation
   Catholic discourse on 112–15
   as a cultural phenomenon 110–11
   defined 104, 106
   and diversity 89
   and government 108
   leadership issues 115–17
   and mission 94
   of morality 111–12
   and narrative 8
   narrative of 107–8
   and the new wilderness 3
   theory 108–9
secularism
   Catholic discourse on 112–15
   defined 104, 105, 106
   hard and soft 106, 109–10
   and modernisation 112
   perspectives on 109–10
   pragmatic 110
secularity
   Catholic discourse on 113–15
   defined 104, 105, 106
   principle of 107–8, 111, 112
Sedmak, Clemens 25, 35–6
"see, judge, act" methodology 29
self-absorption 69
self-control 185
Senior, Donald 155, 160–1, 164, 169
A Sense of the Sacred 181–3
sensus fidelium 28, 74
settlement image 2, 3
Shenk, David 127, 128

Shorter, Aylward 44, 48, 60
signs of the times
  discerning the 15–17, 39, 80
  methodology 17
  theology 16, 17
sinners 173
social differentiation 111
social environment 49
social identity 47–8
social imaginary
  and Catholic education 14
  defined 13
social imagination 53, 56, 100
social institutions 69
social networking 97
social order 80, 81, 82, 105
social systems 49–50
sociological exploration 16
South Africa, collapse of apartheid 149
spirituality 89, 158
St Anselm 75
St Augustine 157
St Francis Xavier 121
St Paul
  form of writing 163
  and the person of Jesus 171
  sense of mission 64, 145
  usage of the term "church" 142
  use of the term "Kingdom" 172
staff, educating 2
stages of faith, Fowler's 186
Stark, Rodney 108
The Structure of Scientific Revolutions 74
Stuhlmueller, Carroll 155, 160–1, 164, 169
sub-cultures 41
subsidiarity 99
superstition 83, 120
Syllabus of Errors 83, 90
symbolic system 50, 51
Synod on Evangelisation (1974) 140–1, 143, 147–8
synoptic writers see Luke; Mark; Matthew
synthesising information 97, 101
Syria 164

T

Tanner, Kathryn 5, 101
Taylor, Charles 13, 76, 81, 83, 104, 115, 128, 133
Taylor, Mark 68–70, 87
teaching–learning relationship 183
technoliteracy 70
technological system 49–50
technology 81, 97, 98, 112
terrorism, global 87, 94
theological exploration 16
theological method 16–17
theological reflection
  art of 29–32
  attitudes people bring to 30
  in Christian ministry 27
  and culture 36–8, 43, 62–3
  defined 29
  and human experience 28, 29, 30, 36–8
  and the imaginal horizon 15
  as a learning process 29, 193
  as a means of reading the signs of the times 24
  and missiological imagination 8, 12
  and mission 19
  model for 36–8
  processes 11
  as a resource 8
  scripture as a personal and communal resource in 158
  systematic 10
theology *see also* local theology
  academic 4–7
  anchored by missiology 19–20
  contextual nature of 11, 25, 32–5, 86
  doing 4, 10, 16, 22, 35–6, 39
  of inculturation 141
  misconceptions 4–5
  narrative see narrative mission theology; narrative theology
  and paradigms 75
  of the signs of the times 16, 17
The Thirty Years War 81, 107
time
  and meaning-making 64–5
  and space, compressed 96
Titus 159

Tomlinson, John 96
Torah consciousness 188, 188fn289, 189
tradition see religious tradition
transcendent, the 115, 178, 186
travel, cheap 95
trust 183
truth
   belief that God is the source of all 126
   and beliefs 119
   Biblical claim to 156
   claims to absolute 75, 109
   and errors 90
   as eternal verities in the Gospel stories 163
   God's 158
   and ideological pluralism 125–6, 132–3
   and meta-narratives 129
   and the mind of God 123
   in modernity 129
   nature of 76
   no such thing as 86
   and the person of Jesus 123–4
   in post-modernity 129–30
   and pre-modern society 120
   and the principle of contingency 121
   sceptical of claims to 69
   and science 125
   scientific 74
Turner, Frederick 3

U
United Kingdom
   Catholic education in 6, 116, 187–8
   and community cohesion 109
   new migration 100
United States of America
   Catholic education in 6
   and the founding fathers 109–10
   frontier image 2–3
   global recession of 2008–09 96
urbanisation 100, 102

V
value systems 69
values, Catholic school 166, 181–3
Vatican Congregation for Catholic Education 20

W
Walls, Andrew 61
White, Dan 184–5, 192
Whitehead, James and Evelyn 24, 27–9, 39
wilderness image 2, 3, 53, 94
wisdom consciousness 189
witness, proclamation by 148, 151, 173–4, 185
word, proclamation by 148, 151
world culture 98
worldview
   of the age 65, 66, 73
   and Catholic schools 66
   Christian 79, 123, 131, 135, 177–8
   as a concept 72–3
   and culture 60, 61–2, 65, 66, 73, 83, 119
   defined 57–8
   dominant 76
   of the faith 65, 66, 73, 83
   and human aspiration 65–6, 84
   of humanism 83
   and identity 73, 76, 77
   interpretive map 72–5
   macro and micro levels 73
   of modernity 68, 77, 79, 83, 84
   and narrative 65, 73
   a new whole coherent 131–2
   paradigm shifts within a 75–6
   and paradigms 74
   pre-modern 76–8, 85
   religious 65
   and the second modernity 88, 132
   truth in the post-modern 129–30
Wostyn, Lode 24, 31

Y
Young Adult Catholics: Religion in the Culture of Choice 70
Young Christian Workers' movement 29
youth culture 101–2

www.ingramcontent.com/pod-product-compliance
Lightning Source LLC
Chambersburg PA
CBHW061348300426
44116CB00011B/2035